EDUCATION THEORIES FOR A
CHANGING WORLD

EDUCATION THEORIES FOR A
CHANGING WORLD

KARL AUBREY AND ALISON RILEY

Sage

1 Oliver's Yard
55 City Road
London EC1Y 1SP

2455 Teller Road
Thousand Oaks, California 91320

Unit No 323-333, Third Floor, F-Block
International Trade Tower Nehru Place
New Delhi 110 019

8 Marina View Suite 43-053
Asia Square Tower 1
Singapore 018960

Editor: James Clark
Editorial Assistant: Esosa Otabor
Production Editor: Neelu Sahu
Copyeditor: Diana Chambers
Proofreader: Clare Weaver
Indexer: KnowledgeWorks Global Ltd
Marketing Manager: Lorna Patkai
Cover Design: Naomi Robinson
Typeset by KnowledgeWorks Global Ltd
Printed in the UK

Library of Congress Control Number: 2023931627

British Library Cataloguing in Publication data

A catalogue record for this book is available from the British Library

ISBN 978-1-5297-6415-4
ISBN 978-1-5297-6414-7 (pbk)

CONTENTS

ABOUT THE AUTHORS

Karl Aubrey has recently retired from his post at Bishop Grosseteste University where he held posts as a visiting tutor, senior lecturer and Programme Leader on the Professional Studies in Education. He does however continue to follow and write about his research interests. Prior to this, Karl was the Programme Leader for a range of initial teacher education and professional development programmes at a large city Further Education college. Between 2003 and 2005 he was seconded to the DfES Standards Unit as a learning and teaching practitioner in the East Midlands. His doctoral thesis explored the reforms in Further Education teacher education from 2000 to 2010, from the viewpoint of teacher educators. Karl's research interests include inclusion, education policy, pedagogy and work-based learning.

Alison Riley is the Academic Co-ordinator for the BA (Hons) Early Childhood Studies degree at Bishop Grosseteste University. She has also worked on a number of education-related programmes at the university, including ITT courses. Prior to joining Bishop Grosseteste University, Alison spent 16 years working in Primary Education as a classroom teacher, deputy head teacher and finally head teacher of a large junior school. Alison has been involved in a number of collaborative projects and has recently been involved in an EU-funded project researching 'Creativity in Early Science and Mathematics Education'. Alison has recently commenced doctoral studies in which she is researching the journey of students entering Higher Education with alternative qualifications.

INTRODUCTION

WHY A BOOK ABOUT EDUCATIONAL THEORIES FOR A CHANGING WORLD?

The aim of this book is to present a case for a compassionate, democratic and inclusive form of education that enables students to cope and thrive in times of change and uncertainty. The reader will explore the current key themes that are evident in society as they affect education. In doing so, we have sought to invite the reader to consider a socially just form of education in an ever-changing world by offering alternative theoretical and practical notions to reflect upon.

The state of flux in the world is very evident as events and crises become ever more frequent. Sherwood (2022: 9) lists 'Brexit, war, climate disasters, a tanking economy, political instability, global insecurity, … [and] … a sense of doom' as examples of some of the major changes that are now almost commonplace. Such is the rate of recurrence of events that the *Collins English Dictionary* word of the year for 2022 was 'permacrisis'. *Collins English Dictionary* has defined permacrisis as 'an extended period of instability and insecurity' that succinctly encapsulates how dire the experiences have been for many people in recent years, particularly 2022 (*Collins English Dictionary*, cited in Sherwood, 2022). Arguably, it is as if the notion of permacrisis has been normalised, yet such events and crises can, and have, a profound impact on education, especially when policies and practice appear to be increasingly fixed in ideas of traditional, instrumental and didactic principles of the past. It is contested that to prepare young people for such uncertain times, an alternative outlook is needed.

We feel that this book, *Educational Theories for a Changing World*, is timely in that it challenges the traditional aspects of educational thinking and practice in a time of uncertainty, crises and amid some key societal issues. Unlike our other books, in this volume we look at how education can be used as a vehicle for social change by exploring key themes through an educational lens on how these could/can be addressed. It does so by considering seven themes and by interweaving theories, ideologies and philosophies that seek alternative ideas for the future. Therefore, the aim of this volume is threefold. First, to explore the various aspects that influence educational thinking, policy and practice. Second, to offer readers the opportunity to examine the major themes and to analyse the impact they have on education. These major themes are: the curriculum, education as a vehicle for social mobility, the rise of right-wing populism, the Black Lives Matter movement, the COVID-19 pandemic, LGBTQ+ and the climate crisis. Finally, it proposes ideas and aspirations to strive for in the creation of an education in a changing world. Underpinning these ideas and aspirations we include concepts, including social justice, democracy, inclusion, emancipation and compassion, all of which we hope will prepare learners for the challenges they face in uncertain times. Our overall ambition for this book is to evaluate the ways in which education can be a transformational activity to tackle crises and changes in society. We should clarify that this book is not a comprehensive account of each of the themes explored; rather, it is an introduction and overview that we hope acts as a helpful and informative starting point for readers that will enable them to delve deeper into the themes that interest them.

The book takes into account education from an international perspective when considering each of the themes, as well as employing the ideas of educational thinkers from around the world as the themes themselves are of global concern. It is argued that the impact of these themes affect all sectors of education. The scope of the book somewhat limits us, for the most part, to the UK and compulsory state education. The school systems in the four nations of the UK have differed for some time, even before devolution in 1999 when Scotland, Wales and Northern Ireland were formally given powers to set their own education policy agenda. However, since the Conservative and Liberal Democrat Coalition formed in 2010, and under the direction of Michael Gove as the Secretary of State for Education, the English school curriculum was reformed with the emphasis on subject-specific knowledge. Subsequently, however, the Scottish curriculum (Curriculum for Excellence) prioritised the application of knowledge, which the Welsh Government (2022) in their new curriculum has also embraced. There are also divisions regarding the use and promotion of standardised testing, and the compiling and publication of league tables between the devolved nations (Institute for Government, 2020). These differences are, for the most part, ideological in nature, which in turn could affect the way that each nation thinks about and formulates education policy which influences learning and teaching. Therefore, in the following chapters we will refer to the UK if the context is broad enough to cover all four nations. Otherwise, if the contextual point is specific to a devolved nation, we will refer to that nation individually.

CONTEMPORARY DEVELOPMENTS IN EDUCATION

To give background and context to the current picture of education from our point of view, we offer the following brief outline of contemporary historical worldwide events.

Up until the 1950s and the early 1960s, education was still very much viewed and prac-tised as a knowledge/skills-based, hierarchical and examination-driven activity. How-ever, the 1950s witnessed huge variations in world order following the horrors of the Second World War and there was a rush of people calling out for a fairer society. Many European nations, such as France, Belgium, Holland and Portugal, rapidly started to give up their colonial responsibilities. The Cold War focused people's minds regarding the frightening possibility of a cataclysmic nuclear conflict. That was until the fall of the Berlin Wall in 1989 and subsequent opening of the border between Soviet-controlled East Berlin and the Western-occupied West Berlin, bringing an end to the commu-nist regime in the region and marking the symbolic ending of the Cold War. In the United States of America, there was an upsurge of interest and involvement in the civil rights movement, mass protests against the Vietnam War and increased calls for gender equality. Furthermore, in the UK it was not unexpected that the highpoint of 'British state-sanctioned progressivism contained in the Plowden Report [1967] coincided with the decriminalization of homosexuality and [the end] of capital punishment, [and] the legalization of abortion' (Howlett, 2013: 3). These major changes were in keeping with the social open-mindedness of the UK in the 1960s, and in particular with Harold Wil-son's Labour government (Howlett, 2013; Aubrey and Riley, 2021, 2022).

Starting at the end of the last century, there was, however, some disquiet about the perceived poor state of education. Thomas (2013) argues that this disquiet was notice-able on both sides of the Atlantic where there 'was a new political awakening, and politically inspired changes affected the way education would develop for the next thirty years' (2013: 60). This political awakening corresponded with a new economic concept called neoliberalism. Thomas (2013) defines neoliberalism as a

> brand of economics that put markets and individual choice at the core of economic suc-cess.... The neoliberal turn gathered speed in the early 1980s, happening alongside the ramping up of the Cold War rhetoric that had emerged as part of the Thatcher–Reagan alliance. There was an invigorated narrative about the failure of state-run systems and a focus on the contrasting economic models in use on either side of the Iron Curtain.
>
> (p. 61)

This focus on a neoliberal model has consequently led to the marketisation of educa-tion, promoted by right-wing agendas both in England and in other neoconservative governments in different parts of the world, with the idea of shrinking the role of state in education 'and opening up the provision of educational services to the com-petitive discipline of the marketplace and private providers' (Coffield and Williamson, 2012: 35). The results of this marketisation of education has produced a proliferation of quasi-markets in the form of parental choice and competition between schools. In these quasi-markets, students and their parents are seen as customers or purchas-ers and schools as 'providers'; the more well-liked schools would prosper, while the schools that were less well liked would lose pupils and possibly even close (Thomas, 2013: 65). Together with quasi-markets and increasingly evident competition between schools, marketisation has also increased emphasis and frequency of testing, and the publication of the results of this testing in league tables. The emphasis on testing and choice is also of concern in the USA and is powerfully expressed in the seminal work of the renowned academic and educationalist, Diane Ravitch, *The Death and Life of the Great American School System: How Testing and Choice are Undermining Education* (2010).

Marketisation, testing and choice feature heavily in business and also play their part in affecting the competition between schools, each trying to succeed in the race to the top of the league table. The burden of this pressure to attain top results 'is not just on staff, but on the children themselves' (Thomas, 2013: 67). Marketisation also plays a part in creating and promoting a curriculum, the content of which prepares students for employment rather than their holistic personal development. The choice of subjects mostly prioritises the science, technology, engineering, and mathematics (STEM) subjects, usually to the detriment of the arts. This competition and prioritising of STEM subjects is by no means exclusive to schools; universities are also witnessing funding cuts for arts subjects.

NEED FOR CHANGE

We have already briefly outlined what we consider is the picture of education, including a fleeting overview of how educational thinking and practice has changed over the last 75 years or so. Education, we suggest, needs to be forward-looking and helping learners to take an active part in society by fostering such values as hope, building aspirations and courageous advocacy, encouraging harmony, dignity and respect. There are optimistic steps being planned and implemented which will help learners prepare for these uncertain times – for example, the Ofsted (2019, updated 2021) Education Inspection Framework under the element of *Personal Development* looks to see if educational establishments are preparing learners for life in modern Britain by equipping learners to be responsible, respectful and active citizens who will contribute positively to society. But the Statutory Inspection of Anglican and Methodist Schools (SIAMS) (2018) goes even further, seeking wisdom as well as knowledge and skills, as they look for evidence of fostering values such as hope, building aspirations, courageous advocacy, communities and living well together, dignity and respect. These positive comments, although well-meaning, require more substance and a complete change of direction in the way that education in all sectors is viewed, legislated for and practised. This, we feel, will require more than just educational reform; it will need a radical transformation.

A detailed evaluation of the transformation needed to address the key issues will be analysed later in the book, particularly in the final chapter about realigning education with social justice in changing times. However, as a brief foretaste at this early stage, it is fitting that we indicate where some of these needs may be focused. Our wish is that education should be at the forefront of personal development and aspiration. With this in mind, we will consider the range of barriers and difficulties that learners might encounter in achieving their ambitions. Ideology, particularly when aligned with populism, is a thread that we contest runs deeply throughout this book. In the UK and in other countries, populism is a powerful and, we argue, a degenerating force. It will also consider the Black Lives Matter movement in relation to education. Furthermore, we reflect on the disruptive effect on learning and teaching resulting from the tragic global impact of COVID-19, which, while resulting in some innovative practice through the application of e-learning, also highlighted some significant inequalities such as the lack of internet access and appropriate devices for some students. Moreover, the considerable disruption to teaching through extended lockdown periods, school closures and the exam results fiasco will surely have an impact on this generation of students in years to come. The book will also appraise issues of inclusivity, in particular LGBTQ+, since, while it is heartening that progress in this area has been made to some extent, we acknowledge that much still needs to be done in all sectors of education to ensure inclusivity for all. Finally, the current and looming crisis of climate change is an area where education has, and can, play a major role for the future of the planet.

OPPOSING NOTIONS OF THINKING ABOUT EDUCATION

Trying to define and categorise the different notions of how we think about education is a risky undertaking because not only are grey areas involved in such a task, but also there are many overlaps and contradictions, and the way we think about education evolves with time. However, as a starting point, broadly speaking there are two opposing ways of thinking about education: traditionalism and progressivism, which will be explored later. Although this book focuses on the key themes featured in each of the chapters, which have and will have an impact on education, at this point it is fitting to reflect on how we endeavoured, and to some extent struggled, to place educational thinkers' ideas into categories of thought. Our previous two books focused on individual theorists, their concepts and a critique of their thinking, and offered ways of putting their ideas into practice. For example, in *Understanding and Using Educational Theories* (2022) we attempted to group the thinkers' ideas into the three broad psychological schools of thought: behaviourism, constructivism and humanism. In *Understanding and Using Challenging Educational Theories* (2021), although the thinkers included could, to some extent, be classified in either the constructivist or humanist schools of thought, they were all, to varying degrees, progressive in their thinking. All the thinkers in this volume advocated a progressive learner-centred approach, bolstered by their persuasive awareness of social justice and democracy; for them, education was an emancipatory, active and a transformative process. We attempt to offer our own groupings for these thinkers here, although we acknowledge there are limitations in doing so. These groupings are: freedom in childhood, home schooling and deschooling; social class, race and gender; the relationship between power and knowledge; caring education; critical and transformative education. We acknowledge that these groupings are eclectic in nature, but we hope they will be evident and useful when analysing the major themes covered in each of the chapters of this book.

The problematic task of grouping and categorising ways of thinking encountered in our attempts mentioned above is also apparent when trying to differentiate the two seemingly obvious distinctive educational notions of traditionalism and progressivism. Superficially, it might appear a simple division between the traditionalist way of thinking being knowledge centred and the progressive being learner centred. However, the difference is more complex. For example, the debate on the divide between the two philosophies has been a long-standing and profound concern not only for educators, but also for politicians and the public, although such concern may be more of a perception than a reality at times. Furthermore, there is an argument for adopting a neutral and blended approach rather than either a 'child-centred *or* a teacher-centred one is appropriate for *all* children' (Carr, 2000: 137). In short, and as a starting point, traditionalists can be associated with a knowledge-based, product-based, teacher-centred and subject-centred approach, while progressives can be aligned with a child-centred, learner-centred, radical or experimental approach (Carr, 2000; Howlett, 2013). Each of the two notions have their own educational thinkers who support either traditionalism or progressivism. For example, traditionalism is mostly associated with the works of B.F. Skinner and his fellow behaviourists, as well as Barak Rosenshine and other like-minded cognitive psychologists. While progressivism is aligned with thinkers who have a more holistic notion of learning and teaching where social justice and democracy are to the fore; thinkers include, for example, John Dewey, A.S. Neill, Carl Rogers, bell hooks and Henry Giroux. These thinkers and their ideas will be explored in further depth.

WHO WOULD FIND THIS BOOK RELEVANT?

Our aim is that this book will be useful for both undergraduate and postgraduate students, and as a valuable professional development resource for practitioners who are involved with learners in all sectors of education, particularly as the themes are matters of current and future concern. The contemporary nature of the content links key societal issues with education. It is also felt that those involved within youth work and the broad field of social sciences would find this book of use and interest. We fully recognise that this is a wide remit. However, similar to our two previous books, we are keen to include a broad scope of readers whose practice does, or will, involve work with learners in formal education, such as in schools, further education (FE) colleges and universities, as well as informal education, such as early years, youth work and offender education. It also includes initial teacher education for teaching in schools and FE colleges, education studies and youth work undergraduates. Our aspiration is also to refresh, and perhaps introduce for the first time, readers to alternative educational concepts and ideas proposed by progressive thinkers. Hopefully, it will be of interest to those seeking ideas and theories for how education can prepare learners for the current permacrisis we encounter in education and society at large.

ORGANISATION AND STRUCTURE OF THIS BOOK

Chapters are presented in a way that we feel is logical in respect of the purpose for the book. Each chapter has similar features, as they all list the learning outcomes that indicate what the reader should be able to do having read the chapter; this is then followed by the key words that are relevant to the specific chapter. The Introduction sets the scene for the chapter. The structure of the chapter differs according to the theme being explored. Each chapter closes with a summary of the content and a glossary of terms of the key words. The key words are emboldened in the text on their first mention. Every chapter finishes with ideas for further reading, which readers can extend their in-depth study, as well as a reference list of the sources cited in the chapter.

Chapter 1 explores the different influences on educational thinking, policy and practice. This includes a further analysis of educational thinking through the three key schools of thought and how these have evolved to support our knowledge of learning and instruction in a changing world. This we do with the goal of promoting a democratic, socially just and inclusive environment for learners, communities and practitioners. In so doing, this opening chapter also acts as an antecedent to provide the reader with food for thought on how the way we think about education can improve the outcomes for learners, teachers and communities in relation to the eight key themes explored in the subsequent chapters.

In Chapter 2, the curriculum Part 1 considers a brief historical perspective up until the current times, as well as reviewing curriculum influences and the theoretical curricula models. In Chapter 3, the curriculum Part 2 explores the notion of the curriculum from the 1944 Education Act, including the increasing influence of politics on shaping the curriculum content. The chapter also considers the diverging curriculum implementation of the devolved UK nations. Chapter 4 evaluates the notion of education as a vehicle of social mobility by analysing the complexities and challenges involved. The chapter also draws upon the work of Pierre Bourdieu and Basil Bernstein regarding social class, as well as outlining some of the initiatives designed to tackle inequality in education. Chapter 5 contemplates the rise in populism internationally as well as in the UK, and its impact on education, including the language and division created in the ensuing culture wars. We look at the Black Lives Matter movement in Chapter 6, while highlighting the inequalities currently evident in society, including ideas to improve learning opportunities and decolonise the curriculum. Chapter 7 evaluates the impact that the COVID-19 pandemic has, and is having, on students, staff and education as a whole. The chapter highlights errors made during the pandemic by governments and underscores the positive innovative pedagogical practices during lockdown. Chapter 8 considers LGBTQ+ equality and the notion of education and inclusion, and the role of education as a positive vehicle for social change. The last key theme at Chapter 9 focuses on the climate crises and how education can create a platform for raising awareness. Finally, Chapter 10 offers the reader ideas for changing and uncertain times by challenging current educational thinking and opting for a new radical approach.

All chapters include matters of historical context, political/social/cultural influences and impacts, theoretical thinking that underpins (and challenges) the topic, and, where relevant, ideas for practice and possible case studies.

USING THE BOOK

There are a number of ways in which you could use this book. You could, if you wished, start with the Introduction and read straight through, or you could go straight to whichever key theme you are interested in, or the theme which is the topic of your assignment. We do hope, however, that even if you skip the thematic chapters, you start with the Introduction and the following next chapter, as well as finish with the final chapter to give you a greater depth of context to support the theme of your choice and consider progressive ideas in how to strive for better educational outcomes. Furthermore, although Chapters 2–9 are presented as individual key themes, we argue that they are significant contemporary phenomena and that they are mainly connected with each other in a number of ways. Making these connections, we feel, will help you construct critical and analytical synthesis between the themes. For example, Chapters 2 and 3, the curriculum Parts 1 and 2, and Chapter 6, the Black Lives Matter movement, and Chapter 5 Populism, could be aligned with most other chapters. You could also use the References and Further Reading to explore topics of interest in more depth. Irrespective of the way you use the book, it is our sincere hope that it will help with your understanding of the educational perspectives of the key themes, and the influences, ideologies and theories that affect them. In doing so, we also hope that it will help stimulate a deeper perception of the issues faced in current state of education and help prepare for future events and crises.

REFERENCES

Aubrey, K. and Riley, A. (2021) *Understanding and Using Challenging Educational Theories* (2nd edn). London: Sage.

Aubrey, K. and Riley, A. (2022) *Understanding and Using Educational Theories* (3rd edn). London: Sage.

Carr, D. (2000) *Professionalism and Ethics in Teaching*. London: Routledge.

Coffield, F. and Williamson, B. (2012) *From Exam Factories to Communities of Discovery: The Democratic Route*. London: Institute of Education, University of London.

Howlett, J. (2013) *Progressive Education: A Critical Introduction*. London: Bloomsbury.

Institute for Government (2020) *Devolved Public Services*. Available at: www.institutefor government.org.uk/publication/devolved-public-services-schools (accessed 9 March 2023).

Ofsted (2019, updated 23 July 2021) *Education Inspection Framework 2019*. Available at: www. gov.uk/government/publications/education-inspection-framework (accessed 9 March 2023).

Ravitch, D. (2010) *The Death and Life of the Great American School System: How Testing and Choice are Undermining Education*. New York: Basic Books.

Sherwood, H. (2022) Permacrisis named Collins' word of 2022 as global disasters pile up. *The Guardian*, p. 9, 2 November.

SIAMS (2018) An evaluation schedule for schools and inspectors. Available at: www. churchofengland.org.sites/%20Evaluation%20Schedule%202018_O-pdf (accessed 9 March 2023).

Thomas, G. (2013) *Education: A Very Short Introduction*. Oxford: Oxford University Press.

Welsh Government (2022) *Education is Changing*. Available at: https://gov.wales/education-changing (accessed 9 March 2023).

1

HOW THEORY HAS SHAPED PRACTICE

LEARNING OUTCOMES

Having read this chapter, you should be able to:

- identify how educational theory has helped to shape practice;
- recognise key educational theories and associated theorists;
- understand how theories can be applied to developments in educational practice including through digital technology.

KEY WORDS

accommodation; advance organisers; assimilation; classical conditioning; empiricism; networks; nodes; operant conditioning; rationalism; zone of proximal development.

INTRODUCTION

While this text seeks to examine the way in which theories can be applied to an ever changing world, it is important to note that this is not a new idea. Arguably, it can be suggested that the work of theorists have had a significant influence on policy and practice, most significantly in education where the work of key theorists such as Piaget, Vygotsky and Skinner have shaped educational practice. Moreover, significant to this text is the way in which these early thinkers have influenced the work of the more contemporary theorists detailed in the chapters.

Educational psychology in particular seeks to help us understand why humans think and behave in the way they do and thus provides a secure framework from which to develop theories on learning. Kimble (1961), cited in Long (2000: 10), defines learning as an experience 'which produces a relatively permanent change in behaviour, or potential behaviour', thus excluding those changes that occur naturally as part of development or growth. MacBlain (2014) observes that learning is more than simply acquiring new information and knowledge within a classroom situation, and argues that it is a complex concept for which multiple views are held, particularly when trying to help us understand how children learn. From a psychological perspective, general principles have been derived stemming from the different ways in which theorists approach the phenomenon of learning (Phillips and Soltis, 2009). Ertmer and Newby (1993, 2013) argue that learning theories stem from an attempt to illuminate the timeless debate of how people acquire knowledge and how they come to know, suggesting that two opposing positions exist: **empiricism** and **rationalism**. They go on to observe that these positions are evident in the 'modern learning viewpoints' commonly used today, which they categorise as behaviourism, constructivism and cognitivism, a view supported by Yilmaz (2011) who posits that typologies of learning can be categorised into these three main schools of thought.

The aim of this chapter, therefore, is to examine how these schools of thought were developed and how they influenced practice, both at the time of their inception and in the period subsequently. Furthermore, the chapter will seek to identify how these theories have evolved through the development of new theories and in response to developments in the field of education.

HISTORICAL CONTEXT: TYPOLOGIES OF LEARNING THEORIES

This section will detail the evolution of the three main theories of learning, commencing with behaviourism, and then examining the development of cognitivism and constructivism as a response to some of the criticisms of behaviourist theory.

BEHAVIOURISM

Influenced by the empiricist view of learning that sees experience as the primary source of knowledge, and reflecting the philosophy of John Locke who argued that the mind at birth was a *tabula rasa* (blank slate) to be filled with ideas as the world is experienced through the five senses, behaviourism purports that behaviour is shaped through forces in the environment. Furthermore, behaviourists expound the view that changes in behaviour are determined by others who shape the desired behaviour through providing stimuli which act as reinforcers for the behaviour to occur. Behaviour can be explained as everything that a person says or does, and it is the study of these overt behaviours and how these can be observed and measured that provided the basis of behaviourism (Ng'andu et al., 2013). It was behaviourism that provided the foundations for learning theories and their influence on modern curriculum development and classroom practice (Cunningham et al., 2007; Yilmaz, 2011; Ertmer and Newby, 2013; Ng'andu et al., 2013). Thus, it is pertinent to explore the foundations of behaviourism before considering how it made, and continues to make, such an impact on practice.

Behaviourism originated through the work of Russian psychologist, Ivan Pavlov, who established the branch of behaviourism known as **classical conditioning**. Through his experimental work on salivation in dogs, in which he observed that the natural responses of dogs to salivate on the sight of food could be conditioned through the unnatural stimulus of the ringing of a bell, Pavlov developed his theory of conditioned reflexes, the precursor to classical conditioning. According to MacBlain (2014) this subsequently provided the impetus for other theorists to examine the nature of learning, one of whom was John Watson who is credited with establishing the school of behaviourism in 1913 (MacBlain, 2014).

Watson proposed that all behaviours were acquired through the process of conditioning, expanding on Pavlov's work with animals to explore how classical conditioning might be used to shape human behaviour. Watson is perhaps best known for his experimental work involving children, the most well known being the case of Little Albert for whom he conditioned a fear response. Establishing that Albert showed fear in loud sharp noises, Watson paired this with a white rat for which Albert had previously shown no fear. Watson repeatedly made the noise that had previously startled Albert, while at the same time showing Albert the rat. Eventually, Albert cried at the sight of the white rat even when no sound was present, leading Watson to conclude that he had conditioned the fear response in Albert. This work led Watson to claim:

> Give me a dozen healthy infants, well-formed, and my own specified world to bring them up in and I'll guarantee to take any one at random and train him to become any type of specialist I might select – doctor, lawyer, artist, merchant-chief and, yes, even beggar man and thief, regardless of his talents, penchants, tendencies, abilities, vocations and the race of his ancestors. (Watson, 1928: 82)

This view resonates the empiricist view of learning and the previously referred to ideas of John Locke that promote a view of learning as a passive rather than active process (MacBlain, 2014).

In contrast, another proponent of classical conditioning, Edward Thorndike, theorised that learning was an active process. From his position as Professor of Educational Psychology, Thorndike adopted the principles of classical conditioning, while at the same time developing his own theory of connectionism which built on the stimulus response framework observed by Pavlov. For Thorndike, however, learning was a result of trial and error, in which a behaviour could be strengthened if rewarded, leading to his law of effect which stated that a response followed by a rewarding state of affairs is likely to be strengthened and repeated in a similar situation. Moreover, Thorndike suggested that where a response failed to gain an expected reward, then connections became weaker.

It was Thorndike's work which inspired perhaps the most well-known behaviourist, B.F. Skinner, who, drawing from this work, established his own branch of behaviourism, **operant conditioning**. Like Pavlov, Skinner conducted his experimental work in a laboratory with animals, but with the specific intention of using his work to learn more about the behaviour of humans. While this has been the source of much criticism of his theories, Feeley argues that his work should not be discounted on this basis, as it 'led to important findings regarding how humans behave and thus learn' (2023: 132). Feeley (2023) goes on to observe that Skinner was one of the most influential psychologists as his findings have been applied to enhance learning in a variety of environments.

From his work with pigeons and rats, Skinner was able to establish important behavioural principles that led to his theory of operant conditioning, this being the systematic application of a stimulus to condition a desired response (Feeley, 2023). In his work, Skinner designed a box, known as the Skinner Box, in which rats were placed. Skinner then used a system of levers and switches to condition the rats to undertake certain actions to release food, which he called positive reinforcement. Subsequently, electrical circuits were introduced to the box as a form of negative reinforcement, again to elicit a response from the rats.

As we will see later in the chapter, principles of behaviourism were consistently applied to thinking and practice in educational settings for three decades in the fifties, sixties and seventies. However, as seen in the next section, a shift from this way of thinking was seen as new theories began to emerge.

COGNITIVISM (COGNITIVE CONSTRUCTIVISM)

A criticism of behaviourism was its focus solely on those behaviours that were observable, thereby negating any internal thought processes or the impact of emotional responses in a given situation (Yilmaz, 2011). This notion that not all behaviour is observable and that learning is not simply a change in behaviour, paved the way for a new way of thinking from theorists who claimed that prior knowledge and mental processes were more important than stimulus in eliciting a behaviour or response. Consequently, cognitivism, otherwise known as cognitive constructivism, was established.

Yilmaz (2011) observes that the cognitive revolution began in the 1950s with a number of theorists emphasising the importance of cognitive processes on learning. Cognitive processes were defined as mental structures, including memory, attention, concept formation and information processing, which were seen as a way in which to understand how knowledge is acquired. Like behaviourists, cognitive theorists still emphasised the need for observation, but as a vehicle by which to infer the internal mental processes. From the cognitivist perspective, learning is an active process in which the learner is an active participant in the drive for knowledge acquisition. Important in cognitivism is the knowledge already held by the learner, which should serve as a foundation on which to build subsequent knowledge. Thus, learning should be meaningful, allowing learners to code, organise and build on the structures that already exist (Ally, 2008).

While American psychologist Edward Tolman can be credited with initiating the cognitive movement (Yilmaz, 2011), it is Swiss psychologist Jean Piaget who is most commonly associated with cognitive theory. Golder (2018) observes that Piaget's theory of cognitive constructivism comprises two key elements – ages and stages – which help to predict what learners can and cannot understand, depending on their age and stage of development. Piaget identified four stages of development in children, commencing with the sensorimotor stage (0–2 years), through the preoperational stage (2–7 years) and concrete operational stage (7–11 years) and ending with the formal operational stage (11–15 years) (Aubrey and Riley, 2022). In his original work, Piaget observed that children must pass through each stage successfully before moving on to the next, although in his later work he did acknowledge that children developed cognitively at different rates and recognised that some may be able to access advanced learning at a younger age than others (MacBlain, 2014).

In addition to his stage theory, Piaget also posited that in order to process new information, it was necessary for young children to build on already constructed understanding and knowledge gained from their interactions with their environment. These internal mental representations, which he theorised existed in the brain, he referred to as 'schemas', adopting the ideas of one of the original pioneering cognitive psychologists, James Mark Baldwin. Piaget explained the formation of schemas through the dual processes of **accommodation** and **assimilation** (MacBlain, 2014). Piaget then saw learning as an active process, and while his early work was conducted in a laboratory setting, much like behaviourism, latterly he observed children in their natural settings, interacting and listening to them as they engaged in activities. This led to

Piaget emphasising practice which focused on the 'whole child', presenting the notion of 'child-centred' education that was seen as a viable alternative to the behaviourist approach.

Nonetheless, Piaget was not without his critics, which subsequently paved the way for the final influential theory of learning – social constructivism.

SOCIAL CONSTRUCTIVISM

Ertmer and Newby ([1993] 2013) identify similarities between behavioural and cognitive theories as being 'primarily objectivist', suggesting that the world is real and external to the learner (p. 54). They go on to argue that this had resulted in some theorists questioning such a basic, objectivist approach in which the goal of instruction is to map the world to the learner, instead adopting a more constructivist approach (Jonasson, 1991, cited in Ertmer and Newby, [1993] 2013). In constructivism, knowledge is not seen as independent to the knower, but rather the learner constructs their own knowledge from their interactions within their environment. While Piagetian theory is considered a constructivist theory – hence often referred to as 'cognitive constructivism' – it should be noted that there is a discrete difference between this and social constructivism. As seen above, Piaget saw children as constructors of their own knowledge through assimilation and accommodation, which he saw as a continuous process (Dagar and Yadav, 2016). However, Piaget did not see learning as a social process and posited that with the right environment, learning would proceed with minimal interaction. This was in opposition to the later theories of social constructivists who viewed knowledge as socially constructed between the learner and a more knowledgeable other.

A key social constructivist theorist is Russian psychologist, Lev Vygtosky, known as the father of social constructivism (Dagar and Yadav, 2016). Vygotsky believed the origin of knowledge construction to be the social intersections of people, through interactions that involved sharing, comparing and debating. Vygotsky saw child development as a construct which was 'driven by a complex interplay of biological maturation, societal expectations and the child's own active participation in culturally determined activities and social interactions' (Bodrova and Leong, 2023: 62). To this end, child development was culturally situated and depended on the social context of each child. Learning then, for Vygotsky, commenced in the home prior to formal schooling and proceeded by way of experiential learning. Vygotsky emphasised the importance of culture in knowledge construction and referred to the social patterns of behaviour and beliefs passed down through generations by way of cultural tools such as stories, rhymes and art (MacBlain, 2014).

Underpinning Vygotsky's social constructivist approach was the importance of language as a means by which meaning is transmitted, and at the core of his work was the reciprocal nature of language with children taking an active role in interpreting what they hear and responding accordingly. Moreover, Vygotsky believed that children are born with innate cognitive abilities such as attention, memory and visual recognition which enable them to learn through the guidance of others. The guidance of others was central to Vygotsky's notion of the **zone of proximal development** (ZPD) and the role of the more knowledgeable other (MKO) in this. Vygotsky saw the ZPD as a 'theoretical space of understanding that is just above the level of understanding of a given individual' (Pritchard, 2018: 28). Vygotsky theorised that this was the area of learning that the learner would move on to next, and in which, with the support of the MKO, they could work effectively. The role of the MKO could be undertaken by an adult, such as parent or teacher, or even a sibling or peer who had already achieved that level of learning. In supporting the learner to their next stage of development, the MKO adopts a scaffolding approach, a concept that another social constructivist theorist, Jerome Bruner, developed from Vygotsky's work.

Like Vygotsky, Bruner saw learning as a social process, whereby learning and thinking were progressed through interactions with those around them (MacBlain, 2014). Bruner viewed these interactions as a form of scaffolding, which he believed was everywhere in the lives of children. Scaffolding is a flexible approach, tailored to the needs of the individual child, and requires providing support to the learner, at an appropriate level of sophistication, and targeted at just the right time. Scaffolding might occur through discussion or through the provision of specific resources, but importantly, it should support the learner in achieving the next stage of development according to the theory of ZPD (Pritchard, 2018). As we will see in the next section, the work of both Bruner and Vygotsky have had a notable influence on current classroom practice.

APPLICATION OF LEARNING THEORIES TO PRACTICE

This section will discuss the influence of the three identified learning theories on practice. Commencing with behaviourism, which was the first of these learning theories to influence practice, the section will examine the evolution of subsequent theories in the light of an increased understanding in how children learn.

MacBlain (2014) posits that behaviourism can be seen evidenced in classroom practice on a daily basis. Furthermore, since it is a theory so firmly embedded, he goes on to suggest that for most practitioners this practice is predominantly carried out on an unconscious level. Setting aside the Skinner-inspired use of reward systems in settings, which sees practitioners utilise a variety of strategies to mould a desired behaviour while employing sanctions to discourage unacceptable behaviours, behaviourism can also be seen in other aspects of curriculum delivery. Pritchard (2018) observes that teachers might use verbal praise and encouragement to motivate children to complete work, or in some cases more tangible rewards such as stickers or team points might be utilised. For Skinner, reinforcement strengthens the behaviours of individuals, so the child is likely to repeat the behaviour in anticipation of the offered reward, thus learning proceeds.

Skinner's interest in applying his behaviourist theory to education followed a visit to his daughter Deborah's fourth grade school in 1953 (Buxton-Cope, 2020). On observing Deborah's maths class, Skinner remarked that 'through no fault of her own the teacher was violating almost everything we knew about the learning process' (B.F. Skinner Foundation, n.d., para. 10). From his laboratory work, Skinner established that a successful learning process should be personalised, starting from the learner's current level of understanding, and broken down into small steps, in which success should be rewarded and reinforced regularly. Furthermore, feedback should be given as immediately as possible after learning had proceeded, giving the learner the opportunity to rectify any errors. However, contrary to this Skinner noted that all students were expected to complete the same work, resulting in some learners being unable to complete the work due to the tasks being out of their reach, while for others the task was well below their ability level, meaning that learning was not extended. Furthermore, since the teacher was unable to provide immediate reinforcement, which Skinner had previously established was most effective in strengthening behaviour, feedback therefore lacked impact. Skinner's response to this was to design his first teaching machine.

While Skinner was not the first psychologist to develop a teaching machine, he was the first person to advocate them as a means by which to personalise learning. Skinner recommended that each child had their own machine which they could work on at their own pace, with the machine only allowing them to proceed to the next stage, having successfully completed the preceding stage. Skinner referred to this as 'programmed instruction'. Skinner spent ten years working as part of the teaching machine movement, and programmed instruction particularly held appeal for educationalists. Nevertheless, from a practical perspective, the teaching machine proved too complex to be viable and, despite its potential benefits, content soon reverted back to a book format (Buxton-Cope, 2020).

Nevertheless, it could be argued that Skinner was a theorist who was ahead of his time since teaching machines could be considered as the precursor to Integrated Learning Systems (ILS) commonly used in schools today, which maximise the processing power of modern computers (Pritchard, 2018). Semple (2000) observes that the principles of the teaching machine were replicated in these more traditional computer-based systems which adopted the fundamental principles of behaviourism – namely, drill and practice tutorial programmes. Early programmes were sequenced such that the learner could practise and master simple concepts before being allowed access to more complex problems, with regular and positive feedback motivating the learner to engage in the programme. Furthermore, from a diagnostic perspective, the teacher is able to keep track of the progress made by each learner.

Semple (2000) argues that the advantage of drill and practice is through their ability to teach new skills by way of rote learning, as well as strengthening pre-existing associations and reinforcing knowledge. Furthermore, since the application can employ different levels of difficulty and variation it remains stimulating for the learner. Nevertheless, the application of behaviourism and associated learning systems is not without its criticisms, heralding a rise in the application of alternative theories to the learning process. Most significantly, behaviourism contends that learning can be explained through observable behaviour, without accounting for the mental processes that underpin this, thus leading to the suggestion that this was too limiting to explain learning. Moreover, Pritchard (2018) argues that a cause for concern lies in the apparent lack of understanding engendered by the process alongside the criticism of the solitary and individualistic style of learning promoted by the ILS which fails to acknowledge the importance of social interactions in the learning process. Pritchard (2018) contends therefore that while behaviourism has a place in the planning which teachers undertake it should not be used in isolation since other theories might be better suited to understanding and promoting learning.

It was cognitive constructivism that provided a viable alternative to behaviourism and which subsequently influenced the learning process from the late 1950s onwards (Ertmer and Newby, 1993, 2013). The appeal of cognitive constructivism over behaviourism was its emphasis on the acquisition of knowledge through the application of mental structures. Rather than emphasising observable behaviours, cognitivists sought to establish a conceptual understanding of the learning process, examining how information is received, organised, stored and retrieved. It was through an understanding of this process which then underpinned the learning experience provided.

Reflecting Piaget's stage theory, a cognitivist approach to learning acknowledges the importance of ensuring that teaching reflects the age of the child. While it is important to note that Piaget later modified his views, acknowledging that children did develop at different rates, it can be seen that the national curriculum in England still loosely reflects the ages and stages identified by Piaget. Since its inception in 1988, the national curriculum in England applies to children from 5 to 16 years of age, divided into four key stages; subsequently, provision for children in the age group 0–5 years was articulated through the Statutory Framework for the Early Years Foundation Stage (EYFS) in 2006. As can be seen from Table 1.1 below, there is some correlation between these stages and those identified by Piaget.

Piaget also advocated for an approach that not only emphasised the importance of how a child reached a correct answer, but also why incorrect answers were given. He was particularly interested in readiness, suggesting that if learning was accelerated beyond what the child was capable of, they would not have the required building blocks to complete the task; as such, teachers should engage children in tasks

Table 1.1 The relationship between Piaget's ages and stages, and the national curriculum

Age	Key Stage	Piaget's Stage
0–5 years	Early Years Foundation stage	Sensori motor stage (0–2 years) Pre-operational stage (2–7 years)
5–7 years	Key Stage 1	Pre-operational stage (2–7 years) Intuitive stage (4–7 years)
7– 11 years	Key Stage 2	Concrete operational stage (7–11 years)
11–14 years	Key Stage 3	Formal operational stage (11–15 years)
14 –16 years	Key Stage 4	

appropriate to their stage of development. This too can be seen reflected in the national curriculum, which states that:

> The national curriculum provides an outline of core knowledge around which teachers can develop exciting and stimulating lessons to promote the development of pupils' knowledge, understanding and skills as part of the wider school curriculum.
>
> (DfE, 2013: 6)

The nature of the national curriculum is such that concepts are revised and revisited, allowing learners to build on previously learned knowledge reflecting a constructivist approach which emphasises the importance of 'making knowledge meaningful and helping learners organise and relate new information to existing knowledge in memory' (Ertmer and Newby, [1993] 2013: 54). Bruner referred to this as a spiral curriculum, in which topics or subjects are revisited throughout a child's school career with the complexity of the material increasing on each revisit. In this way, new learning has a relationship with previous knowledge and thus has a context. Bruner advanced the notion that even young children can learn complex material provided that it is properly structured and presented (EPI, 2012).

It can be seen then that the application of cognitivist theories is underpinned by current thinking in education, with Ertmer and Newby ([1993] 2013) emphasising delivery which draws on the learner's previous experience when planning activities. Furthermore, delivery style should be tailored to individual learning styles with a focus on how new information is organised and structured; consideration should also be given to how new information might be assimilated and accommodated to the learner's existing mental structures. Cognitivist theory then supports learners as active participants in their own learning, since it is through these first-hand experiences that mental structures are developed. Piaget emphasised the importance of the whole-child and posited that children have a natural propensity to learning, provided the environment supports these natural tendencies.

The active application of cognitive theory in learning includes enquiry learning, discovery learning and problem-based learning, affording the opportunity for learners to gain mastery of the subject matter through drawing from the structures that already exist. Moreover, similar to behaviourism, advances in technology have also seen the principles of constructivism reflected through computer applications. As seen above, cognitivists see learning as an internal process, involving memory, thinking, reflection, abstraction, motivation and metacognition. Therefore, the view of learning is from the information processing point of view through accessing different types of memory (Ally, 2008). Ally (2008) observes that information is received through the senses where it is processed in the sensory store; this information remains in the sensory store for a very short space of time, during which it is retained in the working memory. Any information not retained in the working memory is subsequently lost, while information in the working memory is transferred to the long-term memory, allowing for assimilation and accommodation to proceed. Appropriately designed Information Technology applications can support this process through presenting materials which maximise sensory experiences and order information in a logical manner. Ally (2008) suggests locating information centrally and minimising the amount of information to proceed is most effective for ease of processing. Furthermore, design should pay close attention to attributes of the screen including colour, graphics and text size, while at the same time pacing information and varying modes of delivery.

Information technology from a behaviourist perspective was criticised for the emphasis on rote learning, reflecting convergent thinking by which answers were restricted and predetermined. However, from a constructivist perspective, applications could be responsive to the information already held by the learner in which divergent thinking could be stimulated. Ally (2008) advises the use of prerequisite test questions in order to activate the required knowledge structure needed to access new materials, capitalising on the flexibility of learning systems which allow learners to choose their own path to develop new knowledge. Once a baseline has been established, learners are encouraged to follow their own line of enquiry – for example, through the use of the internet. A further benefit of this style of learning is the responsiveness to different learning styles, defined as how a learner perceives, interacts with and responds to the learning environment (Ally, 2018).

Additionally, another benefit of computer application from a constructivist perspective lies in the use of programming tools whereby the learner becomes 'part of the construction of new knowledge' (Waite-Stupiansky, 2023: 16). This involves especially designed, child-friendly computer programming tools such as LOGO, a turtle robot, which allows the learner to tinker and make their own creations. Nevertheless, while the cognitivist approach presents a learning experience which is tailored more to the individual needs of the learner, there remains a concern that learning is still a somewhat solitary experience. Waite-Stupiansky (2023) observes that a dilemma for teachers today is the way in which technology isolates learners from each other through their connection to technology over face-to-face interactions, going on to suggest that interacting through the internet could well be marginalising children in respect of the importance of real-life, first-hand experiences.

Semple (2000) notes that Piaget's theory of cognitive constructivism has been criticised for the lack of emphasis on social interaction and cultural transmission, especially when relating to supporting learners. This then lends credence to the work of Vygotsky and Bruner, which will be the focus for the final part of this section. In contrast to Piaget's stage theory, Vygotsky believed that readiness to learn could be determined and promoted through the teaching and learning process which he argued should be child led. Vygotsky (1997) states that:

> The old point of view ... assumed that it was necessary to adopt rearing to development (in the sense of time, rate, form of thinking and perception proper to the child, etc.). It did not pose the question dynamically. The new point of view ... takes the child in the dynamics of his development and growth and asks where must the teaching bring the child.

(p. 224)

This then led to the development of the aforementioned ZPD theory which emphasised the role of the adult, or MKO, in moving the child's learning outside of their current level of development to their learning potential. Thus, learning proceeds faster than it otherwise would, and as the child performs more complex tasks, a new level of assisted performance emerges, hence leading to a cycle of increasingly more complex skills and competencies (Bodrova and Leong, 2023). Vygotsky promoted the notion that learning should be targeted at the highest level of a child's ZPD, which presupposes a personalised learning approach for each child, and while logistically this may prove challenging, Bodrova and Leong (2023) suggest that classroom practice has evolved around this. They contend that assistance from the MKO in supporting the ZPD does not necessarily need to be an adult, and settings have instead utilised learning in social contexts through group working and peer mentoring. Moreover, advances in technology have also facilitated provision by way of specifically designed materials and tools that allow the child to self-assist.

Semple (2000) suggests that computer simulations present opportunities for learners to draw from their sociocultural backgrounds, which is also a key feature of social constructivist theory. In this way, a community of peers is built in which children start to view one another as a resource for learning. In this respect, technology may be viewed as the cultural tool of their generation, with collaboration, either face-to-face or online, being seen as fundamental to the learning process. Furthermore, through adopting a multimedia approach, educational and cognitive processes can be developed through co-operative learning, problem solving, critical thinking and reflection.

Ultimately, the social constructivist approach seeks to help children make the transition from assisted to independent performance (Bodrova and Leong, 2023) involving the use of scaffolding. Scaffolding is a process by which support is offered when a new or more complex concept is being taught, with the intention of gradually removing the support until it is no longer required. It was Bruner who popularised scaffolding as a construct, and argued that scaffolding should be observed in all aspects of a child's learning experience, both formal and informal. In classrooms today, scaffolding can be seen through the breaking down of tasks into smaller steps, modelling how tasks or problems can be solved, or through creating groups of mixed ability children to solve problems. Moreover, scaffolding might exist through classroom displays or resources available which might serve as an additional prop for those children who need it. MacBlain (2014) observes that this way of working to progress learning is a powerful motivator for many children.

INFLUENCE OF TYPOLOGIES ON CURRENT THINKING

As seen above, theoretical thinking has informed practice since its inception and continues to do so. Furthermore, as will be discussed in this section, modern-day thinkers have also utilised the principles of these theories in advancing ideas to meet the needs of a learning society.

As noted earlier in the chapter, behaviourism has been used in settings as a means of modifying behaviour. Arguably, since the abolition of corporal punishment in England in 1986, schools have sought ways in which to manage pupil behaviour, underpinned by a number of government acts and legislation, the most recent of which sets out that:

> Using positive recognition and rewards provides an opportunity for all staff to reinforce the school's culture and ethos. Positive reinforcements and rewards should be applied clearly and fairly to reinforce the routines, expectations, and norms of the school's behaviour culture.
>
> (DfE, 2022: 16)

This resonates with the work of B.F. Skinner, as outlined in the preceding section. Furthermore, the document goes on to outline that challenging behaviour should be addressed through the implementation of a range of possible sanctions that should be clearly set out and made clear to the pupils. Alongside this, and in acknowledgement of a rise in challenging behaviours in settings, Skinner's work has been further advanced to address specific behaviour problems in learners – namely, through the application of Applied Behaviour Analysis (ABA). ABA was pioneered in the 1960s by Ole Ivar Løvaas, and was aimed at improving the lives of children with autism and their families (Smith and Eikeseth, 2011). Underpinned by an understanding of the science of learning and behaviour, ABA has three main principles: first, it contends that behaviour is affected by the environment, and second that this behaviour can be strengthened or weakened by consequences. Finally, reflecting a behaviourist approach, changes to behaviour are more effective when positive over negative reinforcement is used. Specific to ABA is the personalised approach to the application of rewards, with rewards being offered having specific meaning to the learner (Autism Speaks, 2022). Smith and Eikeseth (2010) observe that children receiving early ABA interventions made significant gains in development.

In contrast, a behaviourist who rejected the principles of positive reinforcement was Edward Tolman who challenged the idea that people are passive learners and instead developed his own cognitive branch of behaviourism, referred to as 'latent learning'. Conducting his own experiments on rats, Tolman's theory of latent learning proposed that organisms can still learn even if immediate reinforcement is not received (Tolman and Hoznick, 1930). Furthermore, Tolman (1930) expressed that learned behaviours were not immediately obvious since the learner may choose not to display learned behaviours until motivated to do so, which was a departure from traditional behaviourist theory that held that learned behaviour was directly observable following stimulus reinforcement. In explaining this, Tolman believed that learners develop their own cognitive map – or mental map – a structure to be stored until such times as it is needed. Pell (2020) observes that latent learning is challenging to see in the classroom, largely because it is a phenomenon which is happening all the time, but by its very nature not immediately obvious. Nevertheless, he proposes that children can be encouraged by allowing them to conduct their own research into topics, as well as providing opportunities to develop skills and knowledge which has previously been learned.

The idea of drawing from skills and knowledge previously learned also reflects the principles of constructivist theory and, as with behaviourism, contemporary thinkers have sought to develop the work of constructivists such as Piaget and Vygotsky to better reflect learners today. One such thinker is Ernst von Glasersfeld who referred to himself as a radical constructivist (Phillips and Soltis, 2009). Glasersfeld rejected the idea that the individual learner receives knowledge through an external reality and believed that all knowledge is constructed rather than perceived through the senses (Macleod, 2019). In this sense, Glasersfeld argues that knowledge is invented not discovered and only helps the learner to function in their own environment. Moreover, each individual has their own reality; thus, it is wrong to assume that all understandings are the same as this is based on the learner's personal construction. Applying his work in an educational context, Glasersfeld suggests that teachers should not present 'sacred truths' (p. 10) to learners, but instead should present opportunities that allow learners to trigger their own thinking. Furthermore, rather than just developing knowledge around a set curriculum, Glasersfeld (2001) recommends 'a repertoire of didactic situations in which the concepts that are to be built up can be involved. And these situations should be such that they evoke the students' spontaneous interest' (2001: 10). Glasersfeld (2001) further recommends that as opposed to emphasising right or wrong answers, teachers should be more concerned with how learners reached the answer they have given. He expounds that:

> Students rarely produce a random solution. They have worked at it, and if the result which they consider to be right at the moment is not what the teacher thinks it should be, their effort must nevertheless be acknowledged. Disregarding it, is a sure way to demolish whatever spark of motivation they had. And then it is not surprising that their willingness to tackle new tasks disappears.

> (2001: 11)

While Glasersfeld (2001) acknowledges the challenges of working with the thinking processes of each individual student, he promotes the idea that providing problem-solving activities to learners will promote thinking, while at the same time encouraging a wide range of skills that can be applied to a range of situations.

THE RISE OF CONNECTIVISM

Siemens (2005) observes that the three broad learning theories – behaviourism, cognitivism and constructivism – came to prominence before the impact of technology began to influence learning. While the preceding section has identified some of the ways in which these theories have been modified to fit some of the changes in technology, Siemens suggests that where the underlying conditions have altered so significantly that modifications to existing theories are no longer sensible, then a theory of learning which embraces all that technology has to offer is required. In response, Siemens established the term 'connectivism', which he first used in a blog post in 2004, followed by a 2005 article entitled 'Connectivism: a learning theory for a digital age'. In the same year, Stephen Downes produced a similar article on connectivism, 'An introduction to connective knowledge', which also emphasises the importance of establishing a learning theory that reflects learning in a digital age.

In advocating for a theory specific to the digital age, Siemens (2005) posits that traditional theories focus too heavily on the notion that learning occurs inside the person, emphasising the process of learning over the value of what is learned. He goes on to argue that in an environment where knowledge is in abundance, then it is necessary to focus on how information is acquired, with an emphasis on how that information is evaluated in terms of its relevance. Thus, intrinsic to learning is how information is processed and categorised, particularly in an environment where information is constantly changing and evolving. Siemens states:

In today's environment, action is often needed without personal learning – that is, we need to act by drawing information outside of our primary knowledge. The ability to synthesize and recognize connections and patterns is a valuable skill.

(2005: 3)

Thus, Siemens holds the view that the very nature of learning is changing with the evolution of technology, necessitating a new approach to how we view learners and present learning experiences to them. Arguably, as discussed later in Chapter 7, the need for this was accelerated during the COVID-19 pandemic when education was hastily forced online. It would seem prudent, therefore, to capitalise on this as an opportunity to examine how connectivism might take its place as a dominant theory of learning.

The principles of connectivism lie in a view of learning as a construct which resides outside of the self and is therefore not entirely under the control of the individual. Furthermore, it relies on the connecting of information sets which enhance learning outside the current state of knowing (Siemens, 2005). Siemens (2005) presents that the ever-changing state of knowledge requires the learner to be responsive when making decisions, and draws distinctions between important and unimportant information when acquiring new knowledge. Furthermore, the learner needs to be prepared to alter a course of action promptly when new knowledge becomes available.

Siemens (2005) identifies the following eight principles of connectivism:

- Learning and knowledge rests in diversity of opinions.
- Learning is a process of connecting specialised nodes or information sources.
- Learning may reside in non-human appliances.
- Capacity to know more is more critical than what is currently known.
- Nurturing and maintaining connections is needed to facilitate continual learning.
- Ability to see connections between fields, ideas and concepts is a core skill.
- Currency (accurate, up-to-date knowledge) is the intent of all connectivist learning activities.
- Decision-making is itself a learning process. Choosing what to learn and the meaning of incoming information is seen through the lens of a shifting reality. While there is a right answer now, it may be wrong tomorrow due to alterations in the information climate affecting the decision.

(Siemens, 2005: 5–6)

Applying these principles to the learning environment, Siemens (2005) suggests that learners should be prepared for learning in a digital age, with teaching material reflecting this. Ally (2008) posits that this goes far beyond placing materials on the web or linking the learner to other digital materials on the web, suggesting that online learning requires careful and deliberate planning, encompassing a range of activities that reflect different learning styles. In this way, the learner takes some control over their learning through selecting a mode of learning that best suits them.

Ally (2008) proposes that when delivering online learning, the following components should be considered.

PREPARATION

Learners should be informed of the learning outcomes and be aware of any prerequisite knowledge or skills. Self-assessment tests at the start of the learning module will allow learners to identify whether they have the prerequisite skills. Concept maps are included to establish and activate cognitive structures and **advance organisers** are then used as the means by which to underpin the structure and organisation of learning content. Key to preparation is establishing the purpose and process.

LEARNING ACTIVITIES

Online learning should reflect the potential of digital learning, providing a range of activities capturing different learning styles. This might include reading textual information or listening to podcasts. Visuals or video materials provide an alternative means of content delivery. Research can be conducted online, through the web or links to e-books. Learners should be encouraged to track progress through reflective journals, and carefully planned assessment activities allow the learner to track their own progress and revisit concepts.

LEARNER INTERACTION

Interactions occur in a variety of ways in online learning, predominantly through the interface of the online learning platform. Interaction with the content is an essential component of the learning process and design should be such that it does not overload the learner. Rather, learners should be able to sense the information and thus transfer it to their sensory store before it goes into their short memory. Key to this is the development of social cognition by way of external interactions through the instructor, other learners and experts, affording opportunities for the development of social networks.

LEARNER TRANSFER

Learners need opportunities to apply what they have learned in a real-world context, allowing them to go beyond what they have learned online and add meaning to their learning (adapted from Ally, 2008).

Siemens (2005) advocated that teaching through digital technology captured students' attention more effectively and helped them to learn more easily. Moreover, learning new knowledge was the result of interactions with many rather than being monopolised by a few (Altuna and Lareki, 2015). Learning which proceeds through **networks** and **nodes** allowed for easy access to information, collaboration and the development of learning communities. Moreover, the rapid expansion of new networks and technologies provide ample opportunities for extensive learning opportunities.

Nevertheless, while such developments in technology would lead to an assumption that connectivism is a necessary and obvious way forward it is crucial to proceed with caution. When developing his theory of connectivism, Siemens acknowledged that the field of education has been slow to recognise 'both the impact of new learning tools and the environmental changes in what it means to learn' (2005: 7), and despite his observation that 'connectivism provides insight into learning skills and tasks needed for learners to flourish in a digital era' (ibid.), experiences during the Covid pandemic (see Chapter 7) would suggest that settings still have some way to go before connectivism becomes a viable alternative to the three main theories influencing learning in educational settings.

While acknowledging that connectivism is 'all the rage' in the digital era, Tracey (2009: 8) suggests that rather than viewing instructional design as an evolutionary progression, from behaviourism, through constructivism to connectivism, a more rational consideration would be to view them as complementary. Tracey (2009) argues that all three approaches build on one another in providing a more rounded theoretical toolset for the instructor to exploit. This was similarly observed by Ally who advances the idea that behaviourism, cognitivism and constructivism have, and will continue to be used to develop online learning materials. He suggests that 'behaviorist strategies can be used to teach the facts (what); cognitivist strategies, the principles and processes (how); and constructivist strategies to teach the real-life and personal applications and contextual learning' (2008: 39). Ally (2008) goes on to suggest that connectivism should be used as the means by which to develop online learning, incorporating aspects of other learning theories as applicable. In this way, learning objects that promote flexibility and the development of materials tailored to individual learning styles will become embedded in the curriculum alongside the more traditional and well-established delivery styles.

SUMMARY

This chapter has sought to establish how the three main theories of behaviourism, cognitivism and constructivism have helped to shape educational thinking and practice. Furthermore, it seeks to demonstrate how these theories have stood the test of time in terms of some of the changes to curriculum delivery, which are particularly evident through advances in digital technology seen in recent years. By necessity, the chapter has been limited to the main theorists in the three disciplines, and while briefly considering influence on more contemporary thinkers, it is important to note that this is merely a starting point. While the application of these theories, and others, have been contextualised throughout the themes in this text, we would also urge readers to examine some of the more specialist texts in the recommended reading section to learn more about the theories per se.

It should also be acknowledged that the three theories were chosen specifically because these are widely considered to be the main theoretical perspectives which have guided educational thinking (MacBlain, 2014). Moreover, it is these theories that have arguably influenced subsequent theories such as Bandura's social learning theory, Gardner's theory of Multiple Intelligences and the humanist theories of Carl Rogers and Abraham Maslow. Furthermore, elements of these theories can be seen not only to have influenced curriculum development as seen in the chapter, but also have underpinned thinking in the educational philosophies of key thinkers such as Maria Montessori, Loris Malaguzzi, A.S. Neill and John Holt. Again, while it was not possible to address this through this chapter, we would recommend further reading to this end.

Nevertheless, key to this chapter is the idea that while all three theories are very different in their approaches, fundamentally they all seek to support our understanding of learning, with a particular emphasis on how this learning can be supported to give the best possible outcome for the learner. While it may be tempting to seek to establish the benefits of one over another, it is anticipated that this chapter will demonstrate the importance of seeing all three theories as complementary to one another, each offering their own insight into learning, and providing practitioners with a range of tools by which to support learners. Furthermore, as we embrace the digital age, it can be seen that each theory can offer something different from the design of a technology-based curriculum, thereby providing for the diverse needs of learners in the changing world.

GLOSSARY OF TERMS

Accommodation

The changing of existing schema in order to accommodate new information. Piaget believed that when children could not fit new experiences into existing schema, it was necessary to adapt these in order to make sense of the new information.

Advance organisers

Popularised by David Ausubel, advance organisers refer to a conceptual framework that enables learners to assimilate and retain information. Ausubel suggests that these should be used when a new topic is introduced to help the learner to process the new information.

Assimilation

A cognitive process by which new information is fitted into existing schema.

Classical conditioning

First established by Pavlov, classical conditioning refers to the reinforcement of a natural reflex that occurs following a specific, sometimes unnatural stimulus. In the case of Pavlov, the ringing of the bell, the conditioned stimulus, elicited the salivation response in dogs.

Empiricism

A view of learning that suggests that knowledge arises and is validated through first-hand experience. Reflecting on the work of John Locke and John Watson, empiricists view the mind as a blank slate (*tabula rasa*), to be formed and shaped through experience.

Networks

Networks refer to the connections between different entities such as computer networks and social networks. Connections created serve to strengthen learning, although weakness in the connections can cause a ripple effect.

Nodes

In connectivism, a node refers to an object that can be linked to another object through networks; the theory of connectivism is based on the idea that learning proceeds when connections are made between these various nodes, including books, web pages and the learners themselves. Nodes are particularly important in an interconnected world.

Operant conditioning

A theory advanced by B.F. Skinner which holds that if a behaviour is positively reinforced, it is more likely to be repeated. On the other hand, negative reinforcement can prevent an unwanted behaviour from happening. Operant conditioning can then be used to shape behaviours.

Rationalism

Rationalism holds that it is not necessary to have an experience for knowledge to be acquired; rather, it can be acquired through reason and logic. Furthermore, reason acts as both the source and measure of sound knowledge, without the need for any sensory experiences.

Zone of proximal development

Vygotsky referred to the zone of proximal development as the area between the learner's actual development and their potential development which could be achieved through the support of the more knowledgeable other (MKO).

FURTHER READING

Kirscher, P.A. and Hendrick, C. (2020) *How Learning Happens: Seminal Works in Educational Psychology and What They Mean*. London: Routledge.

This text covers 28 works of educational significance in the fields of educational and cognitive psychology. Each chapter focuses on a different seminal study, critically examining its importance and offering suggestions as to how it might be incorporated into practice.

Ross, J. (2022) *Digital Futures for Learning: Speculative Methods and Pedagogies*. London: Routledge.

Aimed at higher education, the text examines the potential for technology as a learning resource in post-compulsory and informal learning settings. It provides a vision for how learning spaces might look in the future through adopting theories and pedagogy across a range of disciplines.

Schunk, D. (2019) *Learning Theories: An Educational Perspective*. London: Pearson.

An introduction to the key theoretical principles with a chapter dedicated to each of the major theories of learning in addition to chapters on other aspects of learning, including neuroscience, motivation and contextual influences.

Stephen, C. and Edwards, S. (2018) *Young Children Playing and Learning in a Digital Age: A Cultural and Critical Perspective*. Abingdon: Routledge (European Early Childhood Education Research Association: Towards an Ethical Praxis in Early Childhood).

An examination of how digital development has influenced pedagogy. It provides a history of technological developments before considering how traditional pedagogy has evolved for the digital age.

Thompson, C. and Edwards, L. (2021) *Learning Theories for Everyday Teaching*. London: Learning Matters.

A text that applies learning theory to everyday practice in a critical and meaningful way. It offers suggestions as to how teachers can incorporate theory into practice through the use of case studies and scenarios.

REFERENCES

Ally, M. (2008) Foundations of educational theory for online learning. In: T. Anderson (ed.) *The Theory and Practice of Online Learning*. Athabasca, AB: Athabasca University Press, (pp. 15–44). Available at: www.aupress.ca/books/120146/ebook/01_Anderson_2008-Theory_and_Practice_of_Online_Learning.pdf (accessed 14 March 2023).

Altuna, J. and Lareki, A. (2015) Analysis of the use of digital technologies in schools that implement different learning theories. *Journal of Educational Computing Research*, 53(2): 205–27.

Aubrey. K. and Riley, A. (2022) *Understanding and Using Educational Theories*. London: SAGE.

Autism Speaks (2022) *Applied Behaviour Analysis (ABA)*. Available at: www.autismspeaks.org/applied-behavior-analysis (accessed 13 March 2023).

Bodrova, E. and Leong, D. (2023) Vygotskian and post-Vygotskian approach: Focusing on "The Future Child". In: L. Cohen and S. Waite-Stupiansky (eds) *Theories of Early Child Development: Developmental, Behaviourist and Critical* (2nd edn). London: Routledge.

Buxton-Cope, T. (2020) *Who the Hell is B.F. Skinner: And What are his Theories All About?* Suffolk: Bowden & Brazil.

B.F. Skinner Foundation (n.d.) Brief biography of B.F. Skinner. Available at: www.ufrgs.br/psicoeduc/chasqueweb/behaviorismo/biography-skinner-fundation.htm (accessed 13 March 2023).

Cunningham, T., Gannon, J., Kavanagh, M.B., Greene, J., Reddy, L. and Whitson, L. (2007) Theories of learning and curriculum design – Key positionalities and their relationships. Working Paper, DIT, 2007. DOI: 10.21427/taah-e493.

Dagar, V. and Yadav, A. (2016) Constructivism: A paradigm for teaching and learning. *Arts and Social Sciences Journal*, 7(4): 1–4.

Department for Education (DfE) (2013) *The National Curriculum in England*. London: Crown copyright.

Department for Education (DfE) (2022) *Behaviour in Schools: Advice for Headteacher and School Staff*. London: Crown copyright.

Downes, S. (2005) An introduction to connective knowledge. Available at: www.downes.ca/cgi-bin/page.cgi?post=33034 (accessed 13 March 2023).

Education Partnerships, Inc. (EPI) (2012) The spiral curriculum. Available at: https://files.eric.ed.gov/fulltext/ED538282.pdf (accessed 13 March 2023).

Ertmer, P.A. and Newby, T.J. ([1993], 2013) Behaviorism, cognitivism, constructivism: Comparing critical features from an instructional design perspective. *Performance Improvement Quarterly*, 26(2): 43–71.

Feeley, K. (2023) The work of B.F. Skinner: Effective practice within early childhood education. In: L. Cohen and S. Waite-Stupiansky (eds) *Theories of Early Child Development: Developmental, Behaviourist and Critical* (2nd edn). London: Routledge.

Glasersfeld, E.V. (2001) Radical constructivism and teaching. Available at: www.vonglasersfeld.com/244.2 (accessed 13 March 2023).

Golder, J. (2018) Constructivism: A paradigm for teaching and learning. *International Journal of Research and Analytical Reviews*, 5(3): 678–86.

Long, M. (2000) *The Psychology of Education*. London: RoutledgeFalmer.

MacBlain, S. (2014) *How Children Learn*. London: SAGE.

Macleod, S. (2019) *Constructivism as Theory for Teaching and Learning*. Available at: www.simplypsychology.org/constructivism.html#:~:text=The%20notion%20of%20radical%20constructivism,foundations%20of%20their%20existing%20knowledge (accessed 13 March 2023).

Ng'andu, K., Hambulo, F., Haambokoma, N. and Tomaida, M. (2013) The contribution of behaviourism theory to education. *Zambia Journal of Education*, 4(1): 58–74.

Pell, R. (2020) Latent learning: What it is and how to use it in the classroom. Available at: www.emergingedtech.com/2020/12/latent-learning-what-it-is-and-how-to-use-it-in-the-classroom/ (accessed 13 March 2023).

Phillips, D.C. and Soltis, J.F. (2009) *Perspectives on Learning*. New York: Teachers College Press.

Pritchard, A. (2018) *Ways of Learning*. Oxford: Routledge.

Semple, A. (2000) Learning theories and their influence on the development and use of educational technologies. *Australian Science Teachers Journal*, 46(3): 1–19.

Siemens, G. (2005) Connectivism: A learning theory for the digital age. Available at: www.itdl.org/Journal/Jan_05/article01.htm (accessed 13 March 2023).

Smith, T. and Eikeseth, S. (2011) O. Ivar Lovaas: Pioneer of applied behavior analysis and intervention for children with autism. *Journal of Autism and Developmental Disorders*, 41(3): 375–8.

Tolman, E.C. and Honzik, C.H. (1930) Introduction and removal of reward, and maze performance in rats. *University of California Publications in Psychology*, 4: 257–75.

Tracey, R. (2009) Instructivism, constructivism or connectivism? *Training and Development in Australia*. Available at: https://ryan2point0.wordpress.com/2009/03/17/instructivism-constructivism-or-connectivism/ (accessed 13 March 2023).

Vygotsky, L. ([1960] 1997) The history of the development of higher mental function. In R.W. Richer (ed.) *The Collected Works of L.S. Vygotsky* (Vol. 4). New York: Plenum Press, pp. 1–259.

Waite-Stupiansky, S. (2023) Piaget's constructivist theory of learning. In L. Cohen and S. Waite-Stupiansky (eds) *Theories of Early Child Development: Developmental, Behaviourist and Critical* (2nd edn). London: Routledge.

Watson, J.B. (1928) *Psychological Care of Infant and Child*. New York: W.W. Norton & Co.

Yilmaz, K. (2011) The cognitive perspective on learning: Its theoretical underpinnings and implications for classroom practices. *The Clearing House*, 84: 204–12.

2

THE CURRICULUM PART 1: KNOWLEDGE AND CURRICULUM MODELS

LEARNING OUTCOMES

Having read this chapter, you should be able to:

- understand the historical, ideological, philosophical and political influences on the curriculum;
- recognise and critically analyse the different types and models of the curriculum;
- understand and evaluate the various terms applicable to the curriculum;
- recognise and apply aspects of social justice and democracy in curriculum provision;
- critically evaluate and make connections between official knowledge and curriculum design.

KEY WORDS

collection and integrated models of curriculum; epistemology; hidden curriculum; objectives (or product) curriculum model; official knowledge; praxis curriculum model; process curriculum model; spiral curriculum.

INTRODUCTION

The concept of the curriculum is complex and ever-changing. Although we shall briefly consider the historical developments of the curriculum, at this early point it is fitting in relation to the aim of the book to explore the comparatively recent changes that the curriculum has undergone, including the influences behind these changes. These changes are aptly reflected upon by A.V. Kelly whose seminal book on the political and philosophical scope of the curriculum, *The Curriculum: Theory and Practice*, was in publication for six editions from 1977 to 2009; in the Introduction of the last edition, he highlighted two reasons for the changes between these dates. These changes were not only evident in the United Kingdom but in other countries also, particularly in the United States of America. The first reason he maintains is the demise of teacher independence and judgement, which has hindered the development of the curriculum by means of evidence-based educator research. The second reason he believes was the ever-growing politicisation of education. Kelly (2009) contests that the impact of conflicting ideologies has had a negative effect on education, especially with the increasing focus of testing and inspection regimes. It is argued that his unease about the changes has become even more of a subject of concern since the publication of his last edition in 2009.

Explaining the meaning of curriculum depends to a certain degree on whether the source comes from a progressive or a traditionalist viewpoint. For example, two contrasting meanings are offered here: the first (progressive) is quite open, but also involves a degree of challenge, and the second (traditional) gives examples of the models of curricula, but is more prescribed on what they should all contain.

The first by Lawrence Stenhouse, a curriculum scholar and researcher, comes from his classic 1975 text, *An Introduction to Curriculum Research and Development*:

> A curriculum is an attempt to communicate the essential principles and features of an educational proposal in such a form that it is open to critical scrutiny and capable of effective translation into practice.

(p. 4)

The second definition is from David Scott's 2008 text, *Critical Essays on Major Curriculum Theorists*:

> A curriculum may refer to a system, as in the national curriculum: an institution, as in a school curriculum; or even to an individual school, as in a school geography curriculum. Its four dimensions are aims or objectives, content or subject matter, methods or procedures, and evaluation or assessment.

(p.19)

The concepts advocated by a number of curriculum thinkers will be explored in this chapter. But to give some context of what follows, a brief preview of the key ideas of some of the more influential scholars whose thoughts on the curriculum have been inspired by their individual philosophy of education are offered in Table 2.1.

Table 2.1   Brief overview of some influential curriculum scholars and their key ideas

Curriculum scholar	Key ideas
John Dewey (1859–1952)	Doyen of democratic education who promoted the value of experience in the process of learning and stressed the need for parity in the academic and vocational curriculum.
Ralph Tyler (1902–1994)	Advocate for behavioural objectives and their evaluation, which still is in place in most curricula, in the guise of the objectives curriculum model.
Jerome Bruner (1915–2016)	Managed the implementation of a radical project to create a refocused school curriculum; he also promoted the spiral curriculum.
Basil Bernstein (1924–2000)	Combined his interest in social class, language codes and pedagogy with the curriculum, particularly the two models of curricula: collection and integrated models of curriculum.
Lawrence Stenhouse (1926–1982)	A prolific writer and researcher on curriculum development and a champion of the process curriculum model. He led the Humanities Curriculum Project, and aligned curriculum development and research with teacher professionalism.
Michael Apple (1942–)	An exponent of critical pedagogy who argued against the use and influence of what he termed the 'official knowledge' of the curriculum.
Henry Giroux (1943–)	Another critical educator who advanced the notions of the praxis curriculum model (which is an extension of Stenhouse's process curriculum model) and the hidden curriculum.

Although we will consider the different curricula models further on in this chapter, a brief overview of these models deserve a very short mention here; these are the **objectives (or product) curriculum model** and the **process curriculum model**, both of which were the focus of Lawrence Stenhouse's work. Like Stenhouse, Bernstein also offered two contrasting curriculum models – the **collection and integrated models of curriculum**. The final model considered is the **praxis curriculum model**, which gained prominence from the advocacy of the critical educator Henry Giroux and fellow radical thinkers. Although not strictly a curriculum model, the spiral curriculum was a concept promoted by Jerome Bruner where learners are introduced to a particular theme which is then revisited to enhance their understanding and give them confidence in using that knowledge.

There are a number of influences on what shapes, and who has a say, on the content and process of the curriculum. Furthermore, the curriculum of all formal sectors of education 'has a powerful legal basis and represents an important social requirement, which is regulated and kept under strict control' (Bartlett and Burton, 2020: 105). It is contested that, and in accordance with Kelly (2009), the biggest influence is related and driven by political ideology, which he argues not only has an effect on 'education itself but also for the very notion of democracy and the concept of "free society"' (Kelly, 2009: 3). Along with this political ideology is the growing marketisation of education with its business terminology and competitive edginess which promulgates test results, placing a huge testing regime on schools. In doing so, the curriculum becomes slanted towards testing and achieving the best results in this competitive environment (Thomas, 2013).

In summary, then, this chapter will begin with a brief overview of the historical context of the curriculum before exploring the concept of knowledge and **official knowledge**. The contrasting curriculum models will be examined, including aspects of class, language and inclusion. The decolonisation of the curriculum will be dealt with as a part of Chapter 6 – the Black Lives Matter (BLM) movement.

HISTORICAL CONTEXT

Exploring the historical context of the curriculum can help illuminate some of the origins of the strains and frictions in current education (Bartlett et al., 2001). It is perhaps surprising that the curriculum has existed since early history 'more or less in its current form, as a product mainly of habit and tradition' (Thomas, 2013: 93). Starting in the 6th century BCE, Confucius, the Chinese philosopher, thought that pupils should learn manners. Ancient Greeks developed a more expansive curriculum, which included arithmetic, geometry, astrology, rhetoric and music. However, education was very intensive, disciplined and physically brutal. In Plato's *Republic*, he wrote about creating what he considered was needed for a model state and stressed the importance of education in such a concept. In the *Republic*, Plato called for a more balanced approach to the curriculum, which argued for a less brutal, intensive and didactic approach to learning that was more relaxed and even learner-centred – an approach that is mirrored by many contemporary progressive educators and curriculum scholars (Thomas, 2013).

The Roman curriculum pursued a similar path in form and content as the Greek model, and both were particularly keen on rhetoric. Roman education prepared boys for high public office. First they attended schools that focused on the teaching of grammar, then they progressed to rhetoric schools, which concentrated on preparing them for public speaking. The medieval period in Europe is broadly considered to have been between the first century CE after the fall of the Roman Empire until the fourteenth century. The medieval curriculum was first developed by Alcuin of York on the order of Charlemagne, King of the Franks. Alcuin of York initially created the *trivium* – grammar, logic and rhetoric – then the *quadrivium* – arithmetic, astronomy, geometry and music (Thomas, 2013). It is interesting and pertinent, regarding the aim of this volume, that Bernstein (2000) aligns the subjects included in both the *trivium* and *quadrivium* with the term 'official knowledge' and social control, which we shall be considering in further detail. It is noted that the *trivium* was studied first, then the *quadrivium*. Furthermore, Bernstein suggests that there is a division between the 'trivium as the exploration of the word and the quadrivium as the exploration of the world; word and world held together by the unity of Christianity' (2000: 120). However, this unity, and the domination of religion in matters of knowledge and education, became a source of tension as medieval scholars gained an increasing understanding of science. This was especially the case as a growing number of Greek and Roman philosophical and scientific writings became translated and accessible.

Jarman (1963) described the European Renaissance period, which lasted approximately between the fourteenth and seventeenth centuries, as the start of modern education. It was a time of enthusiastic European cultural, literary and political resurgence, and the wider discovery of classical philosophy, literature, art and science. The invention of the printing press in the fifteenth century made literacy accessible for many more people. Moreover, Thomas (2013) stays with Shakespeare to make some broad and pertinent comparisons with the current curriculum and education in general. Students were taught in large classrooms, each of which were separated into age groups, and the curriculum content was decided by what adults thought was important. Learning was to become resolutely subject-centred and not child-centred. The Renaissance was also where a new stimulus was given to contemporary thinkers of the time who added further to the knowledge of the time relating to mathematics and science, and to the rebirth of classical literature.

The European Enlightenment period started in the late seventeenth century and finished early in the nineteenth century. It was a period when authority was challenged, and in particular the authority of God, regarding the certainty of knowledge. Thomas (2013) argues that the Enlightenment was the beginning of the empiricist philosophers who were courageous enough to propose that valid knowledge could only be gained through actual experience and experiments (Thomas, 2013). Many of these philosophers' published works had an influence on education and the curriculum, and their ideas were the focus for many educational thinkers who followed. These include Johann Pestalozzi, a disciple of Rousseau, and Friedrich Froebel. However, the work of John Locke and Jean-Jacques Rousseau are noteworthy in this historical synopsis because they have become very influential in shaping the thoughts of others (Raftery, 2012). Locke argued that when children started life, their minds were a blank slate and all new learning and experience had to be established. He therefore advocated individual instruction and the use of rewards and punishments. Conversely, Rousseau considered that children were born with ability and flair, and with a natural awareness of what is right and wrong. These two contrasting ideas are still talked about and even practised in classrooms (Bartlett et al., 2001).

In Britain and other developed nations, the nineteenth-century systems of education progressed in line with the changes occurring in society, particularly due to the massive increase of industrialisation. This intensification of industry and the inherent commerce required a workforce that was both literate and numerate. Britain's world economic standing started to be tested by other industrialised nations such as the USA, France and Germany. Furthermore, in 1867 most British working-class men were given the right to vote and education became important to facilitate their understanding of the issues they would be voting for (Bartlett and Burton, 2020). The Elementary Education Act of 1870, or Forster's Act, made it mandatory for all children in England and Wales between the ages of 5 to 10 to attend school. Before this, only approximately half of the population attended school. But, as we have already seen, the stimulus for giving greater access to education for many more children came not from 'the feeling that the populace needed to have its mind opened ... [or] ... from the love of learning. Rather, the stimulus came from the worry about the nation losing its competitive edge' (Thomas, 2013: 13). The 1870 Education Reform Act contained provision for a curriculum that focused on reading, writing and arithmetic. It did not make attendance compulsory at first, and children still had to pay a small fee to attend. The school leaving age was raised to 12 in 1899. The advent of this state education (just elementary education at this stage), accompanied with the view of school as a major institution, was an enormous shift in social order. The Act was originally intended to generate future citizens who were 'basically literate ... trained how to behave and had learned some rudimentary facts about the world' (Bartlett and Burton, 2020: 82). There were many changes to the curriculum and to education in Britain, particularly during and after the First World War. However, the major changes to the curriculum came about during and after the Second World War, which will be explored in the next chapter.

KNOWLEDGE, POWER AND THE CURRICULUM

Human knowledge plays a significant role not only in understanding, but more importantly, in critically analysing the relationship between power and the curriculum with regard to pedagogy, content and assessment. Kelly (2009) contends that in England and Wales, the designers of the national curriculum simply presupposed that when planning the curriculum all that was needed was to 'outline the knowledge content to be "delivered" and imbibed' (p. 20). Yet, to gain a greater understanding of how curricula are created, and for what purpose, we need to explore the nature of human knowledge to challenge and seek alternative democratic ideas that enable learners to thrive in such uncertain times. Similar to the creators of the national curriculum mentioned above, perhaps many students, no matter which curriculum they are following, consider that knowledge for their particular programme is just taken as a set reality and accept it without challenge. However, knowledge is a complex phenomenon as it has a much more nuanced meaning depending on a number of different viewpoints, including ideological, religious, cultural, class, as well as personal experience.

Human knowledge is socially constructed and is better comprehended and evaluated through a sociological lens relating to the circumstances in which the knowledge is created (Kelly, 2009). The understanding and evaluation of knowledge is the focus of **epistemology** (the theory of knowledge). Epistemology is concerned with what is, or is not, valid as knowledge; it also differentiates between knowledge that is considered as 'implicit or explicit; practical or theoretical; of things or of people; and of skills or of facts' (Wallace, 2008: 94). Furthermore, it takes into account how we understand reality and what shapes our perspectives of knowledge (Ritchie et al., 2014). Epistemology during the Enlightenment and modern era can be illustrated by the advancement of scientific knowledge. René Descartes (1596–1650) is often alluded to as the first scholar to challenge the relationship between knowledge and consciousness, and for Descartes it is self-consciousness that assures knowledge. Conversely, Immanuel Kant (1724–1804), intrigued by the thinking of the time that knowledge could not be assured or certain, challenged the explanation of knowledge offered by Descartes and others. Kant's rational approach to knowledge became entrenched in Western thought. Rationalism came to underpin the thinking of those who followed, such as Darwin who discovered, through his law of natural selection, the evolution of the species (Bartlett and Burton, 2020).

A rational approach to knowledge acquisition appears logical and straightforward because it draws upon knowledge that has been known and established by others. However, using such existing knowledge should inspire us to query the authority and power that underpins the knowledge acquisition process. Although children, from an early age, are urged to discover for themselves as part of the learning process, some knowledge and skills cannot be acquired by discovery alone, such as reading, which must first be acquired from a pre-existing authority. Apart from the use of such pre-existing knowledge, Bartlett and Burton (2020) outline the intricacies involved in knowledge acquisition:

> Our knowledge of the world is a product of a complex network of factors: family background, formative experience, cultural identity, social class, gender and language are all contributory to our sense of who we are but also our sense of what the world is like and what constitutes significant knowledge. Different ways of life and belief systems will inevitably produce different knowledge and different orientations towards it.

(p. 110)

Knowledge, then, is shaped by many diverse elements rather than by a series of facts and statistics. Even so, knowledge included in many curricula, and in particular the national curriculum in England, pays little attention to the diversity of knowledge explored above. Essentially, it is argued that knowledge included in the curriculum is at odds with the reality of the current diverse social context; instead, curriculum knowledge has become official knowledge.

The role of official knowledge in the curriculum and in education generally has been examined by a number of educational thinkers such as Basil Bernstein, Pierre Bourdieu and Michael Apple. The concept of official knowledge has a number of aspects, none of which can be understood in isolation from the political perspective (Craske, 2021). Knowledge has become a commodity, packaged together in a curriculum and supported by the accompanying textbooks, which has been created and promoted by the dominant culture of society. Bernstein (2006) argues that knowledge has drifted away from its human-centred origins and has transformed into official knowledge. It has become a market-driven product where knowledge flows 'like money to wherever it can create advantage and profit. Indeed knowledge is not like, it *is* money. Knowledge is divorced from persons, their commitments, their personal dedications' (Bernstein, 2006: 122). Bourdieu, who, like Bernstein, had a particular interest in sociolinguistics, thought that knowledge was formed from habitus – knowledge acquired from personal experience and the environment in which children grow up. Families who pass on their cultural capital to their children, such as visits to the theatre and discussions around current affairs and literature, give them an advantage in the education system. Bourdieu believed that the more cultural capital people accrue, the more powerful they become (Aubrey and Riley, 2021). Apple, an American progressive educational thinker and prominent critical theorist on the curriculum, also considered that the language used in the curriculum and textbooks reflected the dominant culture, particularly from a New Right ideological perspective. Moreover, for Apple, official knowledge reinforces inequality and the subsequent endorsement of marketisation has led to education values being conceded to commercial priorities (Apple and Oliver, 1998).

To recognise how official knowledge can have an impact upon inequality in society, we need first to return briefly to the concept of cultural capital. Bourdieu and Passeron (1990) argue that the reproduction of cultural principles and behaviours of the dominant social class groups advantage middle-class students over those from the working-class. Children from middle-class families, even before they start their compulsory schooling, are familiar with the accepted values, behaviours and systems of schooling; on the other hand, many working-class students are unlikely to be similarly aware (Bartlett and Burton, 2020). Such reproduction of cultural capital further promotes the proliferation of the inequities for certain sectors of society. Gewirtz and Cribb (2009) summarise Apple's viewpoint regarding this ideologically driven and covert process:

> School knowledge is taken to be an ideological production which contributes to the reproduction of inequalities in society (around the social axes of class, race and gender) whilst simultaneously concealing its own role in processes of social reproduction by masquerading as neutral and universal.
>
> (p. 114)

Apple (1979) argues that schools sustain such inequity by implicitly structuring learning into different types of knowledge evident in the curriculum. In doing so, schools are creating an assembly line of 'technical cultural "commodities" and to the sorting or selecting function of schools in allocating people to the positions "required" by the economic sector of society' (p. 43).

The powerful impact that knowledge in the curriculum can have in sustaining the motives of the dominant culture at the expense of others is very apparent. Yet, Apple argues that considerable progress has been made in education regarding the origin of knowledge by 'transformation of the question of "What knowledge is of most worth?" into "Whose knowledge is of most worth?"' (2020: 14). The transposition of the question enables educators, to a limited degree, to confront existing inequities and to seek a fairer alternative. However, Apple maintains it is educational establishments, driven by increasingly controlling government policies, that advocate dominant culture ideology through what he calls the 'selective tradition: ... that is always passed off as "the tradition," *the* significant past' (1979: 6). What is termed 'the tradition' is often used to promote, but not dispute, the dominant cultural and political discourse. This is evident in the United States schools where:

> knowledge and ways of seeing the world of dominant white (male) elites in U.S. society are validated by being included in the school curriculum, and students study the lives of presidents and generals, but not the working class, blacks, or women.
>
> (Anyon, 2011: 34)

It is not just USA schools that sustain the dominant cultural and political ideology. It is an increasing phenomenon in neoconservative countries, especially those with governments that could be considered to have populist inclinations. For example, in the UK, the Department for Education (DfE) has sought to control the content of the curriculum in attempting to ban what they consider as anti-capitalist content, as well as promoting the imperial aspects of British history. Moncrieffe and Harris (2020) argue that the inclusion of Black history in the national curriculum 'is not … to "rewrite history" – rather, it is to recognise that certain forms of historical experience have been conspicuously absent from the curriculum' (p. 15). It is contended that these politically driven motives of what is, and what is not regarded as knowledge and subsequently included in the curriculum are a warning of the powerful authority that can advantage those of influence, yet be detrimental to others in society.

Apple is a renowned critical curriculum scholar, particularly with regard to the relationship between authority in the form of the dominant culture and the power it can wield. There are, however, two other earlier contemporary thinkers who deserve a mention at this stage while considering the links between knowledge, power and the curriculum. They are the Italian Marxist Antonio Gramsci (1891–1937) and the French philosopher Michel Foucault (1926–1984). In Italy during the 1920s, Mussolini carried out a radical review of the curriculum with the view of controlling knowledge. This action was challenged by Gramsci, who considered that 'the control of the knowledge preserving and producing sectors of a society is a critical factor in enhancing the ideological dominance of one group of people or one class over less powerful groups or classes' (Apple, 1979: 57).

Gramsci's idea of hegemony is a discreet method of power where the dominant leaders of a self-assured society gain the approval 'of the governed to their own domination' (Apple, 2020: 41). The powerful nature of this idea with regard to promoting and sustaining a ruling social dominant class is emphasised by Gramsci as a warning, since it would result in 'each social group … [having] … its own type of school, intended to perpetuate a specific traditional function, ruling or subordinate' (Gramsci, 1971: 40).

Gramsci's ideas on the relationship between power and knowledge are in many ways shared by Foucault. They both thought that state institutions, in an effort to gain popular approval of their authority, used covert methods to conceal their status of dominance (Barry, 2002). Foucault's book, *Discipline and Punish: The Birth of the Prison* (1979), is of particular interest to education and is closely associated with the relationship between power and knowledge. Foucault contends that meanings, which he called 'discourses', are aligned with power and deeply rooted in dominant social and political establishments. These discourses vary in the type of language used to reflect the values and principles of discrete organisations and professions. As such, discourses can have the power to exclude those from outside their own groups. Discourses are frequently linked with powerful and prominent professions such as law and medicine, where the language used is often inaccessible to an outsider. In relation to education, the style of discourse used in the language of matters of the curriculum, assessment and standards also has the power to exclude (Oliver, 2010). This persuasive nature of discourse, warned Foucault, was in danger of creating a disciplined society that could be controlled. Foucault argued that the human body was being entrapped in a process of the

> 'mechanics of power' ... [which] defined how one may have hold over other bodies, not only so they may do what one wishes, so they may operate as one wishes, with techniques, the speed and the efficiency that one determines. Thus discipline produces subjected and practiced bodies, 'docile' bodies.
>
> (1979: 138)

However, Kelly (2009) argues that education in an open society must be based on a free and democratic view of knowledge. With this in mind, the idea of creating docile bodies being controlled in such a way as Foucault articulates provides the reader with ample points to consider when exploring the theoretical curriculum models and other related concepts of the curriculum.

Following what we have explored about knowledge, power and the curriculum, to give a rational context of the main contrasting theoretical curriculum models, it is now fitting to briefly consider the powerful agencies that create the curriculum. The control of education, particularly the curriculum, is in effect a mix of influences from political ideological viewpoints to matters of operational delivery of the curriculum itself. Bartlett and Burton list a number of stakeholders who have differing degrees of influence in how the curriculum develops in the official and taught curriculum in English schools:

- Civil servants drew up and politicians voted upon the legal framework of the curriculum and this remains at the centre of political debate and policy.
- Ofsted inspectors influence how the curriculum is taught because inspection grades affect public league table positions, which in turn impact on parents' choice of school.
- Employers are involved with schools through governance, attendance agreements, work placements and so on, passing opinions on to head teachers, governors, and local and national politicians.
- Local authorities (previously local education authorities) support schools in their authority, offering professional development courses for teachers and other school personnel as well as support services for pupils with a range of needs.
- Parents have a vested interest in the school and the quality of the learning experiences for their children.
- Teachers deliver the curriculum and pupils will respond to this in different ways.

(2020: 109)

Moreover, for Brighouse and Waters (2021), there is a duality to the curriculum as it both influences, as well as is influenced, through 'factors such as pedagogy, leadership, qualifications, testing, parental engagement and pupil disposition to learning' (p. 174).

CURRICULUM MODELS

There are a number of curriculum models to analyse. Although there are many blurred boundaries, each model can be aligned to a certain extent to notions of either the traditionalist or with the progressive educational thinkers. To gain a better overview of the curriculum, and before we delve into the curriculum models and other associated concepts, it is pertinent to look briefly at the meaning of education and how it differs from other often used pedological words. Kelly (2009) invites us

> To see 'education' as a concept which is distinguishable from the other kinds of teaching such as 'training', 'instruction', 'conditioning', 'indoctrination' and so on, one of the features which must distinguish it from these other teaching activities is that it must be focused on intrinsic value, it must be an activity we engage in for its own sake rather than as instrumental to some extrinsic purpose or purposes. This is an important distinction and one which has been largely lost in current policies and practices.
>
> (pp. 57–8)

Kelly's plea that education should be of intrinsic value and be distinguishable from various teaching methods is very much aligned with the idea that education and the curriculum are a force for democracy and social justice.

This section will first consider the facets of the objectives (or product) and the process curriculum models before briefly exploring other curricula such as the collection, integrated and praxis models. It will also look at some of the terms employed in the discourse surrounding matters of the curriculum. Where fitting, concerns for social justice will be raised.

OBJECTIVES CURRICULUM MODEL

The objectives curriculum model is the most common type used in education and is evident in the English national curriculum. It is very prescribed in its framework and the content is usually subdivided into subject-specific areas. The focus is centred on lists of learning objectives, or learning outcomes, that students are required to achieve. Overall, the model is mainly about the training of skills and behaviours along with the assessment of the curriculum learning objectives. The model tends to be somewhat instrumental in nature in that it also informs what teaching methods should be used to enable students to achieve the learning outcomes, in doing so limiting the scope that teachers have in reflecting on practice and making up their own minds about their preferred learning and teaching strategies (Aubrey and Riley, 2021). The objectives model was promoted to a varying degree by two curriculum scholars – W. James Popham and Ralph Tyler. Popham advanced the technicist notion that the specification of behavioural objectives should be core to the curriculum. He further argued that objectives should be differentiated in line with the modes of behaviours they were planned to encourage. As such, Popham promoted the use of Bloom's taxonomy of educational objectives. Although Tyler also argued for using objectives as a rational way of defining learning experiences, he did not advocate that the objectives should be too detailed as he thought that would limit the teachers' flexibility (Scott, 2008).

This model focuses predominantly on targets (or objectives) and is the cornerstone of the national curriculum in England, which is similar to the curriculum in many other countries. The curriculum structure with regard to subject content in secondary schools narrowly follows that which is used in academic fields in higher education. On the other hand, the subject structure in primary schools is more aligned to a cross-curricula approach with topics covering arithmetic, reading and language. When people ask about a school's curriculum, they are invariably asking for a breakdown of the subjects taught (Connelly and Xu, 2012). As will be evident in the next section on the process model, there is considerable criticism in a subject-specific focus to the curriculum.

The objectives model advanced by Popham can be perceived as an efficient model for curriculum designers, which would also make teaching straightforward for teachers. Broad aims are decided first and these are divided into more specific objectives from which the curriculum is created so the objectives can be achieved. Then the curriculum is evaluated in practice to enhance the process of learners achieving the objectives through repeated testing. The objectives model has quite an enduring history, which includes the 'experience gained in training personnel such as radar operators and gunners during the Second World War and on a long-established objective testing of student attainment' (Stenhouse, 1975: 50). Objectives then form a coherent and collective focus for teaching and specifically for testing. As mentioned, Popham had endorsed the use of Bloom's taxonomy as a source of forming the objectives to change the behaviour of learners. Over time, Bloom developed three domains of learning objectives which he considered would help students develop over a range of fields of study. The three domains were cognitive, affective and psychomotor; each of these contained hierarchical level objectives from simple to more complex for students to attain (Huddleston and Unwin, 2002).

Kelly (2009) posits that the objectives model continues to be an appealing option for many curriculum planners. However, he also offers some quite critical points about the model such as a passive view of learning; the difficulty in approaching controversial issues; questioning the appropriateness with special needs learners; view of learning as a linear process; the loss of freedom for teachers and learners; inadequate conception of education; and instrumentation (Kelly, 2009: 71–83). These criticisms centre on the matter of education being a complex and multifaceted endeavour. To a great extent, this model is contrasted by the process curriculum model, promoted by Lawrence Stenhouse, which we will now consider.

PROCESS CURRICULUM MODEL

The process curriculum model was advocated by Lawrence Stenhouse as an alternative to the objectives model, which he considered 'uneducational as it assumed knowledge as a given and discouraged wider questioning' (Burton and Bartlett, 2005: 35). Overall, the process model centres on the learning experience as well as the parts played by teachers, students and the classroom environment, instead of relying on proscribed learning outcomes. The teacher's role is to encourage personal development and embrace student contributions and enquiry rather than passively accepting given knowledge. Students and teachers work together in a manner that enables them to seek further learning prospects. Stenhouse argues that the model fosters student empowerment and emancipation, while also allowing teachers to develop professionally through research and evaluation into their own practice (Aubrey and Riley, 2021). To get a sense of the process model, we return to the very start of this chapter which gave a couple of definitions of the curriculum, in the first of which Stenhouse defines his idea of the curriculum as

> an attempt to communicate the essential principles and features of an educational proposal in such a form that it is open to critical scrutiny and capable of effective translation into practice.
>
> (Stenhouse, 1975: 4)

Therefore, for Stenhouse the curriculum is focused on an active 'learning experience which is open to criticism and ongoing evaluation – a process curriculum model' (Aubrey and Riley, 2021: 185). Despite Stenhouse's enthusiasm for the model, particularly in comparison with the objectives model, he cautions readers about the possible problems of using the process model because it

> rests on teacher judgement rather than on teacher direction. It is far more demanding on teachers and thus far more difficult to implement in practice, but it offers a higher degree of personal and professional development. In particular circumstances it may well prove too demanding.
>
> (Stenhouse, 1975: 96–7)

Stenhouse's caution is understandable because the fundamental practice underpinning the process model is enquiry-based pedagogy where the teacher becomes the 'neutral chair' rather than the 'teacher as expert ... placing them as equals within the arena of debate' (Schostak and Schostak, 2008: 131). This is quite a demanding prospect, yet Whitty (1985) argues that it could attract teachers 'who see their work in education as contributing to a quest for greater democracy and social justice in society' (p. 57).

Stenhouse's notion of the process model attracted a positive response from many educators in the 1960s and early 1970s, at a time of progressive thinking about the curriculum and education in general in the UK. It was the 'golden age' of education, a period that 'was open for experiment and change, and the influence of the so-called "Great Educators" and of "progressivism" generally began to be felt' (Kelly, 2009: 191). The golden age culminated, and arguably exemplified it, with the publication of the Plowden Report (1967). Around the same time as the Plowden Report, the curriculum for initial teacher education was underpinned by the 'foundation disciplines – the psychology, sociology, philosophy and history of education'; these combined disciplines became 'education theory' (Thomas, 2007: 5). It is of note that although the golden age did not bring about many ground-breaking positive changes, nevertheless changes for the better did occur, and 'unlike today, were motivated by a genuine desire to improve the quality of the educational experiences ... rather than by a concern merely to win the approval of the electorate' (Kelly, 2009: 192).

The process model, then, is a curriculum that promotes the development of both student and teacher. It gives the teacher the freedom to develop their professional practice through research and evaluation. Stenhouse believed that teachers would make model researchers because they were continually striving to improve their teaching through reflection. As such, Stenhouse promoted action research as the preferred method to be used in classrooms; in so doing, teachers become 'reflective practitioners employing and developing their own "tacit theories", "personal theories" or "theories-in-use"' (Thomas, 2007: 5). Stenhouse thought that the role of the teacher as a researcher would establish or re-establish teacher professionalism. He was critical of the perceived demise of teacher professionalism brought about in the form of the teacher proof which is presented in the objectives model (Aubrey and Riley, 2021).

The process model, similar to the objectives model, has also drawn a number of critical commentaries. Some of the criticisms levied against the process model have been acknowledged by Stenhouse, such as the problems with assessment and its use in preparing students for success in examinations. Another issue is that the model relies very heavily on the demands of the teacher, which, as we have seen, he also recognised. If teachers lack the open responsive skills required for classroom discussions in their role as 'senior learner' rather than the expert, they will have deficient resources and direction available to them than they would have with the prescribed objectives model (Smith, 2000). Stenhouse's promotion of the teacher as researcher is probably not a realistic option for many teachers with the increasing demands on their time.

This is especially when they attempt to balance the demands of the national curriculum, Ofsted and assessment with the time to produce acceptable research methodology which will pass the expected scrutiny. Kemmis also argues that Stenhouse was not altogether clear whether their research was 'to contribute to public knowledge by writing about their work or whether it was enough that they deepen their own understanding' (1995: 4). Nevertheless, the process model is seen by many as a beacon for learner and teacher, and empowerment, and its ethos is associated with other progressive curriculum concepts discussed below.

COLLECTION AND INTEGRATED MODELS OF CURRICULUM

The collection and integrated models of curriculum were the creation of Basil Bernstein and detailed in his 1996 work *Pedagogy, Symbolic Control and Identity: Theory, Research and Critique*. He was a distinguished British social theorist in the field of the sociology of education; he died in 2000 and his work is of great substance and significance. There are interesting similarities and contrasts between the two models advocated by Bernstein, and with the process and content models considered earlier. For example, Bernstein's collection model is the most predominant curriculum model globally and is focused on behavioural objectives. Conversely, with the integrated model, learners have a degree of influence regarding the content and rate of curriculum progress (Scott, 2008). His ideas have particular cognisance with the socially just and democratic ways of thinking about and practising education. Although the scope of Bernstein's work was wide ranging, he mainly concentrated on three areas: language and social class, the development of knowledge, and the curriculum.

What was also important for Bernstein was the relationship between education and democracy, which is very evident throughout his work. In his last key work, *Pedagogy, Symbolic Control, and Identity: Theory, Research, and Critique*, he clarifies his rationale for the importance of the relationship:

> Education is central to the knowledge base of society, groups and individuals. Yet education also, like health, is a public institution, central to the production and reproduction of distributive injustices. Biases in the form, content, access and opportunities of education have consequences not only for the economy; these biases can reach down to drain the very springs of affirmation, motivation and imagination.

> (Bernstein, 2000: xix)

Bernstein (1971) deemed that the key principles that shape the curriculum vary depending on the social beliefs that control what he called the classification and framing of knowledge offered by educational establishments. Classification and framing are two significant terms that underpin his ideas on the curriculum, particularly his thoughts on the collection and integrated models of curriculum. Classification describes the boundaries between the curriculum models. A strong classification indicates a curriculum which is clearly separated into a collection of traditional academic subject knowledge. Conversely, a weak classification indicates an integrated curriculum with very loose boundaries between subject domains. The term 'framing' is concerned with the transmission of what matters in educational knowledge through pedagogical practice. Framing, then, is about the range of control that both teachers and learners have regarding the selection and organisation of knowledge and the tempo of learning and teaching that takes place. A strong framing limits the control and choices available to teachers and students. On the other hand, a weak framing means more choice for teachers and students regarding the content, options for flexibility and the tempo of learning (Goodson, 2001; Scott, 2008). Bernstein contended that the stronger the classification and the framing, the more the relationship between the teacher and student had a predisposition to shift to a more hierarchical and traditional stance; the student then becomes an ill-informed passive recipient of knowledge with little status or rights (Gewirtz and Cribb, 2009).

Using classification and framing as a conceptual framework, we can now see how they relate to Bernstein's two models of curriculum. The collection model is strongly classified and has clearly defined subject boundaries. Students are expected to meet certain programme entry requirements and select their modules of study. In the collection model, the framing is also strong, students have scant choice in the what and how are being taught or in the tempo of the learning process. On the contrary, the integrated curriculum model subjects and the content are interrelated, and the borders between subjects are weak (Atkinson, 1985). The integrated curriculum is closely associated with cross-curricula practice used in primary schools in England, where 'teachers have sought to establish their claims to expertise around notions of pedagogy, such as child-centred enquiry' (Robertson, 2000). The framing in primary schools is to a degree also weak, yet this is increasingly being strengthened by the limitations of the national curriculum and by Ofsted. The collection model is a traditional approach and is mainly evident in secondary education.

PRAXIS CURRICULUM MODEL

The central concept of the praxis curriculum model is the idea of social transformation and the link between theory and practice. Advocacy for the praxis model came from the supporters of critical pedagogy educators, mainly from America, such as Michael Apple, Ivan Illich, Paulo Freire and Peter McLaren, but arguably the main promoter of the model is Henry Giroux, one of the most notable radical educational thinkers of current times. For Giroux and his fellow critical educators, education is the practice of democracy which endeavours to empower and give voice to all members of society. This view of education as a practice of democracy is part of an American progressive legacy 'stretching back to Dewey, which saw education as a mechanism by which the composition of society could be continually re-structured and reconstituted' (Howlett, 2013: 266). Morrison emphasises Giroux's ideas and the purpose of schools in that they should be:

> Sites of cultural production and transformation rather than reproduction; they should be sites of empowerment and emancipation of individuals and groups within a just society, enabling individual and collective autonomy to be promoted in participatory democracies that embrace a diversity and plurality of cultures and social groups. This is a view of democracy as a celebration of difference and diversity rather than as serving the agenda of an elite, powerful minority or ideology.
>
> (Morrison, 2001: 280)

The concept of praxis comes from Freire who gave the term 'prominence' as 'action and reflection upon the world in order to change it' (hooks, 1994: 14). Unlike Stenhouse's product model and Bernstein's collection model, the praxis model is certainly not prescribed in any way, or indeed driven by behavioural objectives, or focused on the notion of the passive transmission of knowledge – quite the opposite. From what we have already discovered about different curriculum models, the praxis model can be perceived, to some extent, as aligned to Bernstein's integrated model, particularly regarding its connections with inequalities with social class and inclusion. However, it is argued that it is more of an extension of Stenhouse's process model. Curtis and Pettigrew explain the critical, democratic and hopeful nature of the model:

> The praxis model conceives of knowledge as tentative and open to critique: often challenging taken-for-granted knowledge as the voice of the powerful and the source of oppression. According to this model, a curriculum is only worthwhile in as much as it has direct relevance to the real lives and experiences of learners. The aim of the praxis model is to raise critical consciousness: the cultivation of informed and committed action as a foundation for hope in the future.
>
> (2010: 38)

Giroux (1998), when writing about the role of university teachers, stressed the importance of teachers offering students opportunities to learn about how the relationship involving both knowledge and power can lead to emancipation. He further argued that students' past experiences are important in the overall effort to challenge the current controlling privileges in order to re-create their interactions and transform, where possible, their world (Giroux, 1998: 49). Accordingly, the curriculum (the praxis curriculum) should be:

Organized around knowledge that related to the communities, cultures, and traditions of students, which in turn provide them opportunities to negotiate a critical sense of history, identity, and place.

(Giroux, 1998: 49)

Teachers require radical teaching methods that promote positive and trusting teacher–student relationships, so discussions, negotiations, self-reflection and challenge can be embraced by all who are involved (Giroux, 2011). It is intriguing to note that when we consider the qualities required of Giroux's transformational intellectuals, such as reflection and challenge, they are similar to Stenhouse's notion of the teacher as researcher (Goodson, 2005). Giroux's idea of teachers as transformative intellectuals is a powerful prospect of their democratic role in classrooms and beyond. Yet he railed against the increasing business modes of management, punitive restrictions and commercial processes that teachers were exposed to where they:

are reduced to a subaltern class of technicians; and students are positioned as mere recipients of the worst forms of banking education and, in the case of students marginalized by race and class, treated as disposable populations deserving of harsh punishments and disciplinary measures modelled after prisons.

(Giroux, 2011: 12)

Giroux contended that this prevailing dominance of powerful corporate thinking and processes towards the school curriculum damaged the democratic aspirations of a wide spectrum of students. He relates this to his notion of the '**hidden curriculum**', a term we have previously briefly considered, as a way that authority implicitly implants its own beliefs and values to ensure orderly and structured school routines and processes. As such, the hidden curriculum in school is a form of social control that prepares students for their working lives where corporate firms and institutions use comparable processes and means for financial gain (Bartlett and Burton, 2020). Furthermore, he argues that the hidden curriculum is an interposition to advance 'social control, one that functions to provide differential forms of schooling for different classes of children' (Giroux, 1983: 47). For some, the hidden curriculum may have positive outcomes in preparing students for adult life. Giroux, however, considered that the hidden curriculum rewarded passivity and compliance, rather than striving for social transformation (Anyon, 2011).

Unlike the more structured product and collection models, the praxis model is somewhat abstract in nature and has attracted criticism accordingly. It has been censured for being too idealistic and lacking on explaining the effects on teaching practice (Morrison, 2001). As well as being difficult to teach, it risks exposing learners to a limited and excessively critical view of the world (Curtis and Pettigrew, 2010). Although Giroux has passionately promoted the praxis curriculum and emphasised its use into concrete classroom action, there is little evidence of any Western government endorsing the curriculum model as a framework for learning and teaching. Furthermore, Giroux did not specify how the model, and indeed critical pedagogy, would help learners gain the transferable skills needed for employment (Howlett, 2013). Regardless of the criticisms, it will be useful to compare and contrast all these models with the different UK and comparative curricula considered in the next section.

SUMMARY

The curriculum has existed since early history, starting with the Chinese philosopher Confucius in the sixth century BCE, followed by the Greeks and Romans. In medieval Europe, the curriculum was at first dominated by Christianity, before the Greek and Roman philosophical and scientific writings were discovered. During the European Renaissance period, the curriculum was mainly subject-centred, but the scholars became bold enough to seek new knowledge through experience and experiment, and many of these had, and still have, an influence on education in general. In nineteenth-century Britain and in other developed nations, education progressed in line with changes to society and increasing industrialisation. Britain realised the importance of education for economic growth and the 1870 Elementary Education Reform was the beginning of compulsory education in England and Wales. Although there were subsequent changes in the British curriculum, major change did not occur until after the Second World War.

Human knowledge plays an important part in understanding and analysing the association between power and the curriculum. Understanding and evaluating knowledge is the function of epistemology, or the theory of knowledge, which explores what is valid or not valid, taking into account these diverse perspectives. It is argued that the knowledge included in many curricula pays inadequate attention to these different perspectives, nor do they reflect the reality of the diversity of society; rather, the curriculum knowledge has become official knowledge. For Craske (2021), official knowledge is closely linked with political ideology because knowledge has developed into a commodity and packaged into a curriculum, which is reinforced by textbooks created and advanced by the dominant culture in society.

There are a number of theoretical curriculum models that have been developed and critically evaluated by curriculum scholars from both traditional and progressive standpoints. The objectives (or product model) is the most common model and is evident in the English national curriculum. It is focused on learning objectives, and mostly about the training of skills and behaviours, along with assessment of the pre-set learning objectives. The model has attracted considerable criticism which centres on passive learning and its instrumental approach. The process curriculum model was advocated by Stenhouse as an alternative to the objectives model, focusing on the learning experience, and the parts played by teachers and students; it also fosters student empowerment and emancipation, and professional teacher development.

Bernstein identified two contrasting curriculum models. The collection model is very similar to the objectives model. He argued that this model is strongly classified and separated into different subjects. There is also, what he termed, a strong framing where teachers and learners have little choice in what is taught and at what speed. On the other hand, Bernstein's integrated model is weakly classified with fewer divisions between subjects, and the framing is also weak with more teacher and student choice of what is taught and at what speed. Henry Giroux's praxis curriculum was a development of Stenhouse's process model. At its core, the praxis model is about social transformation, and acknowledges that human knowledge is conditional and should be open to critical commentary.

GLOSSARY OF TERMS

Collection and integrated models of curriculum

Bernstein outlined two types of curriculum which are aligned with classification and framing. First, the collection type of curriculum is strongly classified and has defined and separated subjects. There is also a strong framing with the collection curriculum, teachers and students have few options in the manner and the rate at which knowledge is taught. Second, the integrated curriculum is less defined and has less prescribed separation between subjects and is similar to the cross-curriculum model evident in English primary schools. Framing in the integrated curriculum is relatively weak.

Epistemology

The study of and the understanding of knowledge, epistemology 'addresses the issue of what counts as knowledge ... [and draws] ... distinctions between knowledge understood as being, for instance, implicit or explicit; practical or theoretical; of things or of people; and of skills or of facts' (Wallace, 2008: 94).

Hidden curriculum

The hidden curriculum implicitly embeds sets of values and beliefs by way of ordered and structural school procedures and routines. The implicit outcomes may be positive through students gaining social attributes from teachers. Conversely, the hidden curriculum could also be seen as an imposition to advance 'social control, one that functions to provide differential forms of schooling for different classes of children' (Giroux, 1983: 47).

Objectives (or product) curriculum model

Contrary to the process curriculum model, the objectives curriculum model is generally more prescribed in its formation and content. Its use is widespread in education and relates mainly to subject-specific curricula; it is also centred on the prescribed lists of learning outcomes that students must submissively achieve. It concentrates mainly on the training of skills and in modifying behaviours; it also focuses on assessment and the testing of learners' achievement. This model is mainly involved with specific and set instructional methods instead of giving teachers the freedom to make their own decisions about learning and teaching approaches.

Official knowledge

Knowledge that is constructed by those responsible for creating education policy which seeks to replicate the status quo in society to the detriment of those people not of the dominant culture and social class. It is endorsed and legitimised in the school curriculum and in school textbooks. Official knowledge stresses the requirement of competence and, as such, places education as a prerequisite of the industry and business sectors.

Praxis curriculum model

The praxis curriculum model is an extension of Stenhouse's process curriculum model. Giroux, like other critical pedagogy thinkers, advanced the praxis curriculum model, which has at its core the idea of social transformation and the link between practice and theory. It recognises knowledge as provisional and accessible to criticism; it challenges traditional notions about knowledge, as well as the view of authority and oppression.

Process curriculum model

Stenhouse argued that the process curriculum model nurtured student empowerment and emancipation; it also gave teachers the freedom to develop their professional practice by way of research and evaluation. It focuses on the learning experience, and the roles and activities of both the student and the teacher, as well as the classroom environment. The teacher welcomes active student enquiry rather than students passively accepting given knowledge. It supports teachers and learners to work in accord and to allow students to access further opportunities. However, Stenhouse emphasises that the model is more challenging than the objectives curriculum model in practice.

Spiral curriculum

A concept where students are introduced to topics and then revisit these later to bolster their knowledge and understanding. Every time the topic is revisited, students enhance their depth of understanding and their confidence in applying that knowledge.

FURTHER READING

Apple, M., Ball, S. and Gandin, L-A. (eds) (2010) *The Routledge International Handbook for the Sociology of Education.* Abingdon: Routledge.

A thorough collection of essays from progressive educationalists with a variety of issues related to the curriculum, theory and practice, as well as the struggles over oppression and social justice.

Brown, A. and Wisby, E. (eds) (2020) *Knowledge, Policy and Practice in Education and the Struggle for Social Justice: Essays inspired by the work of Geoff Whitty.* London: University College London Press.

Another excellent compilation of essays from progressive educators such as Michael Apple, David Gillborn, Michael Young, Sharon Gewirtz and Alan Cribb among others who celebrate the life and work of Geoff Whitty.

Elliott, J. and Norris, N. (eds) (2012) *Curriculum, Pedagogy and Educational Research: The Work of Lawrence Stenhouse.* London: Routledge.

A comprehensive exploration of Stenhouse's work on the curriculum and pedagogy, with informative perceptions his notions for practical ideas for practice.

REFERENCES

Anyon, J. (2011) *Marx and Education.* Abingdon: Routledge.

Apple, M. (1979) *Ideology and Curriculum.* Boston, MA: Routledge & Kegan Paul.

Apple, M. (2020) Social mobilizations and official knowledge. In: A. Brown and E. Wisby (eds) *Knowledge, Policy and Practice in Education and the Struggle for Social Justice: Essays Inspired by the Work of Geoff Whitty.* London: University College London Press.

Apple, M. and Oliver, D. (1998) Becoming right: Education and the formation of conservative movements. In: M. Apple and D. Carlson (eds) *Power/Knowledge/Pedagogy: The Meaning of Democratic Education in Unsettling Times.* Boulder, CO: Westview Press.

Atkinson, P. (1985) *Language, Structure and Reproduction: An Introduction to the Sociology of Basil Bernstein.* London: Methuen.

Aubrey, K. and Riley, A. (2021) *Understanding and Using Challenging Educational Theories* (2nd edn). London: SAGE.

Aubrey, K. and Riley, A. (2022) *Understanding and Using Educational Theories* (3rd edn) London: SAGE.

Barry, P. (2002) *Beginning Theory: An Introduction to Literary and Cultural Theory* (3rd edn). Manchester: Manchester University Press.

Bartlett, S., Burton, D. and Peim, N. (2001) *Introduction to Education Studies.* London: Paul Chapman Publishing.

Bartlett, S. and Burton, D. (2020) *Introduction to Education Studies* (5th edn). London: SAGE.

Bernstein, B. (1971) *Class, Codes and Control: Theoretical Studies Towards a Sociology of Language*, Vol. 1. London: Routledge & Kegan Paul.

Bernstein, B. (1996) *Pedagogy, Symbolic Control and Identity: Theory, Research and Critique.* London: Taylor & Francis.

Bernstein, B. (2000) *Pedagogy, Symbolic Control, and Identity: Theory, Research, and Critique* (revised edn). London: Rowman & Littlefield.

Bernstein, B. (2006) Thoughts on the Trivium and Quadrivium: The divorce of knowledge from the knower. In: H. Lauder, P. Brown, J.-A. Dillabough. and A. Halsey (eds) *Education, Globalization and Social Change*. Oxford: Oxford University Press.

Bourdieu, P. and Passeron, J-C. (1990) *Reproduction in Education, Society and Culture* (2nd edn). London: SAGE.

Brighouse, T. and Waters, M. (2021) *About Our Schools: Improving on Previous Best*. Carmarthen: Crown House Publishing.

Burton, D. and Bartlett, S. (2005) *Practitioner Research for Teachers*. London: Paul Chapman Publishing.

Connelly, M. and Xu, S. (2012) Curriculum and curriculum studies. In: J. Arthur and A. Peterson (eds) *The Routledge Companion to Education*. Abingdon: Routledge.

Craske, J. (2021) Logics, rhetoric and 'the blob': Populist logic in the Conservative reforms to English schooling. *British Educational Research Journal*, 47(2): 279–98.

Curtis, W. and Pettigrew, A. (2010) *Education Studies Reflective Reader*. Exeter: Learning Matters.

Foucault, M. (1979) *Discipline and Punish: The Birth of the Prison*. London: Penguin.

Gewirtz, S. and Cribb, A. (2009) *Understanding Education: A Sociological Perspective*. Cambridge: Polity Press.

Giroux, H. (1983) *Theory and Resistance in Education: A Pedagogy for the Opposition*. London: Heinemann Educational.

Giroux, H. (1998) Education in unsettling times: Public intellectuals and the promise of cultural studies. In: D. Carlson and M. Apple (eds) *Power, Knowledge, and Pedagogy: The Meaning of Democratic Education in Unsettling Times*. Oxford: Westview Press.

Giroux, H. (2011) *On Critical Pedagogy*. London: Bloomsbury.

Goodson, I. (2001) Basil Bernstein, 1925–2000. In: J. Palmer (ed.) *Fifty Modern Thinkers on Education: From Piaget to the Present*. Abingdon: Routledge.

Goodson, I. (2005) *Learning, Curriculum and Life Politics: The Selected Works of Ivor F. Goodson*. London: Routledge.

Gramsci, A. (1971) *Selections from the Prison Notebooks*. London: Lawrence & Wishart.

hooks, b. (1994) *Teaching to Transgress: Education as the Practice of Freedom*. London: Routledge.

Howlett, J. (2013) *Progressive Education: A Critical Introduction*. London: Bloomsbury

Huddleston, P. and Unwin, L. (2002) *Teaching and Learning in Further Education* (2nd edn). London: RoutledgeFalmer.

Jarman, T.L. (1963) *Landmarks in the History of Education: English Education as Part of the European Tradition*. London: Murray.

Kelly, A. (2009) *The Curriculum: Theory and Practice* (6th edn). London: Sage.

Kemmis, S. (1995) Some ambiguities in Stenhouse's notion of 'the teacher as researcher'. In: J. Rudduck (ed.) *An Education that Empowers: A Collection of Lectures in Memory of Lawrence Stenhouse*. Clevedon: Multilingual Matters/BERA.

Moncrieffe, M. and Harris, R. (2020) Repositioning curriculum teaching and learning through Black British history. *Research Intelligence* (BERA), Autumn, 144, 14-15.

Morrison, K. (2001) Henry Giroux, 1943–. In: J. Palmer (ed.) *Fifty Modern Thinkers on Education: From Piaget to the Present*. Abingdon: Routledge.

Oliver, P. (2010) *Foucault – The Key Ideas*. London: Hodder Education.

Plato (1993) *Republic*. Oxford: Oxford University Press.

Plowden Report (1967) *Children and their Primary Schools: A Report of the Central Advisory Council for England*. London: HMSO.

Raftery, D. (2012) History of education. In: J. Arthur and A. Peterson (eds) *The Routledge Companion to Education.* London: Routledge.

Schostak, J. and Schostak, J. (2008) *Radical Research: Designing, Developing and Writing Research to Make a Difference.* London: Routledge.

Scott, D. (2008) *Critical Essays on Major Curriculum Theorists.* London: Routledge.

Smith, M. (2000) Curriculum theory and practice. *The Encyclopedia of Informal Education.* Available at: www. infed.org./biblio/b-curric.htm (accessed 9 March 2023).

Stenhouse, L. (1975) *An Introduction to Curriculum Research and Development.* Oxford: Heinemann.

Thomas, G. (2007) *Education and Theory: Strangers in Paradigms.* Maidenhead: Open University Press.

Thomas, G. (2013) *Education: A Very Short Introduction.* Oxford: Oxford University Press.

Wallace, S. (2008) *Oxford Dictionary of Education.* Oxford: Oxford University Press.

Whitty, G. (1985) *Sociology and School Knowledge: Curriculum Theory, Research and Politics.* London: Methuen.

3

THE CURRICULUM PART 2: CURRICULUM APPLICATIONS

LEARNING OUTCOMES

Having read this chapter, you should be able to:

- understand the current political influences on the curriculum;
- recognise the different applications of the curriculum;
- understand the national and cultural reasons underpinning the design and content of the curriculum;
- recognise and apply aspects of social justice and democracy in curriculum provision;
- consider the approaches to apply democratic, inclusive and socially just values to a set curriculum.

KEY WORDS

Curriculum for Excellence; devolution; Education (Butler) Act 1944; Education Reform Act 1988; Every Child Matters; Head Start; Plowden Report; Rose Report.

INTRODUCTION

This chapter follows on from Chapter 2 which explored the concept of knowledge and curriculum theoretical models. It delves into the different applications of the curriculum in the UK, including the English national curriculum and the curriculum available in the devolved nations, before discovering some examples of the international curricula offered. The scope is focused mainly around the curriculum for secondary, primary and early years education, although we have attempted to differentiate between the sectors; there are, for obvious reasons, some overlapping between the sectors. Finally, we have listed some ideas for application which could be relevant when considering the theoretical curriculum models.

There is no intention of giving detailed contents lists of what subjects are taught at what stages for each of the mentioned curricula. Furthermore, we ask you to be aware that in the UK education is a devolved responsibility for each of the four nations and as such there are some complex political and cultural differences that also include early childhood education and care in England, Wales, Scotland and Northern Ireland. Although the scope of this chapter limits the opportunity to investigate these differences in great detail, they will be highlighted where appropriate. The shift in the political influence over curriculum matters and the resultant governmental policy and legislation are considered, particularly since the end of the Second World War in the UK, specifically the **Education (Butler) Act 1944** and the **Education Reform Act 1988**. Furthermore, reviews and subsequent reports into the curriculum in the UK, such as the **Plowden Report** and the **Rose Report**, will be explored. Although not perhaps strictly speaking related to the curriculum in a traditional sense, we have included two past programmes that have endeavoured to link education with aspects of child safety, anti-poverty, well-being and health care: **Head Start** in the USA and **Every Child Matters** (from 2003 to 2010: one of the foundations of the English national curriculum) in the UK. This, we argue, is in line with the aim of the book, which is to seek democratic and socially just ways of thinking about the curriculum in such uncertain times. Coffield and Williamson, writing in their perceptive 2012 text *From Exam Factories to Communities of Discovery: The Democratic Route*, challenge the then Conservative-led coalition government about the direction of their education policies:

> The policies that would build wide open-ended and free learning opportunities at all stages of life in order to give meaning to the term 'democratic education' are not even being considered. Instead, the dominant thrust in education debate is to improve competitiveness of the British economy. Our concern is that other, equally important goals – the democratic, social and cultural purposes of education – are being quietly forgotten, because in modern societies economic arguments tend to trump all others.

(p. 8)

Writing over a decade after this was written, we contend that the shift towards competitiveness has, to some extent, increased at the expense of the democratic, social and cultural purposes of education.

UK CURRICULA

The 1944 Education Act, or Butler's Act, which was implemented after the Second World War and related to secondary education, 'is often represented as *the* defining moment in the history of education' (Bartlett and Burton, 2020: 85); it was probably the most significant education policy since the Education Act of 1870. The Act also restructured the education sectors to what we know today: primary, secondary and further education. It extended secondary education for all up to the age of 14, raised to 15 in 1947. As well as providing for free secondary education for all, it was a very segregated 'tripartite' system which, according to Thomas, divided 'the clever from the not-so-clever, with the introduction of a set of tests at the age of 11 – the "11-plus"' (2013: 80). From the results of the 11-plus, children were allocated into one of three different types of school, and curriculum: grammar (academic), technical, and secondary modern (practical). Chitty (2014: 6) suggests that the creation of different systems was the result of

> patronizing attitudes towards the sort of education thought 'appropriate' for working-class children [which] persisted in the types of curriculum provided for the majority of the pupils attending the new secondary modern schools.

It is of interest to note that this segregated system which allocated children according to their 'tested' ability was the result of the findings of two reports, both of which were very influential in the creation of the 1944 Act: the Hadow Report (1926) and the Norwood Report (1943). The Norwood Report outlined three types of curriculum for each type of school:

1   The first type of curriculum is academic in orientation and pursues knowledge for its own sake having an indirect relation to 'considerations of occupation'.
2   The second type of curriculum is directed to 'the special data and skills associated with a particular kind of occupation'. The curriculum would always have a limited horizon and would be closely related to industry, trade and commerce 'in all their diversity'.
3   The third type of curriculum balances training of mind and body and teaches the humanities, natural science and the arts to a degree which enables pupils to 'take up the work of life'. While practical in orientation it would appeal to the 'interests' of pupils and would not have as its immediate aim the preparation for particular types of work.

(Bartlett and Burton, 2020: 84)

The 1944 Act did not give any direction regarding the content of the curriculum, apart from ensuring that religious study was compulsory; rather, it left such decisions to the professional discretion of local teachers as a matter of democracy. The notion of non-intervention from the government concerning the curriculum was regarded as a 'secret garden' not to be interfered with by politicians (Kelly, 2009; Chitty, 2014; Bartlett and Burton, 2020). However, leaving decisions in the hands of teachers soon became a contested and political issue. Increasingly, politicians wanted a say in matters of curriculum content, process and assessment, especially where education and the economic national needs were concerned. Such interest in the curriculum from politicians, Thomas (2013) argues, led to the creation of the national curriculum in the 1980s not only in the UK, but also in some other European nations. There have been many changes to the curriculum, and indeed education, since the 1944 Act, such as the change from selective education towards a comprehensive system for nearly all state-educated secondary pupils, which started in the 1960s. There have been numerous changes in the examinations from GCEs, the CSEs and on to the GCSEs, English Baccalaureate (EBacc) – as well as the introduction of vocational qualifications, much of which is aligned with the evolution of the national curriculum. Following an exploration of the English national curriculum, the different UK and comparative curricula will be considered.

THE ENGLISH NATIONAL CURRICULUM

The 1988 Education Reform Act and the introduction of the national curriculum signalled a remarkable change in education policy for England and, at the time, Wales. It was remarkable because since the Second World War, the government had no say in the direction or content of the curriculum which was left to schools and local authorities to control. Responsibility for school funding began to be taken from local authorities and given to individual schools. Also, further education colleges were removed from the auspices of local authorities, but they had to take into account the needs of local employers. The Reform Act signalled two main themes which have been evident since: the limiting of control by local authorities and the 'introduction of market values into educational provision' (Wallace, 2008: 87). Although the main purpose of the 1988 Reform Act was to ensure standardisation of education, in actuality, prior to the Act, it followed certain features to make sure a measure of standardisation between schools was observed, such as the syllabi of 'GCE Ordinary [O] and Advanced [A] levels, … [and] … school culture and well-established professional habits' (Bartlett and Burton, 2020: 123).

The national curriculum was established by a Conservative government with Margaret Thatcher as Prime Minister as an attempt to reform what was perceived as failing educational standards in schools and, according to Bartlett and Burton (2020), to dismantle what the New Right considered the teachers' subversive influence over the curriculum. It was intended to be compulsory for all children in state-run education between the ages of 5 and 16 years, over the four age-related Key Stages (Key Stage 1, 5–7; Key Stage 2, 7–11; Key Stage 3, 11–14; Key Stage 4, 14–16). The curriculum was to be assessed and the outcomes published in league tables. The principal ideology of the Conservative government was embedded in the belief in traditionalism and the value of marketisation. From the outset, the national curriculum promoted 'a traditional approach to education and, when coupled with other Tory reforms, promoted competition between schools' (Bartlett and Burton, 2020: 124). It should be stressed that successive Labour and Conservative–Liberal Democratic coalition governments have all, with their own changes, kept the national curriculum as a focus of educational provision in schools. Indeed, it was the 1997 Labour government who first exercised their power on pedagogy with regard to the teaching of numeracy and literacy (Brighouse and Waters, 2021). Although the consequences of the national curriculum were dramatic for England and Wales, and even the UK as a whole, it became apparent that the perception of failing educational provision was evident 'throughout the "free world"' (Kelly, 2009: 2).

The national curriculum has had many changes in content, methods of assessment and disputes concerning the value of academic, creative, vocational and experiential learning. In general, though, many educationalists agreed that there was a requirement for a national approach for the curriculum. It is argued that a majority of teachers were captivated by the curriculum and thankful for clarity of what was required of them (Brighouse and Waters, 2021). Despite that general approval, there was, and still is, considerable criticism, including the design used, uninspired structure, prominence of assessment and the 'teaching to test', and the lack of ongoing consultations with teachers and educational researchers. Kelly (2009) laments the loss of freedom of teachers' professional judgements as a reason that the curriculum has stopped evolving and that the visions that emerged from the progressive thinking in the 1960s and 1970s – for example, the 1967 Plowden Report – have been disregarded and suppressed. The lack of consultation with educationalists hampers teachers' professional judgements, which is evident in the attempts to 'teacher proof' the curriculum by government advisers and results in a proscribed curriculum that is over-reliant on assessment. Pressures from competition and accountability drive many teachers to 'teach to the test', which could lead to teaching becoming

> mechanized, stressing the learning of facts and the coverage of material, with scant attention to the real grasp that students had made of that material. Had they understood? Had they gained insights? Did they develop new awareness?
>
> (Thomas, 2013: 97)

Even though the national curriculum was meant to reach a broad spectrum of learners' needs in schools, Brighouse and Waters (2021) contend that this has never been the case, and for some learners, teachers and parents, school and the curriculum is seen as futile. They argue that this is mainly because the accompanying national assessment structure places too much emphasis on testing and examinations as part of the accountability processes on learners and the schools (Brighouse and Waters, 2021: 172). There is also commentary from some that strongly suggests that the national curriculum content disadvantages those from working-class families and from minority ethnic groups, particularly in the history curriculum. History as a subject is too focused on British, mainly English, topics ending at the close of the Second World War and does not consider major events such as the 'Middle East crises, the Cold War, and the decline of the British Empire' (Bartlett and Burton, 2020: 130). Furthermore, little attention is afforded to the contribution from those from the British colonies. We will be exploring this a little later in the book. However, Nesrine Malik states that this lack of recognition has resulted in editing the history curriculum which, she argues, 'can only be down to ideology' (2020: 177).

It is of interest and significance that the national curriculum is not mandatory for academies and free schools. Yet these schools make up the best part of the secondary, and progressively, primary schools in England, which Bartlett and Burton (2020) point out

> constitutes a fundamental structural weakness in the provision of a nationally coherent curriculum. It may be that a rigid national curriculum has become less significant to the government as a means of controlling schooling as the market in education has developed, which has weakened the powers of both LAs [local authorities] and teachers.
>
> (p. 138)

SECONDARY CURRICULUM

The curriculum attracts more attention in primary than in secondary schools. In secondary schools, the emphasis is on examinations and subject syllabi, and consequently these factors tend to manipulate the curriculum with the demands from Year 11 (Brighouse and Waters, 2021). In secondary schools, the curriculum is mostly learned in subject-specific areas, divided into core subjects (English, mathematics and science), and foundation (art and design, citizenship, computing, design and technology, languages, geography, history, music and physical education).

There has been a narrowing of the English national curriculum over the years which has led to more and more children taking no part in foundation subjects, apart from citizenship, computing and physical education, after they have finished Key Stage 3. This narrowing of the secondary curriculum was orchestrated by the then coalition government Education Secretary, Michael Gove, and driven by the accountability and competitive processes. As a result, Key Stage 4 was dominated by GCSEs, and the EBacc (English Baccalaureate) more or less became the English national curriculum (Brighouse and Waters, 2021). EBacc stresses the importance of the perceived academic subjects such as English, mathematics and science at the expense of the practical and creative secondary school subjects (Zafirakou, 2021). This narrowing of the curriculum has become even more limited and, it is argued, ideologically controlled under Gavin Williamson, Conservative Education Secretary between 2019 and 2021 (at the time of writing, there have been five Education Secretaries since Williamson stood down). A number of matters affected education during Gavin Williamson's time as Education Secretary, including the COVID-19 pandemic, which will be explored in Chapter 5. For this curriculum chapter, we will briefly focus on the provision of the arts and the use of anti-capitalist sources.

There has been concern from educators and the arts industry relating to the decline of learners taking art subjects in secondary schools, with many students switching to the more perceived academic subjects. The reason for this, according to Weale (2021), is the gradual reduction in funding for art subjects in schools, similar to plans for cutting funding for art degree programmes at university, as well as prioritising the provision of STEM (science, technology, engineering and mathematics) subjects and the future economic needs of the country. Yet it is contended that the creative arts make a huge contribution to the nation in both fiscal and cultural capital. Davies and Trowsdale's (2021) research, although acknowledging the enrichment the arts can bring to the learning experience, recognised the subordinate position of the arts in relation to the core subjects in both the time and space allotted to them in the subject-specific curriculum. Their work demonstrated the value of emphasising the culture of the arts through a multi-subject curriculum with the core subjects as a 'multicultural frame can facilitate rich and engaging educational experiences' (Davies and Trowsdale, 2021: 1434). Andria Zafirakou (2021), a Global Teacher prize winner and an enthusiastic promoter of the value of art education for children, writes passionately in her 2021 insightful book: *Those Who Can, Teach: What it Takes to Make the Next Generation*. When discussing her award with members of the Department of Education she takes them to task:

> I don't think this government has done enough to support the arts … For example, you introduced the EBacc, which has destroyed textiles. The British fashion industry has some of the best designers in the world, yet you have killed the textiles curriculum for kids. My curriculum. Where will these designers of the future come from now?
>
> (Zafirakou, 2021: xvii)

The second matter for curriculum concern, and one driven by ideology and part of the culture war, focuses on a Department of Education's guidance to English schools, published in September 2020, relating to the use of resources from what they considered anti-capitalist groups. The guidance classified 'anti-capitalism' as an 'extreme political stance' and compared it with opposition to freedom of speech, antisemitism and endorsement of illegal activity (Mohdin, 2020). Although the guidance was later reviewed and not acted upon because of a legal challenge, it attracted some intense criticism from educators, MPs and human rights groups, and those identified by the DfE as 'anti-capitalist groups', one of which was the Black Lives Matter movement.

PRIMARY AND EARLY YEARS CURRICULUM

The primary curriculum has involved considerable discussion and interest, particularly since the publication of the ground-breaking 1967 Plowden Committee Report which, among other recommendations, promoted the notion of the child being at the centre of the education process. Although this does not appear to be too contentious, it did attract criticism from right-wing commentators who argued that it was too progressive; however, this criticism was contested by most educationalists (Wallace, 2008). The discussions and practice of the English primary education during the 1960s was focused on and driven by the child. Bryan (2012) suggests that it was a time when the clear relationship between primary education and the economy was not in the thoughts of educators, their main professional focus being on a child-centred approach to their practice. The report was also aligned with many of the child-centred educational thinkers such as Dewey, Piaget, Montessori and Malaguzzi. The Plowden Report on primary education in England and Wales was indeed progressive with its emphasis on play and active experience; such ideas were perhaps not surprising, as it was still part of the postwar optimism where many people looked to the future and embraced change.

Furthermore, the recommendations from the report called for closer relations between school and home, the use of schools for community purposes and the creation of middle schools, and the ending of corporal punishment. Although not all recommendations were accepted at the time, the report had a lasting influence on primary education in the UK and USA, particularly for its focus on child-centred learning (Rowntree, 1981). However, in the following decade this acceptance of progressive ideas in education was about to end with the 'advent of the right-wing Conservative Thatcher government in 1979, which quickly reaffirmed the more traditional subject-based curriculum' (Aubrey and Riley, 2022: 18). Then, although many of the recommendations of the Plowden Report were jettisoned, the idea of child-centred learning and teaching have for the most part endured, despite the increasing assessment demands, particularly in the Cambridge and Rose Reports of the primary curriculum. Notwithstanding the change in government, when the New Labour government came to power in 1997, it also took a more hands-on approach to the teaching of the curriculum. It initiated a series of national strategies, which included the literacy and numeracy strategies. Teaching of literacy and numeracy came in the form of set hours in the timetable and governed by an advised pedagogy. As a result, the 'government was able to inspect the performance of the pupils and teachers against suggested, if not statutory, practice' (Bryan, 2012: 186). These two strategies were included into the 2003 Primary National Strategy which broadened its remit to incorporate the other areas of the curriculum, but still very much concentrated on the core subjects (Bartlett and Burton, 2020).

There were four reviews of the primary curriculum which followed Plowden, albeit by some decades, which are of significance in understanding how the nature of the curriculum can be shaped by political ideology. As such, it is fitting to briefly consider each of these in turn to appreciate the shift from a child-centred to a traditional knowledge-based approach to the curriculum. The independent Cambridge Review of Primary Education led by Robin Alexander started its work in 2004 and its final report was published in 2010. The report was meant to acknowledge, commemorate and refresh the efforts of the Plowden Report some forty years earlier (Brighouse and Waters, 2021). It was undeniably the most thorough and wide-ranging enquiry into English primary education since Plowden. The review was tasked to account for the strengths and weaknesses of English primary education and to recommend a vision for the future which would raise children's aspirations beyond the requirements of conforming with government policies. However, the independent nature of the review process was hardly likely to be appealing to politicians regardless of their party. The Cambridge Review published a number of interim reports which challenged government initiatives such as assessment, national strategies and the curriculum in general, and drew extensive coverage from the press. In 2007, Ed Balls, the New Labour Education Secretary, uncomfortable with criticisms being aired in the press, asked 'Sir Jim Rose to pre-empt the exercise by undertaking a "root and branch" review of the primary curriculum' (Chitty, 2014: 164).

The Rose Review focused on organising subjects into six broad groups of learning: mathematical understanding; historical, geographical and social understanding; understanding English, communication and languages; scientific and technological understanding; understanding the arts; and understanding physical development, health and well-being (Bartlett and Burton, 2020: 133). Although the report supported the inclusion of traditional subjects as essential to the primary curriculum, it sought to promote these as broad areas of learning rather that stand-alone subjects, with an emphasis on cross-curricula work through projects and during lessons, which was child-centred and reminiscent of the primary curriculum of the 1960s and 1970s. The Rose Report also stressed the importance of developing literacy and numeracy in the early years of education (Chitty, 2014). The Labour government also promoted the curriculum as giving teachers the professional freedom to choose the way they taught skills and knowledge, yet they had previously been accused of micro-managing the curriculum

(Bartlett and Burton, 2020). The Rose Report, published in 2009, was well received by teachers and educators in general, but the researchers did not have the scope afforded to the independent Cambridge Review team. A third curriculum review of 2009 was sponsored by the Department for Children, Schools and Families Committee, led by Professor David Hargreaves, which found that there should be less political control over the curriculum. The Hargreaves Report discarded both the Cambridge and Rose Reports as being overly complex (Chitty, 2014).

Despite the depth of research and the effort of all three reviews, when the Conservative-dominated coalition government entered office in 2010, with Michael Gove as the Education Secretary, the findings of all three reports were rejected and instead they revealed that they would be introducing their new national curriculum in England for 5–16-year-olds based around traditional principles and subject-specific areas (Chitty, 2014). The review of the national curriculum was led by four experts with Tim Oates as the chairperson. The first draft of the primary curriculum was published in 2012 and attracted considerable criticism from the media, which concentrated on four aspects:

> Children being encouraged to recite poetry from memory by the age of 5; the use of officially mandated spelling lists; making a foreign language compulsory from the age of 7; and expecting children to be able to recite the 12 times table from the age of 9 ... [which] ... could be construed as a 'back-to-basics' curriculum, with its emphasis on academic rigor and 'traditional' approaches to learning.
>
> (Chitty, 2014: 166)

The criticism was not limited to the press, but also by many educationalists and academics, including Professor Andrew Pollard who was one of the four experts involved in the review of the new curriculum. Notwithstanding the depth of criticism, when in 2013 the following version of Michael Gove's national curriculum emerged, little had changed from the first draft; moreover, world-related history was 'downgraded in favour of the chronological learning of facts about British history' (Chitty, 2014: 167). Like all curricula, a number of changes have been made since 2013, but these are focused on assessment – for example, from 2020 the removal of national curriculum assessments at the end of Key Stage 1. Hence, all pupils will now be assessed at the start and then at the end of their primary schooling (Bartlett and Burton, 2020). The other national curriculum changes since 2013 are mainly related to specific subject areas which, particularly regarding the primary subjects in mathematics and science, require young children to cover the subjects in too much depth. This could cause pupils problems in their conceptual learning and, as a result, lead them to become disinterested at their early stage of schooling (Bartlett and Burton, 2020; UK Government, 2022). It is argued that by scrapping the findings of the previous reports, especially

Rose, the government dismantled the social justice aspects of education in favour of an education driven by the quest for their view of academic attainment.

The Early Years Foundation Stage (EYFS) was included in the national curriculum in England as part of the Education Act of 2002. In 2008, the EYFS was introduced for 3–5-year-olds. It intended to:

- break the cycle of deprivation;
- provide children a better start in life, regulate early childhood education and care;
- create synergy between research and policy;
- emphasise the 'unique' child, build strong relationships with parents and
- introduce accountability.

Since its introduction, the EYFS has undergone a number of revisions which include amendments to the Early Learning Goals (ELGs) and an increased prominence of matters of assessment, school readiness and safety, as well as improving children's attainment in literacy, language and mathematics. Despite a delay because of the amendments above and the disruption caused by the COVID-19 pandemic, the EYFS has been implemented from September 2021 (Palaiologou, 2022). The EYFS has attracted some positive feedback from academics, practitioners and early years researchers, particularly the need for greater regulation, the importance placed on play-based learning, safeguarding and inclusion. However, it has also drawn a high degree of scepticism from the same group of professions who criticise the bureaucratic way that the EYFS functions with regard to the efforts required to meet targets, the limitation on set standards about learning and development, which hinders professional independence and creativity of practice with early years children. Furthermore, there is disquiet about the government's suggestion that the main purpose of early years education is to make children ready for the formal learning setting that awaits them when they begin school at 5 years old (Palaiologou and Male, 2021a).

EVERY CHILD MATTERS

The English national curriculum turned away from the Every Child Matters agenda, which was thoroughly eradicated with the website shutting down very soon after the coalition government took office in 2010. Every Child Matters was a radical programme which set out to change and improve the lives of all children and young people from birth to 18 years of age. The programme was a reaction to the enquiry and subsequent report from Lord Lamming in 2003 of the tragic murder of Victoria Climbié in 2000. It resulted in the professionals from education, social services, health and the probation service working with a shared purpose to protect children and young people. The aim of Every Child Matters was to enhance education achievement, reduce levels of ill health, teenage pregnancy, crime, anti-social behaviour, and neglect and abuse. The shared five outcomes, or pillars of the programme were: being healthy; staying safe; enjoying and achieving; making a positive contribution; and achieving economic well-being (Wallace, 2008). These outcomes became established as part of the Children Act of 2004 and 'shared across all government services, and underpinned by an integrated inspection framework ... to ensure all services work together effectively and share information' (Wallace, 2008: 97). Through the 2004 Children Act, the Labour government strived to align their future planning initiatives regarding children, young people and families with the United Nations Convention on the Rights of the Child (UNCRC) (Palaiologou and Male, 2021b).

SUMMARY

Since its inception, the English national curriculum has changed. Some of the changes can be considered detrimental to social justice at the expense of competition and marketisation. This is exemplified by the demise of the ECM agenda and the rapid changes to reduce the importance of some of the previous wider curriculum subjects, such as personal social and health education (PSHE), as well as citizenship. Brighouse and Waters (2021) consider this shift in the overall nature of the curriculum away from the aspects of social justice also included:

> The reduction of funding for the arts, culture, libraries and youth services – all presented as part of the austerity agenda – added to many teachers' impression that what Gove wanted to do was to get schooling back under tight government control.

> (p. 185)

Yet on a positive note, and despite the control and changes, most teachers and schools have now adapted to the English national curriculum. The majority of teachers and schools teach to what they perceive the national curriculum is about, how it is assessed, and they teach what they know and like, and what the children enjoy. Brighouse and Waters (2021: 185) found that primary schools continue to employ the '"Rose curriculum" and a lot still use the Cambridge Primary Review work they developed ... [and that they found] ... no amount of central interference can achieve uniformity'.

DEVOLVED NATIONS CURRICULA

Perhaps it is fitting that we explore the term '**devolution**', and in particular in the context to education and the curriculum regarding the devolved nations of the UK. Brighouse and Waters (2021: 523–4) define devolution from an education point of view:

Devolution means the government handing over power, responsibility and significant fundraising powers (which we argue should be called 'equity taxes') to a wholly autonomous lower body to decide policy and practice. (For example, the devolved governments in Wales, Scotland and Northern Ireland can determine their own education strategies and raise their own resources, but they also receive funding from Westminster.)

Devolution for the UK nations occurred in 1997/1998. Wales, Scotland and Northern Ireland were free to take up their own distinctive education ideas, schooling systems, language choices and their own curriculum. It is noteworthy to consider the comments of Brighouse and Waters (2021: 575) again about why devolution is not also being adopted in the English regions:

> We believe that devolution to the English regions will take place, mirroring what has happened in Scotland, Wales and Northern Ireland, but not soon enough; the need to curtail the excessive power of the DfE is urgent. Does it matter if our schooling system is becoming ever more centralised? All democracies understand that, however uncomfortable it may be, decision-making is best when citizens broadly consent. Centralisation can restrict debate, reduce involvement and limit participation, while also allowing governments to exert unwonted [sic] and unwarranted control.

The devolved nations of the UK – Northern Ireland, Scotland and Wales – have each implemented a curriculum that 'promotes cross-cutting areas of learning and significant autonomy to schools and teachers to shape the precise content' (Sibieta and Jerrim, 2021: 3). All three nations are adopting curricula that emphasise a holistic approach to learning and in the development of children as effective members of society. The Northern Ireland curriculum aims to enable children to reach their full potential and make informed choices. By providing learning opportunities, they can develop as individuals, contribute to society, and the economy and the environment. Updated in 2019, it aims to empower young people to develop their potential and make informed and responsible choices and decisions throughout their lives (Northern Ireland Government, 2007). In Northern Ireland, the Foundation Stage (FS) curriculum for all 4–6-year-old children came into effect from 2008. Among the four devolved nations of the UK, Northern Ireland has the youngest statutory starting age. This FS curriculum for Northern Ireland was a huge change from the previous traditional model which gave great emphasis to the subject content and academic attainment. Instead, the FS gave credence through play-based learning, which is termed Playful Teaching and Learning (PLT), which results in children's enthusiasm and motivation, as well as in not being fearful of learning through trial and error. Furthermore, a revised pre-school curriculum guidance document was launched in 2018 which outlines the readiness for children entering formal schooling, and stresses the promotion of the voice of the child and the importance of the interactions between the child and adult (Walsh, 2021).

The Welsh Government has planned to replace what it describes as a:

Narrow, rigid, subject-based national curriculum. The official purpose of the new curriculum is seen as supporting and encouraging children and young people to be:

- ambitious, capable learners, ready to learn throughout their lives
- enterprising, creative contributors, ready to play a full part in life and work
- ethical, informed citizens of Wales and the world
- healthy, confident individuals, ready to lead fulfilling lives as valued members of society.

(Bartlett and Burton, 2020: 139)

The Curriculum for Wales is due to be rolled out from September 2022 for all children in Year 5 and below. The Foundation Phase of the Welsh curriculum for children aged 3–7 is a move away from the UK early years education policy, which was considered an overly formal approach for such young learners. Like the Welsh curriculum for older children, the Foundation Phase is in the process of transformation, but the changes will encompass the four aspects of the vision for whole curriculum outlined above. Emphasis on play-based and outdoor learning is key to the Foundation phase. However, there is some unease from practitioners regarding the 'tension between the play-based pedagogy, underpinned by the developmental approach, and detailed statutory curriculum expectations, especially for Years 1 and 2' (Waters and Macdonald, 2021: 53).

The Scottish curriculum, **Curriculum for Excellence** (CfE), was launched in 2005 and revised in 2019. On its inception, 'the priorities for the curriculum were: achievement and attainment; framework for learning; inclusion and equality; values and citizenship; and learning for life (Brisard and Menter, 2008: 253–4). The CfE aims to support children to become: successful learners, confident individuals, responsible citizens and effective contributors (Scottish Government, 2021). All children and young adults from 3 to 18 years in Scotland participate in the CfE, which has planned experience for all learners across four broad contexts: curriculum areas and subjects; interdisciplinary learning; ethos and life of the school; and opportunities for personal achievement (Scottish Government, 2021). In Scotland, the central aim of education and specifically the early years

is about viewing children holistically, catering for individual need whilst simultaneously raising attainment, and instilling recognition of children's voices and rights in everyday practice .... The four influential factors which encapsulate the Scottish approach

- Holistic children and autonomous educators
- A nation for play: Pushing play in primary

- Environment: intelligent resources
- Planning, reflection and self-evaluation.

(Arnott and Grogan, 2021: 45–6)

The early years curriculum is an integral part of the CfE which attempts to create a seamless transition from early years education to formal school education; however, it is recognised that children do encounter incoherence when transitioning. An initiative is in place, which is supported by the University of Strathclyde, where a smoother transition between early years education and formal schooling can be made through promoting play and by encouraging children's voices (Arnott and Grogan, 2021).

INTERNATIONAL COMPARATIVE CURRICULUM IDEAS

A detailed account of different international curricula would be a huge undertaking and not within the scope of this book. However, we offer a brief introduction of the curriculum as adopted by some countries outside the UK as a starting point for further and deeper exploration. Even though this is a brief introduction, and there are some clear advantages to making comparisons between different nations, there are also some noteworthy drawbacks. These drawbacks particularly include the different cultures in each country and the error of perceiving a curriculum, and even an education system, as superior to another (Bartlett and Burton, 2020). It should also be noted that a number of countries have been in the process of revising their curriculum, but the implementation, like education in general, was put on hold because of the COVID-19 pandemic.

Education in some Asian nations has, in the past, had a reputation of over-use of rote learning. However, most schools are now adopting a curriculum that encourages problem solving, project and group work, and creativity. For example, in 1997 Singapore launched '"thinking schools, learning nation" … to encourage thinking out of the box and risk-taking' (Darling-Hammond, 2010: 185). Similarly, the South Korean curriculum is formally reviewed every 5 to 10 years. The curriculum is heavily influenced by the child-centred notions of John Dewey and Jerome Bruner, particularly in emphasising the significance of discovery and the education of the whole child. The school curriculum in China, Japan and Hong Kong have also adopted integrated subject areas and the encouragement of paired and small group work (Darling-Hammond, 2010). Traditionally, Asian countries stressed the importance of testing and using test scores nationally to stream students. This emphasis on testing has been reduced, especially in China where the explanation for such changes includes the effect of testing on students' lives, the shortcomings of test results as a guide to workforce ability, and the differences between the testing and what is taught (Connelly and Xu, 2014).

Both Asian and European countries have mostly enhanced their curriculum guidance to outline core knowledge and assessment in a manner that seeks to focus on solving problems, applying new knowledge, and analysing and synthesising information to improve student learning (Darling-Hammond, 2010). The approach to the curriculum, and indeed schooling, in Europe is varied. In France, the curriculum is controlled and governed by the state, and schools work to a national standard. But, unlike England where education is considered to be about bolstering the future economy, education in France is understood primarily as intellectual engagement (Bryan, 2012).

Norway and Sweden have recently reviewed their school curriculum. Both countries have set a range of values that encompass democracy, social justice and addressing future social challenges. Norway's new school curriculum (2019) has key features that address the challenges faced by society through three interdisciplinary topics: health and life skills, democracy and citizenship, and sustainable development. Other key features include the development of subject knowledge and understanding through more practical and exploratory learning methods, the importance of play-based learning for the youngest children, adopting more criticality to the approach to sources in different subjects, and fewer subject competencies to allow for more in-depth learning (Eurydice Norway Unit, 2019).

Sweden's revised curriculum goals encourage the development of expressing ethical standpoints based on the knowledge of human rights and basic democratic values, respect for other people, rejection of the subjection, oppression and the victimisation of people, helping and understanding people, showing the respect and care for the environment (Skolverket, 2018). Staying with Scandinavia, Bartlett and Burton (2020) illustrate Finland as an example of the importance of the early years curriculum in children's future development:

> In Finland children go to nursery but don't start formal education until they are seven years old. They have a five-hour school day with 15 minutes outdoor play for every hour. There are no standardised tests until senior year (English equivalent to Year 5). This would appear to be far less formal schooling than many other Western countries, yet Finland scores consistently higher in the Pisa ratings … There is also a smaller gap between the high and low achievers.

(pp. 142–3)

The recent reviews of the curriculum for Australia and New Zealand reflect similar social justice values promoted by Sweden and Norway. The new Australian curriculum, which is due to start in 2023, will now include all young people wherever they are taught in the country. The rationale for the curriculum is to improve the quality, equity and transparency of the nation's education system, which plays a vital part in 'shaping the lives of young Australians and contributing to a democratic, equitable and just society' (Australian Government, 2021). The vision for the 2020 New Zealand curriculum 'is for young people to be confident, connected, actively involved, lifelong learners', and it strives to encourage students to value excellence, innovation, enquiry and curiosity, diversity, equity, community and participation, ecological sustainability, integrity and respect (Ministry of Education, 2020).

In the USA, individual states determine the general core of the curriculum, and the requirements for high school graduation; in addition, students can choose a number of elective and extra-curricula activities (Loo, 2018). It is of interest to note that there have been a number of curricula initiatives that have been offered to the nation as a whole. These have been prompted by the desire to reduce poverty, and to improve health, well-being and the economy; each of these has resulted in varying degrees of success. The 1965 Head Start intervention programme aimed to tackle poverty and provide a good starting point for disadvantaged young children. Head Start was an initiative to provide 3–5-year-old children from low-income families with an array of health and socio enhancement which would allow them 'to learn more effectively once they reach school' (Rowntree, 1981: 113). The Head Start programme was in some ways an inspiration for Every Child Matters, and the setting up of the Sure Start centres in the UK. There were a number of prominent educationalists involved in the planning and implementation of the Head Start programme, including Benjamin Bloom, Urie Bron-fenbrenner and Jerome Bruner. However, Bruner did raise an area for concern about the manner of the implementation of Head Start:

> Compassionate though it undoubtedly was, Head Start did not escape the kind of implicit condescension that goes with reform movements. In most places it did not address the sore issues of … – what it is like being poor and black or poor and Latino, leaving aside what it means to have your kids for part of the day at Head Start with its middle-class child-rearing ideals.

> (Bruner, 1996: 73)

Further US initiatives were forthcoming to stem the issue of poverty and better access to education and a holistic approach to family support, such as A Nation at Risk, (1983), No Child Left Behind (2002) and Race to the Top (2009) which was instigated by President Obama (Ravitch, 2010).

Drawing upon the analysis of a number of studies regarding the effectiveness of different international curricula and education systems, Linda Darling-Hammond (2010) found that

> higher-achieving countries have much leaner standards; teach fewer topics more deeply each year; focus more on inquiry, reasoning skills, and applications of knowledge, rather than mere coverage; and have a more thoughtful sequence of expectations based on developmental learning progressions within and across domains.

> (p. 285)

OVERVIEW OF IDEAS FOR PRACTICE

The points listed below are for you to consider and reflect upon rather than taking them as actual ways to practise; the list is not exhaustive, nor should it be used as a checklist to be ticked. It includes the aspects covered in Chapter 2 on the curriculum, as well as in this chapter. Many of these points are acknowledged as good classroom practice. The ideas come from the works of a number of the curriculum scholars we have explored in the chapter who have promoted a democratic and socially just notion of the curriculum. We appreciate that many of these progressive ideas conflict with formal types of curriculum; however, despite this, Apple suggests that many practitioners, where possible, 'will mediate, transform and attempt to generally set limits on what is being imposed from above' (1988: 26).

- Promote active discovery learning, and where appropriate, discovery play.
- Encourage students to use reasoning to find things out for themselves.
- Foster student participation in making changes to their studies and to their learning environment such as school councils and elections.
- Cultivate critical reflection to develop individual student thought.
- Understand and encourage students to voice their cultural differences.
- Promote student discussion and problem solving to develop their own understanding of new knowledge. Create an environment that stimulates discussion and encourages a sense of cooperation.
- Use reading resources that stimulate critical and active group discussions.
- Make cross-curriculum links wherever possible, but ensure the borders (academic language used) between subjects are made clear to students so they can broaden their understanding of how subjects are linked.
- Encourage students to use their experiences in problem solving to help develop their skills in making decisions; this in turn empowers and emancipates student learning.
- Use wherever possible on-going formative assessment to give students feedback as a diagnostic tool for their progression.
- Use assessment as a developmental tool. Stenhouse, when writing about assessment in relation to the process curriculum model, states: 'the teacher should be a critic, not a marker … improving students' capacity to work to such criteria by critical reaction to work done. In this sense assessment is about the teaching of self-assessment' (1975: 94–5).
- If appropriate, question the interpretation of official knowledge in the form of the texts and the set curriculum.
- Where possible, foster a relationship between teacher and student that involves questioning, negotiation, self-reflection and open communication.
- Avoid teaching to assessment to strive for creativity and stay clear of passivity, particularly where students, because of class or race, feel powerless and without a voice.

SUMMARY

Major changes came about following the 1944 Education Act. The 1944 Act included tripartite segregated types of secondary curriculum and schools. Apart from these three types of curriculum, the government gave scant attention to the content that was left to the professional discretion of local teachers. Although concerned mainly with secondary schooling, the Act also restructured the education sectors we know today: primary, secondary and further education. Giving teachers such discretion soon became a contested political issue, and, through the implementation of the 1988 Education Reform Act, led to the creation of the national curriculum in England and Wales. The curriculum has undergone some wide-ranging changes since the latter part of the twentieth century and in the early part of the twenty-first century. These changes are evident in the UK and in other countries for which Kelly (2009) offers two reasons. First, the demise of teacher independence which has hampered the advance of evidence-based educator research; and second the increasing politisation of education which has had a negative effect on education, particularly with the ever-growing emphasis on testing and inspection regimes.

Each of the devolved nations of the UK has governance over education policy, which includes the curriculum. Generally, each of the three nations has adopted a curriculum that gives schools and teachers a fair degree of autonomy in the curriculum content (Sibieta and Jerrim, 2021). The introduction of the national curriculum in England (and at the time Wales) was the result of a perceived failing in school standards. The curriculum was part of conservative thinking that valued traditional education, marketisation and the importance of assessment and competition. It took away many of the freedoms from teachers' professional judgements and the creative ideas advocated by the progressive educators in the 1960s and 1970s. Furthermore, the English national curriculum saw the demise of the Every Child Matters agenda when the coalition government took office in 2010. Although the curriculum does create a set national educational standard, during the last decade the English national curriculum has attracted critical commentary, which includes a narrowing of subjects on offer, a reduction of funding for the arts and the prioritising of STEM subjects, the disadvantaging of some sections of current multicultural society and the concern that the curriculum is ideologically driven as part of the Conservative government's culture war. The curriculum for the devolved nations with their more holistic approach show a sharp contrast in purpose and application to the English national curriculum, which remains very traditionally academic and overly involved in testing.

Globally, the curriculum is also mostly influenced by dominant ideology and culture. However, many countries are reforming their curriculum to reflect the values of democracy and social justice to enable children to contribute as citizens in an ever changing and uncertain world. For example, apart from the usual subject content, the recent curriculum reforms in Sweden aim to encourage children to express ethical viewpoints based on human rights and democratic values, and a respect for the environment. Similar ideas are being replicated worldwide in many other countries.

GLOSSARY OF TERMS

Curriculum for Excellence

The Scottish curriculum, Curriculum for Excellence (CfE), was launched in 2005 and revised in 2019. Its priorities are achievement and learning, inclusion and equality; values and citizenship; and learning for life' (Brisard and Menter, 2008: 253–4). The aim is to support children to become successful learners, confident individuals, responsible citizens and effective contributors (Scottish Government, 2021), for all children and young adults from 3 to 18 years in Scotland. The CfE has four broad contexts: curriculum areas and subjects, interdisciplinary learning, ethos and life of the school, and opportunities for personal achievement.

Devolution

Devolution for the UK nations occurred in 1997/1998 when Wales, Scotland and Northern Ireland were free to take up their own distinctive education ideas, schooling systems, language choices and their own curriculum.

Education (Butler) Act 1944

Implemented following the Second World War, the 1944 Education Act, or Butler's Act, 'is often represented as *the* defining moment in the history of education' (Bartlett and Burton, 2020: 85), including the Education Act of 1870. The Act restructured the education sectors to what we know today: primary, secondary and further education. It extended secondary education for all up to the age of 14, which was raised to 15 in 1947. As well as providing for free secondary education for all, it was a very segregated 'tripartite' which divided pupils according to ability from their tests at the age of 11 years who were then allocated into one of three different types of school, and curriculum: grammar (academic), technical and secondary modern (practical).

Education Reform Act 1988

The 1988 Education Reform Act saw the introduction of the national curriculum and signalled a remarkable change in education policy for England and Wales. Since the Second World War, the government had very little say in the direction or content of the curriculum, which was left to schools and local authorities to control. School funding began to be taken from local authorities and given to individual schools. Also, further education colleges were removed from the auspices of local authorities, but they had to take into account the needs of local employers. There were two main themes which the Act signalled, and which have been since been obvious: the limiting of control by local authorities, and the 'introduction of market values into educational provision' (Wallace, 2008: 87).

Every Child Matters

Every Child Matters (ECM) was a radical programme which laid out the changes to improve the lives of all children and young people from birth to 18 years of age. The programme was a response to the enquiry and subsequent report from Lord Lamming in 2003 of the tragic murder of Victoria Climbié in 2000. Professionals from education, social services, health and the probation service worked with a shared purpose to protect children and young people. The aim of ECM was to enhance education achievement, reduce levels of ill health, teenage pregnancy, crime, anti-social behaviour, and neglect and abuse. The shared five outcomes or pillars of the programme were being healthy; staying safe; enjoying and achieving; making a positive contribution; and achieving economic well-being (Wallace, 2008).

Head Start

Head Start, instigated in 1965, was an intervention programme to tackle poverty and provide a good starting point for disadvantaged young children in the USA. Head Start was an initiative to provide 3–5-year-old children from low-income families with an array of health and socio enhancement initiatives that would allow them 'to learn more effectively once they reach school' (Rowntree, 1981: 113). It was funded mainly by the federal government. Head Start was the inspiration for a wrap-around support evident in the Every Child Matters agenda, as well as the setting up of the Sure Start centres in the UK.

Plowden Report

The Plowden Report (1967) was also aligned with many of the child-centred educational thinkers. The report on primary education in England and Wales was, even for its time, progressive with its emphasis on play and active experience. Recommendations from the report called for closer relations between school and home, the use of schools for community purposes, the creation of middle schools and the ending of corporal punishment. Although not all of the recommendations were accepted at the time, the report had a lasting influence on primary education in the UK and in the USA, particularly for its focus on child-centred learning (Rowntree, 1981). Its legacy is still evident and is reflected in the succeeding primary curriculum reviews and report findings.

Rose Report (on primary education)

The Rose Report focused on organising subjects into six broad groups of learning: mathematical understanding; historical, geographical and social understanding; understanding English, communication and languages; scientific and technological understanding; understanding the arts; and understanding physical development, health and well-being (Bartlett and Burton, 2020: 133). It also called for developing literacy and numeracy. Although it was in favour of traditional subjects, it sought to promote these as broad groups of learning rather that stand-alone subjects, with an emphasis on cross-curricula and child-centred work reminiscent of the primary curriculum of the 1960s and 1970s. Published in 2009, it was well received by teachers and educators in general, but it was not implemented by the coalition government which came to power in 2010.

FURTHER READING

Ashbee, R. (2021) *Curriculum: Theory, Culture and the Subject Specialisms.* Abingdon: Routledge.

A thorough exploration of the context, culture and the codification of the curriculum. An extremely useful text for teachers and leaders with ideas for practical application, including in the curriculum subjects' areas.

Gillborn, D. (2008) *Racism and Education: Coincidence or Conspiracy?* London: Routledge.

A seminal anti-racist text which explores British education policy and how it sustains race inequality. It does so by looking at major events, challenging the policy and the language used, and the inequity of assessment and critical race theory.

Sharma, L (2020) *Curriculum to Classroom: A Handbook to Prompt Thinking Around Primary Design and Delivery.* Woodbridge: John Catt Educational.

A useful handbook for school leaders and teachers in primary curriculum review and design, drawing from both research and practical experience.

REFERENCES

Alexander, R. (ed.) (2010) *Children, Their World, Their Education: Final Report and Recommendations of the Cambridge Primary Review.* Abingdon: Routledge.

Apple, M. (1988) *Teachers and Texts: A Political Economy of Class and Gender Relations in Education.* New York: Routledge.

Arnott, L. and Grogan, D. (2021) Early childhood education and care in Scotland. In: I. Palaiologou (ed.) *The Early Years Foundation Stage: Theory and Practice* (4th edn). London: SAGE.

Aubrey, K. and Riley, A. (2022) *Understanding and Using Educational Theories* (3rd edn). London: SAGE.

Australian Government (2021) *Australian Curriculum*. Available at: www.australiancurriculum. edu.au/about-the-australian-curriculum/ (accessed 12 March 2023).

Bartlett, S. and Burton, D. (2020) *Introduction to Education Studies* (5th edn). London: SAGE.

Brighouse, T. and Waters, M. (2021) *About Our Schools: Improving on Previous Best*. Carmarthen: Crown House Publishing.

Brisard, E. and Menter, I. (2008) Compulsory education in the United Kingdom. In: D. Matheson (ed.) *An Introduction to the Study of Education* (3rd edn). London: Routledge.

Bruner, J. (1996) *The Culture of Education*. Cambridge, MA: Harvard University Press.

Bryan, H. (2012) Education and schooling 5–11 years. In: Arthur, J. and Peterson, A. (eds) *The Routledge Companion to Education*. London: Routledge.

Chitty, C. (2014) *Education Policy in Britain* (3rd edn). Basingstoke: Palgrave Macmillan.

Coffield, F. and Williamson, B. (2012) *From Exam Factories to Communities of Discovery: The Democratic Route*. London: Institute of Education, University of London.

Connelly, M. and Xu, S. (2012) Curriculum and curriculum studies. In: J. Arthur and A. Peterson (eds) *The Routledge Companion to Education*. Abingdon: Routledge.

Darling-Hammond, L. (2010) *The Flat World and Education: How America's Commitment to Equity Will Determine Our Future*. New York: Teachers College Press.

Davies, R. and Trowsdale, J. (2021) The culture of disciplines: Reconceptualising multi-subject curricula. *British Educational Research Journal*, 47(5): 1434–46.

Department for Children, Schools and Families (2008) *Independent Review of the Primary Curriculum: Final Report. London:* DCSF Publications.

Eurydice Norway Unit (2019) New Norway Curriculum at Primary and Secondary Levels in 2020. Available at: https://eacea.ec.europa.eu/national-policies/eurydice/content/norway-implement-new-curricula-primary-and-secondary-school-levels-2020_en (accessed: 12 March 2023).

Kelly, A. (2009) *The Curriculum: Theory and Practice* (6th edn). London: SAGE.

Loo, B. (2018) *Education in the USA (World Education, News and Reviews*. Available at: https://wenr.wes.org/2018/06/education-in-the-united-states-of-america (accessed: 12 March 2023).

Malik, N. (2020) *We Need New Stories: Challenging the Toxic Myths Behind Our Age of Discontent*. London: Weidenfield & Nicolson.

Ministry of Education (2020) *The New Zealand Curriculum*. Available at: https://parents.education. govt.nz/primary-school/learning-at-school/new-zealand-curriculum/#NZcurriculum (accessed: 12 March 2023).

Mohdin, A. (2020) Rules on anti-capitalist views in schools to be reconsidered. *The Guardian, 16 December,* p. 21.

Northern Ireland Government (2007) *The Northern Ireland Curriculum: Primary*. Available at: www.nicurriculum.org.uk/docs/key_stages_1_and_2/northern_ireland_curriculum_primary. pdf (accessed: 12 March 2023).

Palaiologou, I. (ed.) (2021) *The Early Years Foundation Stage: Theory and Practice* (4th edn). London: SAGE.

Palaiologou, I. (2022) *The Early Years Foundation Stage in Context*. Available at: https://uk. sagepub.com/en-gb/eur/early-years-foundation-stage-in-context (accessed 12 March 2023).

Palaiologou, I. and Male, T. (2021a) Historical developments in policy for early childhood education and care. In: Palaiologou, I. (ed.) *The Early Years Foundation Stage: Theory and Practice* (4th edn). London: SAGE.

Palaiologou, I. and Male, T. (2021b) The Early Years Foundation Stage. In: Palaiologou, I. (ed.) *The Early Years Foundation Stage: Theory and Practice* (4th edn). London: SAGE.

Plowden Report (1967) *Children and Their Primary Schools: A Report of the Central Advisory Council for England.* London: HMSO.

Ravitch, D. (2010) *The Death and Life of the Great American School System: How Testing and Choice are Undermining Education.* New York: Basic Books.

Rowntree, D. (1981) *A Dictionary of Education.* London: Harper & Row.

Scottish Government (2021) What is Curriculum for Excellence? Available at: https://education. gov.scot/education-scotland/scottish-education-system/policy-for-scottish-education/policy-drivers/cfe-building-from-the-statement-appendix-incl-btc1-5/what-is-curriculum-for-excellence (accessed 12 March 2023).

Sibieta, L. and Jerrim, J. (2021) *A Comparison of School Institutions and Policies Across the UK.* London: Education Policy Institution and Nuffield Trust. Available at: https://epi.org.uk/wp-content/uploads/2021/04/EPI-UK-Institutions-Comparisons-2021.pdf (accessed 12 March 2023).

Skolverket (2018) *Curriculum for the Compulsory School, Preschool, Class and School-age EDUCARE 2011 (revised 2018).* Available at: www.skolverket.se/download/18.31c292d516e 7445866a218f/1576654682907/pdf3984.pdf (accessed 12 March 2023).

Stenhouse, L. (1975) *An Introduction to Curriculum Research and Development.* Oxford: Heinemann.

Thomas, G. (2013) *Education: A Very Short Introduction.* Oxford: Oxford University Press.

United Kingdom Government (2022) *English National Curriculum.* Available at: www.gov.uk/government/collections/national-curriculum (accessed 12 March 2023).

Wallace, S. (2008) *Oxford Dictionary of Education.* Oxford: Oxford University Press.

Walsh, G. (2021) Early childhood education and care in Northern Ireland. In: I. Palaiologou (ed.) *The Early Years Foundation Stage: Theory and Practice* (4th edn). London: SAGE.

Waters, J. and Macdonald, N. (2021) Early childhood education and care. In: I. Palaiologou (ed.) *The Early Years Foundation Stage: Theory and Practice* (4th edn). London: SAGE.

Weale, S. (2021) Entire UK curriculum should teach black history, says union. *The Guardian,* 1 April, p. 16.

Welsh Government (2021) *What is Changing?* Available at: www.gov.wales/education-changing (accessed 12 March 2023).

Zafirakou, A. (2021) *Those Who Can, Teach: What it Takes to Make the Next Generation.* London: Bloomsbury.

4

EDUCATION AS A VEHICLE FOR SOCIAL MOBILITY

LEARNING OUTCOMES

Having read this chapter, you should be able to:

- understand the notion of education as a vehicle for social mobility;
- appreciate some of the government policies related to social mobility;
- identify definitions and measures of social class;
- consider the role of educational thinkers in understanding socioeconomic inequality;
- examine the role of educational settings in eliciting social change.

KEY WORDS

absolute mobility; hidden resources; meritocracy; pedagogical discourse; pupil premium; relative mobility; social congestion; social positioning; socioeconomic deprivation.

INTRODUCTION

The recognition of the value and importance of education as a vehicle for social change has been a focus of a number of social movements since the nineteenth century. However, arguably this did not become a governmental concern until the post-war years when education as a human right was adopted by the United Nations (UN) General Assembly as part of the UN Declaration of Human Rights (Bourn, 2022). Since then, further international initiatives have seen an increasing focus on education as a right, including the Education for All (EFA) initiative launched in 1990 which declared that 'every person – child, youth and adult – shall be able to benefit from educational opportunities designed to meet their basic learning needs' (UNESCO, 1990: Article 1), an initiative which has since been strengthened through the UN Sustainable Development Goals (SDG) established in 2015. Sustainable Development Goal 4 reiterates the goal set out in the EFA by affirming an intention to 'ensure inclusive and equitable quality education and promote lifelong learning opportunities for all' (UN, 2015), reinforcing the notion that a quality education helps to reduce inequalities and break the cycle of poverty, empowering people to live healthier and more sustainable lives (UN, 2018).

The ambition to end the cycle of poverty has emerged as a recurrent theme in education policy in the United Kingdom for the past two decades with Labour Prime Minister Tony Blair declaring that his government had a 'new cause and a new ambition: to rebuild Britain as "one nation in which each citizen is valued and has a stake; in which no one is excluded from opportunity and the chance to develop their potential"' (1997: para. 5). Subsequently, the message was reiterated by Prime Minister Gordon Brown who set out a mission to 'fulfil the potential and realise the talents of all our people' (2007: para. 4) and reinforced almost a decade later by Theresa May (2016) who set out an intention to make Britain a country that works for everyone, stating 'when it comes to opportunity, we won't entrench the advantages of the fortunate few. We will do everything we can to help anybody, whatever your background, to go as far as your talents will take you' (GOV.UK, 2016: para. 12).

Remaining with policy designed to end the cycle of poverty, the Conservative government, under the leadership of Prime Minister Boris Johnson, focused policy on the *Levelling Up* agenda, which sought to end geographical inequality through improving economic dynamism and innovation to drive growth across the whole country (HM Government, 2022). In respect of education, the 2022 *Levelling Up* report set out an intention to introduce a new school funding formula to end the postcode lottery and to invest in a lifetime skills guarantee, designed to enable adults to gain A-level equivalency literacy skills and offer adult numeracy programmes and skills bootcamp (HM Government, 2022). Additionally, one of the missions set out in the *Levelling*

Up agenda is to see a significant increase in the number of children achieving the expected standard in reading, writing and mathematics by 2030, with those children in the worst performing areas to see a percentage increase of over one third. Moreover, the agenda highlighted the need to ensure that students have the skills required by employers through utilising the knowledge and skills of local employers in tightening the network of further education colleges, with funding and governance overhauled in line with the needs of employers. Technical skills training was a key focus, with the establishment of nine Institutes of Technology designed to boost skill in STEM subjects (HM Government, 2022).

It can be seen then that education as a mechanism for social mobility is uncontested, with Bukodi and Goldthorpe (2019) observing that ample evidence exists to demonstrate that educational attainment is 'a major, even if not always an overriding, factor in determining who is mobile or immobile' (p. 91). Moreover, as expressed by Bathmaker et al. (2013), a key tenet of UK government policy is the place of education as a route to social mobility and economic prosperity. Bukodi and Goldthorpe (2019) draw together the emphasis of political consensus on the need to increase social mobility alongside the crucial role of education policy in achieving this goal as previously noted. Bukodi and Goldthorpe (2019) argue that this increased focus on raising standards through educational expansion and institutional reform can serve to raise standards and reduce attainment gaps between individuals of different social origins, which in turn leads to an education-based **meritocracy**, whereby position is determined by the degree of achievement in the educational system.

Nevertheless, despite an increased focus on education as a means by which social mobility might be attained, evidence suggests that two decades of policy focused on social mobility has elicited only minimal change (Social Mobility Commission (SMC), 2017). Moreover, as cautioned by the SMC, these policies may no longer be fit for purpose in an ever-changing world, and propose that new approaches are needed if Britain is to become a fairer, more equal country. Education policies across all life stages have fallen short in their overall ambition, and while some successes have been seen, the SMC review of social mobility policies reveal that Britain remains a divided nation, stating that, 'A new geographical divide has opened up. A new income divide has opened up. And a new generational divide has opened up' (SMC, 2017: 8).

This chapter will commence with an overview of what is meant by social mobility in respect of some of the definitions of social class. It will go on to examine some of the education policies related to social mobility and will seek to determine the impact of these from a socioeconomic perspective. Drawing on the work of some of the key thinkers from the field of sociology, the chapter will assess how far education can really be seen as a vehicle for social mobility.

SOCIAL MOBILITY AND SOCIAL CLASS

Bukodi and Goldthorpe define social mobility as 'the movement of individuals over time between different social positions' (2019: 13) and point out that this can be characterised as being in an upward or downward direction – for example, moving from a less to a more disadvantaged position or vice versa. From a sociological perspective, social mobility is largely measured from the perspective of social strata, which is recognised as belonging to a specific social class. In recognition of this, it is pertinent to consider what is meant by social class and examine how perceptions of this have evolved over time.

Social class can be considered as a multidimensional construct, although it can be typified through three defining features:

Economic – measured through wealth, income and occupation.
Political – measured through status and power.
Cultural – measured through lifestyle, beliefs, values and education.

Arguably, of these defining features, economic is that which holds the most significance since a person's social status and power has a strong correlation with their economic position – for example, a person with a professional qualification such as a lawyer or doctor will have higher status and power than a manual worker such as a cleaner. This has implications for culture and lifestyle, since those with greater financial means can arguably afford a more lavish lifestyle acquiring the symbols of social status. It could be suggested that it is for this reason that social status is traditionally measured through occupation, which is also likely to reflect other aspects of class position, such as power, status and lifestyle.

While traditionally, the most recognised categories of social status in Britain fall into the three categories of upper, middle and lower class, various objective forms of measurement have been developed, including both official scales – i.e., those used by the government to measure social class, and unofficial measures more commonly used by sociologists and psychologists for more academic ends. Savage et al. (2013) explain that official analysis of class and stratification is now in its third phase, with the first phase, the Registrar-General's (RG) of Social Class, commencing in 1911 and drawing to an end in the 1980s. This first standard classification system used by the government was a basic two-class model – middle and lower class – and categorised class through occupation type. The middle class comprised professional, intermediate and non-manual skilled workers, while lower class included manual skilled, semi-skilled and unskilled workers. This was a simple and easy to apply tool which ranked occupations on their relative standing in the community and allowed for the collection of a significant amount of data which could be used to make comparisons and monitor trends over a long period of time.

However, critics of this model argue that significant groups of people are omitted from the RG model, including those in the wealthiest brackets who may live off investments, for example, while at the other end of the scale the unemployed, never employed and not employed do not appear in any of the categories. This subsequently resulted in the Conservative government amending the official measurement of class in the 1980s through the introduction of a nine-category scale – the standard occupational classification (SOC). Like its predecessor, this scale measured social class by occupation. However, in this model occupation was ranked according to the qualification or skills required to perform the job rather than on the simple basis of the occupations standing in the community as applied in the RG model. Nevertheless, a level of subjectivity is still necessary in determining how skill levels might be assessed and a further criticism of this model lies in a failure to identify any class structure within the model.

Responding to critiques of these governmental models, in which observers favoured a more sociologically informed approach to identifying class schemas drawing from the theoretical frameworks of sociologists such as Marx and Weber (Savage et al., 2013), the highly influential Erikson–Goldthorpe–Portocarero (EGP) model was developed from the work of Goldthorpe and associates. In this model, seven classes were identified according to a person's employment position. Unlike the RG model, a distinction was drawn between employee and employer, with the former being divided into those on a labour contract with their employer and those in a service relationship. According to Savage et al. (2013), this class schema influenced an overhaul of the UK class system, leading to the National Statistics Socio-Economic Classification (NS–SEC), and was significant in providing opportunities for the comparative analysis of social mobility.

It can be seen, then, that measures of social class are an important component in identifying trends in social mobility and determining the success of government policy designed to improve outcomes for all. The next section of this chapter will therefore provide an overview of how education policy over the past two decades has been designed to address social mobility.

EDUCATION POLICY AND SOCIAL MOBILITY: HISTORICAL PERSPECTIVES

Arguably, the role of education as a means by which to elicit social change first came to prominence in 2001 when Tony Blair, as part of the Labour manifesto for a second term in power, declared that 'our top priority was, is and always will be education, education, education' (*The Guardian*: 2001, para. 2). Included in their manifesto was a pledge to change standards and support at every level from nurseries to schools, colleges and universities. This pledge was subsequently reinforced through a significant number of policies, acts and initiatives, and while this was not unusual in terms of government policy as observed by Smith and Noble (1995), cited in Tomlinson (2003: 195), the difference was that 'Labour was ideologically committed to returning a measure of social justice and equality to a society becoming dangerously divided between rich and poor'. Labour government education policies sought to develop the potential of each and every child through equal opportunities for all, with policies focused on raising standards through increasing the testing regime and encouraging a diversity of schools through the promotion of specialist schools and city academies. Moreover, modernising the curriculum was undertaken through an increased emphasis on literacy and numeracy, and the development of a more coherent 14–19 curriculum which attempted to bridge the divide between traditional and non-traditional qualifications.

Underpinning the Labour government's education policies was Blair's commitment to a system built around *meritocracy* – that is, one that rewards individuals on the basis of academic ability rather than social standing or economics. This was illustrated through Blair's commitment to setting a target of '50 per cent of young adults going into higher education in the next century' (Prime Minister Tony Blair, Labour Party Conference, 28 September 1999), an ambition that was almost realised by 2016 when it was estimated that 49 per cent of 17- to 30-year-olds had entered higher education for the first time (Parliament UK, 2018). Policy discourse around HE study is dominated by an understanding that participation in higher level study has long-term financial benefits, with graduate earnings surpassing those of non-graduates (Bathmaker et al., 2013).

The emphasis on education as a vehicle for social mobility was similarly reflected in the policy agenda of the Conservative–Liberal democratic coalition government formed in 2010 in their proposal for a new 'strategy' for social mobility (Goldthorpe, 2013). The coalition government identified that to increase social mobility it was necessary for government departments to work together in a bid to 'remove barriers in every stage of life, to give people equal access to opportunities and help give second chances to those who need them' (GOV.UK: 2018, para. 3). Like their predecessors, education policy focused on the full range of education provision, including ensuring that children get the best start in life through improving the range and quality of 0–5 childcare and providing 15 hours of free childcare a week for the most disadvantaged 2-year-olds. The coalition government also introduced a **pupil premium** to raise achievement among the most disadvantaged children, as well as improving post-16 opportunities for young people. Reiterating the rhetoric around meritocracy, Liberal Democrat leader, Nick Clegg, stated:

No one should be prevented from fulfilling their potential by the circumstances of their birth. What ought to count is how hard you work and the skills and talents you possess, not the school you went to or the jobs your parents did.

(HM Government, 2011: 5)

The social mobility agenda proposed by the coalition government sought to address some of the inequalities observed in respect of the impact that parental income and social standing had on a child's life chances, acknowledging that children from the poorest background failed to meet the attainment standards expected at key educational milestones. Furthermore, it was acknowledged that these young people were less likely to attend Russell Group universities and inevitably failed to gain employment in professional or managerial jobs. This they identified as being both damaging to individuals, as well as leaving the country's economic standing unfulfilled (HM Government, 2011).

It is notable that while the successive Conservative government, under the leadership of David Cameron, appeared to build on the coalition's vision of creating a more equal playing field for all, with Cameron stating:

Whoever you are, wherever you live, whatever your background, whatever stage of life you are at, I believe this government can help you fulfil your aspirations. And let me be clear, when I say whoever you are, I mean it.

(GOV.UK, 2015: para. 2)

Vizard and Hills (2020) suggest that in the period 2015–2019, inequalities by characteristic, including socioeconomic status, remained a key source of social injustice. They go on to observe that in the period since 2015, social outcomes by **socioeconomic deprivation** widened across a range of indicators, including educational attainment (Vizard and Hills, 2020). Moreover, despite higher education participation continuing to increase, particularly for the most disadvantaged, it was observed that progress in education at age 16 appeared to have stalled, with a fall in participation rates in new apprenticeships, with those in the more disadvantaged areas most effected. Vizard and Hills imply that this can be accounted for by a 'light touch' approach to social policy in this period, particularly in terms of 'major thinking and initiatives to improve social outcomes and to reduce social disadvantage and social inequalities' (2020: 15), which could perhaps be due to an over-emphasis on Brexit plans during this period.

Nevertheless, an overview of two decades of policies designed to improve outcomes and social mobility would suggest only marginal advancement towards any long-term goals. In the latest government policy, the aforementioned *Levelling Up* agenda, author Alun Francis argues that a new approach to social mobility is required (2021) and criticises policy that has previously had as a measure academic achievement and access to professional roles in the job market. While Francis (2021) acknowledges that talent and ability are important factors in social mobility with educational establishments having an important role to play, he also sees a range of wider factors with a part to play, including the working of the labour market, geography, inheritance and place. Nevertheless, Baker (2011) argues that education now has the 'whip hand' of social mobility in that social mobility is effectively mediated by education *and* this situation has widespread political legitimacy (Boliver and Wakeling, 2017). The next section of this chapter will examine what part education might play in social mobility and will examine some of the challenges as outlined by Francis (2021).

EDUCATION AND SOCIAL MOBILITY

Findings from the economic and social research council (ESRC) (n.d.) observed that educational performance appeared to be one of the main barriers preventing people from moving out of poverty, yet, despite the policy rhetoric discussed earlier in the chapter, children from the poorest families still fail to attain their academic potential. The ESRC identify a relationship between poverty and social (im)mobility whereby children living in poverty achieve less well in school, leading to poorer academic outcomes. The research suggests a divide between the rich and the poor in which less investment in educational resources is evident in the poorest sectors of society, commencing in utero and continuing through early childhood, resulting in large socio-economic differences in cognitive functioning (Jerrim and McMillan, 2015). Moreover, income equality between the rich and poor can lead to school and neighbourhood segregation (Harding et al., 2011), meaning that pupils from poorer backgrounds fail to catch up with their more affluent peers who have access to better quality schools. Jerrim and McMillan (2015) suggest that such disparities in educational investment have far-reaching consequences, with the skill gap increasing and notable differences in academic achievement by the end of secondary education. The cumulative effect of this is that those young people from the poorest areas are less likely to access higher education, resulting in less opportunity in the labour market, reflected in unemployment or employment in lower paid, unskilled jobs.

Goldthorpe (2013) outlines that placing education at the heart of social mobility assumes that a rise in the level of educational attainment among those young people from a less advantaged background will automatically lead to greater educational attainment, and in so doing will translate into an increase in **relative mobility**. In order to address this, the ESRC recommend that multiple structural problems need to be addressed, including inadequate school funding in the poorest areas, low-quality teaching and high levels of exclusions in schools located in areas of high socioeconomic deprivation (ESRC, n.d). In this respect, better schools for all would be of high priority, which the ESRC outline as having, 'better teachers and other educational resources, and a better classroom environment, including better behaved pupils and better interactions among pupils and between pupils and teachers' (n.d.: 1). While it would be anticipated that access to better schools would go in some way to closing the attainment gap as observed by Goldthorpe (2013), in reality evidence from research presents a far more complex picture than this would suggest (Breen and Jonsson, 2005; Boliver and Wakeling, 2017; Bowers-Brown et al., 2017).

Goldthorpe argues that a simple change in education policy is an insufficient tool for modifying class mobility since it overlooks the 'self-maintaining' property of class regime. He explains this as 'the capacity of families with greater resources to use these resources specifically in reaction to situations in which some threat to their positions might arise' (2013: 443). Arguably, this relates strongly to intergenerational mobility, defined as 'the relationship between the socioeconomic status of parents and the status their children will attain as adults' (OECD, 2010: 184) or, put simply, how far individuals move up or down the social ladder compared with their parents. In a mobile society, an individual's wage, education or occupation will be seen to be better positioned than that of their parents; thus, they are seen to be upwardly mobile. As seen earlier in the chapter, policies designed to shape access to human capital formation include public support for access to better education at all stages, with policies promoting intergenerational social mobility seeking to utilise the education system as a means by which the future workforce is recruited to key occupations based on their talent rather than social origin (Brown, 2013). This view supports the idea that class structure can be reshaped through meritocratic competition rather than hereditary, which Bell (1973) observed sees education transformed to the role of the arbiter of class position (cited in Brown, 2013). On the other hand, Brown (2013) goes on to suggest that the more recent drive to privatise education has seen a subtle shift from meritocratic competition to one that is driven by market forces. Premised on neoliberal theory, fairness as social mobility supposes that those from more disadvantaged backgrounds will have the opportunity to compete in the market with their more affluent peers.

Nevertheless, evidence suggests that policy agendas have made little impact on intergenerational social mobility, with Brown (2013) arguing that framing the problem of intergenerational social mobility through social policy neglects some of the key lessons from earlier sociological studies. Arguably, the shift from a system based on market, rather than meritocratic, competition has in fact been detrimental to intergenerational social mobility, while neoliberal theories suggest the creation of mobility opportunities through an upgrading of the workforce does not necessarily benefit the most disadvantaged. For example, the Conservative-led coalition government determined in 2011 that there was 'room at the top' for highly qualified graduates from all backgrounds, with demand for skilled workers outstripping supply, while at the same time acknowledging low levels of social mobility compared with the postwar period and against a backdrop of one in five young people not in education, employment or training (NEET). It appeared that, despite the opportunities available, those from working-class backgrounds were still not entering the working domain of their middle-class counterparts, which, as argued by Goldthorpe (2013), would reflect a stagnation of relative social mobility, which can be explained by the observation that individual achievement is competing against a backdrop of positional competition whereby those from middle-class positions are able to mobilise capital in order to maintain their advantage in both the field of education and in the workplace. As observed by Brown:

> Unlike **absolute mobility**, 'relative' mobility is based on a positional competition that determines one's standing (or position) in a hierarchy of academic performance or hierarchy of labour-market entrants, where the key to personal welfare is an ability to stay ahead of the crowd because if everyone advances together it 'increases the crush'.

(2013: 682)

Bathmaker et al. (2013) observe that even where young people hold a degree-level qualification, successful transition into paid employment remains uncertain since labour markets have failed to keep up with an increasing number of graduates – a direct result of the aforementioned policy introduced by New Labour to increase the number of young people accessing higher education. As noted by Boliver and Wakeling, 'education, and especially higher education, has become pivotal for entry to certain well-rewarded occupations, notably the professions, meaning that higher education and social mobility are increasingly intertwined' (2017: 1). However, Boliver and Wakeling (2017) go on to contend that entry to higher education is predicated by social class, and while an increasing number of young people from working-class origins may well be accessing higher education, the nature of that establishment and the degree course taken begins to assume a new importance, or, as Boliver and Wakeling observe, 'As higher education systems expand, inequalities between levels within the system begin to emerge' (2017: 4). Britten et al. (2016) caution that higher education participation rates have resulted in some discrepancy in labour market returns, according to academic discipline and university prestige, with graduates of lower status disciplines and academic institutions finding it increasingly difficult to obtain graduate-level jobs. Since students from working-class backgrounds most frequently apply to the less prestigious post-1992 universities, the power of education to promote social mobility must be called to question. A more disconcerting observation from Britten et al. (2016) is that even in cases whereby students from working-class origins graduate from more prestigious courses or institutions, they still appear to be disadvantaged, particularly in more prestigious organisations.

Bathmaker et al. (2018) suggest a clear correlation between early educational experiences, most specifically choice of schools and higher education choice, arguing that this stratification of the education system is inextricably linked to the workings of the English class system. They go on to suggest that parents in the most affluent classes seek to maintain their position by ensuring that their children secure places in independent, private schools, while those in the middle classes adopt a similar strategy through manipulating the housing market and using the system to ensure that their children attend the best primary schools and higher rated secondary and grammar schools. This, they argue, leaves parents of working-class children with little option but to send their children to the local comprehensive school (Bathmaker et al., 2018). It can be seen then that the middle and upper classes will mobilise their forces in order to maintain their position in society, while at the same time securing their children's future. Brown (2013) refers to this as a form of **social positioning** which occurs in a landscape of **social congestion**, whereby the number of middle-class jobs are out-stripped by demand. Brown posits that social congestion is most prevalent in econo-mies with large middle classes, mass education and wide income inequalities, and in which people use the education system as a means by which to stand out from the crowd (2013: 7). Moreover, as those from more privileged classes seek to sustain their advantage, the working classes see themselves as increasingly socially distanced as they navigate the tension between what is required to do a job against what is required to get a decent job.

It can be seen, therefore, that a divide continues to exist between young people from different socioeconomic backgrounds, and while an increasing number of young people seek places in higher education, they remain disadvantaged in terms of acces-sibility to high-status courses and institutions. Reay (2018) suggests that this reflects a landscape by which class inequalities are not so much about exclusion from the system but from within it, with just 1 in 20 children from the most disadvantaged backgrounds enrolling in the elite Russell Group universities. Thomas and Quinn (2007) posit that young people with non-traditional qualifications find themselves unprepared for university, lacking the sense of entitlement most commonly seen in the middle and upper classes who are more likely to enter higher education with more traditional qualifications (Chowdry et al., 2010; Harrison, 2011; SMC, 2016). Moreover, the preva-lence of young people from working-class backgrounds in post-1992 universities could well be attributed to the seeking of a sense of belonging whereby they choose a uni-versity based on how well they believe they will fit in. In this respect, it can be seen that a relationship exists between the social class from which a young person belongs and their choice of education. Moreover, it can be seen that this relationship is first formed from an early age, whereby middle-class parents who assume an automatic progression to higher education, make education choices which best position their children to attend elite universities (Devine, 2004). Furthermore, while working-class parents may well have a similar ambition for their children, a lack of personal experi-ence in the education system means that they are less able to provide the necessary foundations to support their children in making the most prudent higher education choices. In order to understand the complexity of this relationship between social mobility and education, it is pertinent therefore to consider the ideas of some of the key thinkers in the field of social and cultural capital.

RELEVANT EDUCATIONAL THINKERS

The work of French sociologist Pierre Bourdieu has commonly been employed as a lens by which to gain a better understanding of the educational division between individuals from different socioeconomic backgrounds. For Bourdieu, education policy was seen as a mechanism by which the existing social hierarchy was legitimised, perpetuating socioeconomic inequality through a system that enabled the dominant classes to retain their position in society (Gauntlett, 2011; Edgerton and Roberts, 2014). According to Bourdieu, the education system validates social inequalities, since in order to achieve success within it, there is an assumed possession of cultural capital and higher class habitus (Sullivan, 2002). Bourdieu referred to cultural capital as a familiarity with the dominant culture, resulting from engagement in and with education and culture (Grenfell, 2007), while habitus was seen as the social norms or tendencies that guide behaviour and thinking, which Bourdieu believed involved unconscious action that is reproduced 'without any deliberate pursuit of coherence ... without any conscious concentration' (Bourdieu, 1984: 170).

Bourdieu theorised that those children from working-class families were not in possession of cultural capital or upper-class habitus, making failure in the education system both inevitable and acceptable. Moreover, since educational credentials served to reproduce and legitimise social inequalities, then those in the upper classes were seen to be deserving of their place in the social structure (Sullivan, 2002). Moreover, Bourdieu identified a juxtaposition between family status and education, which, according to Tzanakis, sees 'parents endow[ing] their children with physical, human, social and especially cultural capital whose transmissions create inequalities in children's educational and occupational attainment' (2011, p. 76). Furthermore, this family reproduction can be seen to be transmitted into educational settings, with schools and teachers rewarding those in possession of elite cultural capital through the establishment of elitist standards, often at the expense of those lacking such capital (Atkinson, 2011; Tzanakis, 2011).

Far from seeing education as a mechanism for social mobility, Bourdieu's work presents the education system as a means by which social status might be maintained through both institutional and familial habitus. The influence of socioeconomic status on education choices highlights a relationship between cultural and social capital – that is, the capital accrued from networks of relationships. Bourdieu defined social capital as

> the sum of the resources, actual or virtual, that accrue to an individual or a group by virtue of possessing a durable network of more or less institutionalized relationships of mutual acquaintance and recognition.

> (Bourdieu, in Bourdieu and Wacquant, 1992: 119)

For Bourdieu, social capital expounds 'the cold realities of social inequality' (Gauntlett, 2011: 3), since in simple terms this reflects the notion that who you know is more important than what you know, reflecting a world in which 'the elite jobs go the posh men ... who went to the exclusive schools' (ibid.). Thus, those in possession of social capital are able to make social connections through accessing networks and alliances (Dillon, 2014). From an educational perspective, this enables parents to draw from their own educational experiences, working the system and confidently intervening on behalf of their children (Brooks, 2019). Moreover, as observed by Reay (2018), the self-assured relationship with education observed in upper-class parents is reflected through choice of university whereby these parents 'did not even articulate the divide between old and new universities because going to a new university is not what someone like them does' (p. 132). Moreover, Reay (2018) observed that those from the upper and middle classes increasingly recognise that in an educational landscape in which 50 per cent of the population has a degree, then the institution that awarded that degree assumes increasing importance. Reflecting the work of Bourdieu, Reay (2018) noted that educational success comes easily to such classes, because they have 'the money, confidence, social connections and resources to make it happen without a great deal of effort' (p. 134).

While it can be seen, then, that Bourdieu's work (1984) presupposes that education is a means by which social order might be maintained, it should be noted that his work may lack currency in the current education landscape. As seen earlier in the chapter, the fair access agenda championed by successive governments has arguably encouraged a system that is built around meritocracy, in which entry to higher education in particular is based on the educational talents of the individual, regardless of their class. According to Goldthorpe (2013), when a society proceeds in the direction of an education-based meritocracy, social mobility is enhanced, and where this does not occur, it will be for legitimate meritocratic reasons. However, while the UK education system should be well placed to compensate for the effects of social reproduction, it is apparent that the social imbalance may be too firmly engrained for these measures to be fully effective. As observed by Reay (2018), while there appears to be an upper-class disdain of the lower classes regarding access to elite universities, it can equally be assumed that the socially disadvantaged eliminate themselves from these institutions due to their perceived lack of cultural capital, which Bourdieu referred to as 'the poverty of aspiration' (Devine, 2004). Furthermore, as Boliver (2011) observed, it is unlikely that the socioeconomic inequalities of access to higher education will decline, since those from the most advantaged backgrounds will always be best placed to take advantage of any expansion to the education system. Perhaps the inequalities between social classes are too firmly embedded for the apparent barriers to education to be fully removed.

Bourn (2022) posits that while Bourdieu's work may have some credence in helping to understand the influences on education, he goes on to suggest that this presents a rather dispiriting view of education which could well lead to a sense of disempowerment among educationalists. Moreover, as suggested previously, Bourdieu's work is situated in a different culture and time, making comparisons with current practice challenging. It is pertinent, then, to consider the work of thinkers who approach educational reform from a more current stance and one that is more applicable to the context of this work, one of whom is American educationalist Michael Apple.

In his text *Ideology and Curriculum*, Apple (2019) proposes that 'knowledge that is actually taught in schools, surrounding what is considered to be socially legitimate knowledge, are of no small moment in becoming aware of the school's cultural, economic, and political position' (p. 6). He goes on to argue that this ideology reflects social norms in which students and teachers find themselves unable to challenge social, economic, cultural, political and educational disparity, and instead he states that 'schools latently recreate cultural and economic disparities, though this is certainly not what most school people intend at all' (2019: 33). Apple suggests that 'schools exist through their relations to other more powerful institutions, institutions that are combined in such a way as to generate structural inequalities of power and access to resources' (2019: 65). Moreover, like Bourdieu, Apple proposes that schools are responsible for reinforcing and reproducing these inequalities through everyday school practices – i.e., through the curriculum, pedagogy and daily activities that preserve social inequalities.

As noted earlier in the chapter, the apparent shift from an education-based meritocracy to one that is driven by market forces is criticised by Apple who presents the view that 'under the growing power of neoliberal ideological forms, education is being commodified' (2013: 16). Apple goes on to argue that in an educational landscape which sees institutions as products, subject to market forces, then those who work in them become valued solely by their contribution to the economy measured through test scores and examination results. This, he believes, devalues the true nature of both formal and informal education, and overlooks those important educational activities such as 'the labour of love, care and solidarity' (2013: 16). Apple considers that a society that does not engage in successful struggles over these forms cannot be considered truly serious about equality (2013: 16).

Apple (2019) suggests that the solution to the problem of educational disparity is to be found not in schools but in constructing a social order that is self-critical and focused on social and economic equality. Nevertheless, he does see the role of education as a social good and in his 2013 text *Can Education Change Society?* Apple sets out 'what can and is being done now to create a number of important conditions for critically democratic schooling that participates in social transformation' (2013: 22). These he recommends as

> Bearing witness to negativity—that is, telling the truth about the ways in which current policies and practices may reproduce relations of inequality, dominance, and subordination inside and outside of education;

Showing spaces of contradiction and action where it may be possible to engage in transformational social and educational efforts; and

Being the 'critical secretary' of people and movements already engaged in these kinds of more critically democratic actions and programs.

(Apple, 2016: 131)

Apple argues that a crucial aspect of the task is in bearing witness, in which he proposes that specific cases can be used to examine what has happened and is already happening in schools and communities. Through learning from these cases, he suggests that that 'new educational structures are truly possible within the existing educational systems if social movements and political alliances are built that both challenge an accepted common sense and begin to create a new one' (2013: 127). In his text *Ideology and Curriculum* (2019), Apple turns his attention to the way in which children learn, arguing that rather than focusing on the cognitive domains of learning as proposed by psychological theories, emphasis should be placed on educational issues in the wider context, through the development of democratic citizens of the future, and in this respect the position of schools should be one that minimises the limits imposed by the outside, including anti-democratic practices. In his progressive notion of critical pedagogy, Apple seeks to expose the realities of inequalities in educational structures and encourages critical practice in which practitioners reflect the values and content of their teaching and identify any potential bias in practice (Aubrey and Riley, 2022). In his book *Teachers and Texts: A Political Economy of Class and Gender Relations in Education*, Apple states: 'sometimes, just thinking seriously can be a form of resistance itself' (1988: 182), which reiterates the belief that if educators resist the power of the dominant culture on the use of official knowledge, the standardised curriculum and the return to traditional teaching methods, then they themselves are in a position to contest some of the injustices that could hamper a democratic education.

Another sociologist who was concerned with the disparities in experiences of young people from different social classes was Basil Bernstein whose work focused on the relationship between political economy, family, language and schooling. Bernstein was committed to equity and social justice, which he saw as a means by which to '[prevent] the wastage of working class potential' (1961: 308). Influenced by the work of French sociologist Emile Durkheim, Bernstein is perhaps most well known for his early work on language, communication codes and schooling, which he later applied to a focus on **pedagogical discourse**, practice and educational transmission (Sadovnik, 2001).

Bernstein's work on language, communication and codes proposed that two general types of linguistic codes were in use – elaborated and restricted – which can be defined as follows:

Elaborated code – this tends to be characterised by a high proportion of grammatical features such as subordinate clauses, adjectives, the pronoun 'I' and passives and tends to be used in more formal, educated situations allowing users to apply language creatively.

Restricted – this is used more generally in informal situations and often reflects membership to a group; it tends to lack stylistic range and is meaningful through context – i.e., typified by slang and colloquialism. Use of gesture and intonation supports meaning.

Bernstein proposed that social class differences in the use of these codes were the norm, with those from the middle class more likely to express themselves through the elaborated code, while working-class people used the more limiting restricted code. Moreover, it was also observed that while the working class were often constrained by access solely to the restricted code, those from the middle class were able to exploit both linguistic codes, depending on the situation they found themselves in. This put those from the working class at a distinct disadvantage, limited as they were in language usage. Sadovnik (2001) observes that Bernstein was somewhat criticised in his discussion of social classes through language, with critics labelling it a deficit theory; nevertheless, it did allow for an exploration of how differences in learning among social classes might be affected by the relationship between family and school, and the way in which language was used in different contexts. This, then, enabled Bernstein to make important connections between power and class relations with the educational processes in schools.

Bernstein rejected the criticism that his theory represented a deficit theory, particularly any suggestion that the restricted code used by working-class people was in any way an inferior code. Instead, he argued that 'restricted codes are not deficient, but rather are functionally related to the social division of labour, where context dependent language is necessary in the context of production' (Sadovnik, 2001: 689). Nevertheless, Bernstein did develop his code theory in seeking a connection between communication codes and pedagogic discourse and practice, which enabled him to identify how school processes might foster social class reproduction. In studying different forms of pedagogies, Bernstein drew from Durkheim's work in analysing two types of educational transmission – visible and invisible – suggesting that different rules in classification and framing were applied to each form of pedagogic practice (Sadovnik, 2001). In Bernstein's theory of pedagogic discourse, classification refers to the social division of labour, which at micro level indicates the organisational or structural aspect of pedagogic practice; from the discourse perspective, Bernstein identifies relations between school knowledge and everyday knowledge, as well as the relationship between knowledge within a particular subject area. In the classification of agents, Bernstein considers the demarcation between teachers and learners pedagogic identities, which he considered to be a power relationship, distinguished along strong and weak classifications. Framing, on the other hand, considers how social relations exist within a social division, which, at the micro level of pedagogic practice, can be seen as the location of control over the rules of communication (Hoadley, 2006). This is expressed by Bernstein as 'the degree of control teacher and pupil possess over the selection, sequencing, pacing and evaluation of the knowledge transmitted and received in the pedagogical relationship' (Bernstein 1975a: 88). In short, framing is about who controls what and the nature of that control.

Bernstein related his work on classification and framing to pedagogic discourse in educational practice with a specific focus on social class division. Bernstein was concerned with the transmission of knowledge in educational settings and how this knowledge was related to structurally determined power relations (Sadovnik, 2001). He was particularly concerned with how this impacted on different social groups and was interested in how pedagogic practice differed across schools. Applying his theory to different classroom practices, he identified that pedagogic practice was influenced differently depending on the market for which it served – for example, schools in a working-class area constructed a pedagogy built around a vocational education, serving an economic market. Conversely, settings serving a more middle-class society built a curriculum around an independent and autonomous market, where the autonomy of knowledge was legitimated. Bernstein saw this as the reproduction of class inequalities or, as observed by Sadovnik, 'through a consideration of the inner workings of the types of educational practice, Bernstein contributed to a greater understanding of how schools reproduce what they are ideologically committed to eradicating—social-class advantages in schooling and society' (2001: 691).

Bernstein referred to these different discourses as visible and invisible pedagogies, in which a setting serving a middle-class community will commonly apply an invisible pedagogy, reflected in practice characterised by:

1 Implicit rather than explicit control over the child by the teacher;
2 Reduced emphasis on the transmission and acquisition of specific skills;
3 Relatively free activity by the child in exploring and rearranging an environment arranged by the teacher; and
4 Use of many diffuse criteria to evaluate the pedagogy.

(Bernstein, 1975b: 1)

On the other hand, Bernstein saw visible pedagogy as one that was 'realised through strong classifications and strong framing' (1975b: 9), with more explicit transmission methods and more specific criteria. Arguably, Bernstein's work raised awareness of how educational settings inadvertently allowed conditions for social reproduction through practices that made assumptions about the learning capacity of their pupils.

This chapter has so far considered how education policy has sought to address issues around social mobility, with a reflection on some of the theorists underpinning the potential challenges of tackling inequality through educational policy. Nevertheless, while it is evident through the number of government policies and initiatives designed to address social mobility that this remains a government priority, it should also be noted that measures have been taken to raise awareness. Moreover, evidence from practice suggests that strategies have been developed which have seen some positive results in tackling some of the inequalities discussed in this chapter. Some of these strategies will be discussed in the next section.

IMPLICATIONS FOR PRACTICE

A study undertaken by the Social Mobility Commission (SMC) in 2021 reported some positive outcomes following the implementation of the pupil premium. While the initiative was designed as a financial incentive to provide additional support to those pupils categorised as the most vulnerable in schools, the report highlights that a further consequence of this funding was a change in school culture and policy, particularly in respect of raising staff awareness of some of the challenges that pupils were experiencing (SMC, 2021). The report highlights that a number of secondary schools used the pupil premium funding as a means of boosting students' cultural capital, with teachers in the study observing that a lack of cultural capital presented a causal factor in identifying gaps in attainment. While the teachers' own view of cultural capital diverged from Bourdieu's original definitions, focusing on issues such as lack of opportunity to discuss career choices with parents, limited vocabulary and through geographical limitations, effective measures were put in place to offset these observed inequalities. Such measures included applying a more context-based mathematics curriculum, introducing literacy interventions and paying for educational-based school visits.

In line with Bernstein's work, the SMC (2021) report identified that school context was an important factor when considering inequalities, highlighting that schools in advantaged areas have the benefit of '**hidden resources**', which they define as 'historically strong reputations, high levels of parental engagement, and powerful alumni networks' (2021: 40). In comparison, schools experiencing contextual challenges tend to have high levels of student mobility with many students coming from difficult backgrounds. The report found that school context accounted for large differentials in pupils' attainment, but also identified ways in which setting could mitigate this – for example, through adapting the curriculum and encouraging increased parental involvement. Furthermore, it was identified that schools with hidden resources engendered a sense of belonging in their student body, something that schools in challenging areas sought to foster. Settings identified as demonstrating good practice recommended that teachers pay particular attention to those pupils from the most disadvantaged areas – for example, by employing strategies such as utilising support staff to help pupils with their homework and offer additional interventions.

The revised Education Inspection Framework for the Early Years Foundation Stage (EIF) (2022) restates a focus on cultural capital, that 'cultural capital is the essential knowledge that children need to prepare them for their future success' (Ofsted, 2022: para. 186). The framework advises that inspectors will view provision, considering how far the curriculum is used to enhance experience and opportunities for children, most especially those who are disadvantaged and recognising that children who attend settings will have very different experiences. While again there is a clear distinction with Bourdieu's original definition of cultural capital, there is an acknowledgement that settings may take on some responsibility for allowing children to undertake a range of experiences, some of which they might not otherwise experience. Moreover, the emphasis on cultural capital seeks to build on the children's own personal cultural capital, which suggests a departure from Bourdieu's assertion of a legitimate culture. It could be suggested, then, that a celebration of the cultural capital of all sees a blurring of class boundaries. The Early Years alliance recommends that settings should not over-think cultural capital, but should draw on good practice, which already exists in settings – for example, through providing exciting and stimulating everyday activities such as visits to local attractions and inviting individuals from the community to talk to the children, the aim being to extend and develop cultural awareness.

It can be seen that education has a role to play in addressing some of the socioeconomic inequalities, and some steps have been taken to encourage social mobility through education. Nevertheless, it could be argued that these are small steps and more needs to be done to eradicate the impact of socioeconomic status on social mobility. Indeed, a report by Alun Francis (2021), in response to the Conservative government's levelling up agenda, observes that while there are outliers in both primary and secondary education which have demonstrated what might be achieved in terms of knowledge-based learning and those behaviours required to achieve success, more still needs to be done in respect of translating good practice more widely. Moreover, while the drive to create a 'knowledge economy' has resulted in a mass expansion of higher education, there remains a lack of parity between institutions and courses studied, particularly in respect of outcomes for graduates. Francis suggests that for education to make a difference in social mobility, an understanding of how the education system and the economy currently constrain opportunity needs to be clear, with a focus on 'how they can be made to work together more productively, to identify, cultivate and reward a wider array of talents' (2021: 30).

SUMMARY

This chapter has shown that education as a vehicle for social mobility has been an area of focus for government initiatives for the past three decades at least. Moreover, while the current emphasis for social mobility has shifted to one of levelling up, education remains one of the key initiatives towards providing greater equality. Nevertheless, Francis (2021) suggests that the levelling up agenda proposes a new approach to social mobility, suggesting that the former emphasis on preparing young people for university as a means by which to improve opportunities was not the best proxy measure of social mobility as the agenda seemed to advocate. Instead, the agenda emphasises a much wider range of educational opportunities which Francis (2021) argues is a more accurate representation of the range of pathways which young people might take towards increasing their social mobility, including non-degree routes to higher skills, including a renewed emphasis on apprenticeships.

This current shift in focus is a clear illustration of the challenges of enhancing social mobility and would appear to be one of a succession of policies, which have had varying degrees of success. Moreover, the challenges of measuring social mobility would appear to have added in another layer of complexity with the application of different models of social class, alongside the tension between absolute and relative mobility. Goldthorpe (2013) cites Aldridge who, in his assessment of different forms of mobility, reveals that in absolute terms an upward shift has been seen in intergenerational mobility, although this has occurred as a result of class structural change through the generation of more managerial and professional positions. Conversely, in terms of intergenerational relative mobility, little change has been seen, with class positions of parents and children remaining constant. Moreover, studies undertaken by Blanden et al. (2005) revealed a decline in intergenerational mobility, a decline which was seen to be associated with widening income inequality between social classes. Goldthorpe (2013) notes that this decline might also be attributed to the expansion of higher education whereby middle-class children benefitted disproportionately as their earnings increased.

Reflecting the work of Bourdieu and Bernstein, it could be argued that the social class divide is so heavily entrenched in British culture that the middle-class society will always retain their privileged position, making it increasingly difficult for those from working-class backgrounds to narrow the gap, with Goldthorpe observing that 'education has an effect on *who* is mobile, or immobile, rather than on the overall rate of mobility' (2013: 441). Goldthorpe (2013) goes on to argue that those responsible for education policy have failed to acknowledge the historical evidence of the self-maintaining properties of middle-class society, this being the capacity to react to situations in which threats to their positions might arise. Taking this into consideration, Goldthorpe presents the view that attempts at increasing equality of opportunity, in the sense of a greater equality of mobility chances, would seem unlikely to be effective, whether made through educational policy or otherwise, unless the class-linked inequalities of condition on which class mobility regimes are founded are themselves significantly reduced.

(2013: 445)

However, it should not be overlooked that many of the initiatives designed to address issues of inequality, while not necessarily addressing social mobility per se, have made some impact on children from the most disadvantaged backgrounds, and this in itself must surely be seen as a positive step forward. For example, the introduction of pupil premium funding not only resulted in targeted provision for the most disadvantaged, but also raised awareness among teaching staff of the challenges faced by these young people. Similarly, by including cultural capital as an inspection focus, settings are encouraged to celebrate the unique cultures of their pupils, while at the same time widening their experiences.

Bourn (2022) comments that approaches to education as a vehicle for social change must be underpinned by hope and argues that it is the responsibility of the educator to encourage a sense of a positive future, that change for the better is achievable. Reflected through the work of Apple, a positive step forward might then come from those educationalists wishing to resist dominant ideological influences, addressing issues of class and capital, and making change possible. As stated by Bourn:

If a pedagogical approach is taken within a counter-hegemonic form of education that promotes alternative values bases, then education can become a voice not only of resistance but one of seeking social change.

(2022: 27)

GLOSSARY OF KEY TERMS

Absolute mobility

Absolute mobility refers to the proportion of individuals from a certain class group who are mobile to other class destinations, measured as percentages in one form or another. Absolute mobility can be conditioned by changes to the structure of the class positions between which mobility can occur and by relative rates of class mobility (Bukodia and Goldthorpe, 2019).

Hidden resources

Hidden resources are aspects of school systems that are not immediately obvious, but which are important factors when looking at socioeconomic inequality. Hidden resources include such things as the ethos and reputation of the school, parental engagement, and education and alumni networks. In respect of the pupils themselves, this too would include the knowledge, skill and attributes that pupils already possess when they attend a school, with those from the middle class more likely to be in possession of the hidden resources required to succeed in education.

Meritocracy

A system by which progression is based on ability rather than class. In a meritocratic system, education is presented as a level playing-field by which, provided required standards are met, then access to elite education is available to all. A person is rewarded by merit rather than by wealth or privilege.

Pedagogical discourse

Adapted from Bernstein's work, pedagogical discourse refers to the operation of a set of principles for working that reflects a specific culture. Bernstein viewed this through the discourse of skills and knowledge (instructional), alongside the creation of social order, relations and identity (regulative). In this way, social relations, identities and order are created, maintained and reproduced over time.

Pupil premium

Introduced by the Conservative–Liberal Democrat coalition government in 2011, the pupil premium refers to a sum of money allocated to schools for children from low-income families. Funding was allocated per child based on metrics, including eligibility for free school meals, looked after children and children from forces families. Monies allocated were to be spent entirely on the identified children with the aim of improving educational outcomes for the most disadvantaged.

Relative mobility

Refers to chances of individuals of different class origins being found in different class destinations – for example, how likely it is to see a person from a working-class back-ground appearing in a middle-class position. Measures of relative class mobility would be in terms of how far an adult ranks against their peers or parents in the same social class.

Social congestion

Social congestion occurs through market crowding whereby the number of people qualified in a position exceeds the number of positions available. Brown (2013) describes this as a lack of capacity in the economy to deliver on the opportunity bargain, which can be seen as a result of a flooding of the market with graduates and no more room at the top. Social congestion is prevalent in economies with a growing middle class, mass systems of higher education and wide income equalities.

Social positioning

Social positioning is the act of individuals or groups to maintain their position in the social structure. From the perspective of Bourdieu, this sees upper-class society mobilising their resources to maintain their societal position, particularly in situations where they see their status challenged from those they perceive to be in the middle and working classes.

Socioeconomic deprivation

Socioeconomic deprivation refers to the relative disadvantage of an individual or social group in respect of access to economic, material or social resources and opportunities. Deprivation may be a result of a number of interrelated factors, including poverty, mental illness, limited education and low socioeconomic status, all of which contribute to social exclusion.

FURTHER READING

Ball, S. (2013) *The Education Debate* (2nd edn). Bristol: The Policy Press.

An overview of the past twenty years of education policy, with a focus on how policy has sought to encourage education as a social good, generating social mobility and tackling social inequality. Ball seeks to evaluate whether policy goals are feasible or compatible.

Blandford, S. (2017) *Born to Fail? Social Mobility, A Working Class View*. Melton: John Catt Educational.

Drawing from personal experience, Blandford addresses the educational inequalities of the white working class and considers how change should come from the inside.

Hargreaves, M. (2020) *Moving*. Bloomington: Solution Tree Press.

A personal account of Hargreaves's educational journey from the 1950s to the 1970s. Hargreaves draws from classical and contemporary research in exploring the impact of class movement on his life. Hargreaves considers how his own personal experiences are still reflected today.

Major, L.E. and Machin, S. (2018) *Social Mobility and its Enemies*. London: Pelican Books.

An observation into the effects of decreasing social mobility and the place of education in addressing this. Major and Machin analyse the ways in which social mobility in the UK had changed over the years and the place of education in creating a better future using examples of good practice from other countries.

Reay, D. (2017) *Miseducation, Inequality and the Working Class*. Bristol: The Policy Press.

An overview of the British education system from personal testimonies and statistics, detailing the role of education in the discussion around class, most specifically in the sphere of selective education and the social inequalities it perpetuates.

REFERENCES

Apple, M. (1988) *Teachers and Texts: A Political Economy of Class and Gender Relations in Education*. New York: Routledge.

Apple, M.W. (2013) *Can Education Change Society?* New York: Routledge.

Apple, M.W. (Guest Editor) (2016) Introduction to 'The Politics of Educational Reforms', *The Educational Forum*, 80(2): 127–36.

Apple, M.W. (2019) *Ideology and Curriculum* (4th edn). New York: Routledge.

Atkinson, W. (2011) From sociological fictions to social fictions: Some Bourdieusian reflections on the concepts of 'institutional habitus' and 'family habitus'. *British Journal of Sociology of Education, 32*(3): 331–47.

Aubrey, K. and Riley, A. (2018) *Understanding and Using Challenging Educational Theories*. London: SAGE.

Aubrey, K. and Riley, A. (2022) *Understanding and Using Educational Theories* (3rd edn). London: SAGE.

Baker, D.P. (2011) Forward and backward, horizontal and vertical: Transformation of occupational credentialing in the schooled society. *Research in Social Stratification and Mobility, 29*(1): 5–29.

Bathmaker, A., Ingram, N. and Waller, R. (2013) Higher education, social class and the mobilisation of capitals: Recognising and playing the game. *British Journal of Sociology of Education*, 34: 5–6, 723–43. DOI: 10.1080/01425692.2013.816041

Bernstein, B. (1961) Social class and linguistic development: A theory of social learning. *In:* A.H. Halsey, J. Floud, C.A. Anderson (eds) *Education, Economy and Society*. New York: Free Press, pp. 288–314.

Bernstein, B. (1975a) *Class, Codes and Control Volume 3: Towards a Theory of Educational Transmissions*. London: Routledge & Kegan Paul.

Bernstein, B. (1975b) *Class and Pedagogies: Visible and Invisible*. Centre for Educational Research and Innovation.

Blair, T. (1997) '*Bringing Britain Together*': London 1997. Available at: www.britishpoliticalspeech. org/speech-archive.htm?speech=320 (accessed 13 March 2023).

Blanden, J., Gregg, P. and Machin, S. (2005) Educational inequality and intergenerational mobility. In: S. Machin and A. Vignoles (eds) *What's the Good of Education?* Princeton, NJ: Princeton University Press.

Boliver, V. (2011) Expansion, differentiation, and the persistence of social class inequalities in British higher education. *Higher Education, 61*: 229–42.

Boliver, V. and Wakeling, P. (2017) Social mobility and (higher education). In: *Encyclopedia of International Higher Education Systems and Institutions* (pp. 1–6) DOI: 10.1007/978-94-017-9553-1_43-1

Bourdieu, P. (1984) *Distinction: A Social Critique of the Judgement of Taste*. London: Routledge.

Bourdieu, P. (1989) In: L. Wacquant (1996) (ed.) Towards a reflexive sociology: A workshop with Pierre Bourdieu. *Sociological Theory*, 7: 26–63.

Bourdi, P., and Wacquant, L. (1992) *An Invitation to Reflexive Sociology*, Chicago: University of Chicago Press.

Bourn, D. (2022) *Education for Social Change*. London: Bloomsbury Academic.

Bowers-Brown, T., Stahl, G., Lacey, S., Morrison, A. and Garth, S. (2017) Higher education, social class and social mobility: The degree generation. *International Studies in Sociology of Education*, 26(3): 326–34.

Breen, R. and Jonsson, J.O. (2005) Inequality of opportunity in comparative perspective: Recent research on educational attainment and social mobility. *Annual Review of Sociology*, 31: 223–43.

Britten, J., Dearden, L., Shephard, N. and Vignoles, A. (2016) How English domiciled graduate earnings vary with gender, institution attended, subject and socio-economic background. IFS Working Paper W16/06. London: Institute for Fiscal Studies.

Brooks, R. (2019) *Education and Society*. London: Red Globe Press.

Brown, G. (2007) *In full: Brown speech*. Available at: http://news.bbc.co.uk/1/hi/uk_politics/6246114.stm (accessed 13 March 2023).

Brown, P. (2013) Education, opportunity and the prospects for social mobility. *British Journal of Sociology of Education*, 34(5–6): 678–700.

Bukodi, E. and Goldthorpe, J.H. (2019) *Social Mobility and Education in Britain*. Cambridge: Cambridge University Press.

Chowdry, H., Crawford, C., Dearden. L., Goodman, A. and Vignoles, A. (2010) Widening participation in higher education: Analysis using linked administrative data. *Journal of the Royal Statistic Society*, *176*(2): 431–57.

Devine, F. (2004). *Class Practices: How Parents Help their Children Get Good Jobs*. Cambridge: Cambridge University Press.

Dillon, M. (2014) *Introduction to Sociological Theory*. Chichester: Wiley Blackwell.

Edgerton, J.D. and Roberts, L.W. (2014) Cultural capital or habitus? Bourdieu and beyond in the explanation of enduring educational inequality. *Theory and Research in Education*, *12*(2): 193–220.

Education and Social Research Council (ESRC) (n.d). Evidence briefing: Education vital for social mobility. Available at: www.esrc.ac.uk

Francis, A. (2021) Rethinking social mobility for the levelling up agenda. Available at: https://policyexchange.org.uk/wp-content/uploads/Rethinking-social-mobility-for-the-levelling-up-era.pdf (accessed 13 March 2023).

Gauntlett, D. (2011) *Three Approaches to Social Capital*. Available at: www.makingisconnecting.org (accessed 13 March 2023).

Goldthorpe, J.H. (2013) Understanding – and misunderstanding – social mobility in Britain: The entry of the economists, the confusion of politician and the limits of education policy. *Journal of Social Policy,* 42(3): 431–50.

GOV.UK (2015) PM speech on opportunity. Available at: www.gov.uk/government/speeches/pm-speech-on-opportunity (accessed 13 March 2023).

GOV.UK (2016) *Statement from the new Prime Minister Theresa May*. Available at: www.gov.uk/government/speeches/statement-from-the-new-prime-minister-theresa-may (accessed 13 March 2023).

GOV.UK (2018) 2010–2015 Government Policy: Social mobility. Available at: www.gov.uk/government/publications/2010-to-2015-government-policy-social-mobility/2010-to-2015-government-policy-social-mobility (accessed 13 March 2023).

Grenfell, M.J. (2007) *Pierre Bourdieu: Education and Training*. London: Continuum.

The Guardian (2001) Full text of Tony Blair's speech on education, 23 May. Available at: www.theguardian.com/politics/2001/may/23/labour.tonyblair (accessed 13 March 2023).

Harding, D., Gennetian, L., Winship, C., Sanbonmatsu, L. and King, J. (2011) Unpacking neighbourhood influences on education outcomes: Setting the stage for future research. In: G. Duncan and R. Murnane (eds) *Whither Opportunity: Rising Inequality and the Uncertain Life Chances of Low-Income Children*. New York: Russell Sage Foundation, pp. 277–96.

Harrison, N. (2011) Have the changes introduced by the 2004 Higher Education Act made higher education admissions in England wider and fairer? *Journal of Education Policy, 26*(3): 449–68.

HM Government (2011) *Opening Doors, Breaking Barriers: A Strategy for Social Mobility*. London: Crown copyright.

HM Government (2022) *Levelling Up the United Kingdom*. Available at: https://assets.publishing.service.gov.uk/government/uploads/system/uploads/attachment_data/file/1052046/Executive_Summary.pdf (accessed 13 March 2023).

Hoadley, U. (2006) Analysing pedagogy: The problem of framing. Available at: www.education.uct.ac.za/sites/default/files/image_tool/images/104/hoadley2006.pdf (accessed 13 March 2023).

Jerrim, J. and McMillan, L. (2015) Income inequality, intergenerational mobility, and the Great Gatsby curve: Is education the key? *Social Forces*, 94(2): 505–33.

OECD (2010) *A Family Affair: Intergenerational Social Mobility across OECD Countries*. Available at: www.oecd.org/centrodemexico/medios/44582910.pdf (accessed 13 March 2023).

Ofsted (2022) *Early Years Inspection Handbook for Ofsted Registered Provision*. Crown Copyright.

Parliament UK (2018) *Chapter 1: Post-school Education in the 21st century*. Available at: https://publications.parliament.uk/pa/ld201719/ldselect/ldeconaf/139/13907.htm (accessed 13 March 2023).

Reay, D. (2018) Working class educational transitions to university: The limits of success. *European Journal of Education*, 53: 528–40.

Sadovnik, A.R. (2001). Basil Bernstein 1924–2000. *Prospects: The quarterly review of comparative education*, XXX1(4): 687–703.

Savage, M., Devine, F., Cunningham, N., Taylor, M., Li, Y., Hjellebrekke, J., Le Roux, B., Friedman, S. and Miles, A. (2013) A new model of social class? Findings from the BBCs Great British Class Survey Experiment. *Sociology*, 47(2): 210–50.

Smith T. and Noble, M. (1995) *Education Divides: Poverty and Schooling in the 1990s*. London: Child Poverty Action Group.

Social Mobility Commission (SMC) (2016) *State of the Nation 2016: Social Mobility in Great Britain*. London: HMSO.

Social Mobility Commission (SMC) (2017) *Time for change: An assessment of government policy on social mobility 1997–2017*. London: Institute of Public Policy Research Skills 2030.

Social Mobility Commission (SMC) (2021) *Against the odds: Achieving greater progress for secondary students facing socio-economic disadvantage*. London: HMSO.

Sullivan, A. (2002). Bourdieu and education: How useful is Bourdieu's theory for researchers? *The Netherlands Journal of Social Sciences, 38*(2): 144–66.

Thomas, E. and Quinn, J. (2007) First generation entry into higher education: an international study. *Society for Research into Higher Education*. OUP.

Tomlinson, S. (2003). New Labour and education. *Children and Society*, 17: 195–204.

Tzanakis, M. (2011) Bourdieu's social reproduction thesis and the role of cultural capital in educational attainment: A critical review of key empirical studies. *Educate Journal*, 11(1): 76 –90.

UNESCO (1990) *World Declaration on Education for All*. New York: UNESCO.

United Nations (2015) *Department of Economic and Social Affairs: Sustainable Development*. Available at: https://sdgs.un.org/goals/goal4 (accessed 13 March 2023).

United Nations (2018) *Quality Education: Why it Matters*. Available at: www.un.org/sustainabledevelopment/wp-content/uploads/2018/09/Goal-4.pdf (accessed 13 March 2023).

Vizard, P. and Hills, J. (eds) (2020) *Social Policies and Distributional Outcomes in a Changing Britain: Summary Report*. London: The London School of Economics and Political Science.

5

POPULISM AND EDUCATION

LEARNING OUTCOMES

Having read this chapter, you should be able to:

- appreciate the complexities of populism as a concept;
- understand the position of populism in relation to democracy;
- recognise the influence that populism can have regarding education policy and practice;
- critically appraise, and challenge where necessary, populist educational discourse;
- identify the possible reasons underlining populist thinking in education.

KEY WORDS

critical pedagogy; culture wars; decolonisation of the curriculum; democratic education; the elite; ideology; liberal democracy; neoliberalism; the people; populism; rhetoric.

INTRODUCTION

Populism is a contested and multifaceted concept. Populist, and particularly national populist discourse, has increased since the latter part of the twentieth century and has become increasingly more visible in the UK over the recent past. The concept is positioned firmly with politics, which will be explored in the chapter. Although populism is perceived by many as a right-wing phenomenon, it can, and is, employed by politicians from both the left and right (Mouffe, 2018; Hussain and Yunus, 2021). However, regardless of whether populism embraces right- or left-wing models, it is usually seen as having negative undertones and mainly considered to be 'a threat to contemporary modes of governance' (Sant and Brown, 2021: 410). At this early stage in the chapter, it is worth noting that the link between politics and populism is pertinent in understanding the thinking behind education policy, such as the way that the curriculum and initial teacher education has changed in the UK and other countries. Kelly (2009) argued that the main reasons for these changes were the increasing politisation of education which gave greater emphasis to traditional over the progressive and **democratic education** methods of learning and teaching.

The notion of populism is not new and originally refers to people engaging in the democratic process – for example, those members of the Populist Party in late nineteenth-century USA (Mudde and Kaltwasser, 2017). Currently, there are arguments about the meaning of populism: is it 'discourse, strategy, political logic, **ideology** or political style'? (Hussain and Yunus, 2021); it is suggested that populism could mean, and include, all five of these. However, Mudde and Kaltwasser (2017) define populism as

> [a] thin-centred ideology that considers society to be ultimately separated into two homogeneous and antagonistic camps, 'the pure people' versus 'the corrupt elite', and which argues that politics should be an expression of the ... (general will) ... of the people.
>
> (p. 6)

Mudde and Kaltwasser (2017: 6) refer to populism as a 'thin-centred ideology', which is not like the 'thick-centred' or 'full' ideologies (e.g., fascism, liberalism, socialism); populism tends to attach itself to one of the thick-centred ideologies to bolster its appeal to the public. Scholars of populism agree with the idea of the core message of populism, which appeals to '**the people**' and condemnation of '**the elite**'. As an example of this dualist antagonistic construction, Craske (2021) posits that in the UK politicians have since 2010 activated a planned populist approach to attain their education policy ambition, but which have also had broader political and social consequences. This has been manufactured between 'the people' (commonly, teachers and parents) and the illegitimate 'elite' (an educational establishment) that opposes change. This anti-elite populist **rhetoric**, arguably first tested in the Department for Education (DfE), has now been instituted more widely in our British politics (Craske, 2021: 279).

Another point to stress here in relation to Mudde and Kaltwasser's (2017) definition of populism above, is the notion of the general will of the people. General will (*volonte generale*) is aligned with the eighteenth-century philosopher Jean-Jacques Rousseau. The general will is the idea that people will unite to make laws that reflect their communal interest: 'populism's monist and moral distinction between the pure people and the corrupt elite reinforces the idea that a general will exists' (Mudde and Kaltwasser, 2017: 16). As such, many populist governments will, when they think it is to their advantage, promote the use of referenda as a form of direct democracy, rather than choosing to take the path of representative and institutional legislation (Muller, 2017). From this viewpoint, populism could be seen as a democratic force for good by empowering people who would otherwise have little say in the political process. However, Mudde and Kaltwasser (2017: 18) warn that it can have a more sinister side, because populism implies that the general will is unconditional: 'it can legitimize authoritarian and illiberal attacks on anyone who (allegedly) threatens the homogeneity of the people'.

Jan-Werner Muller (2017), though, cautions that the growth of populism throughout the world poses a significant danger to democracy. Although we have quite correctly stated that populism can be promoted and driven by both right and left political parties, within the context of this chapter on populism and education, the main focus will be on right-wing populism, which is embedded in **neoliberalism**, because that is where the evidence, particularly on its effect on social justice, is most prolific.

The chapter will consider the works of some of the distinguished scholars and writers on populism, as well as those who have undertaken populist research from an educational viewpoint. The main scholars will include Ernesto Laclau, Chantal Mouffe, Jan-Werner Muller, and Cas Mudde and Cristobal Rovira Kaltwasser; many of these populist scholars 'understand populism to indicate a crisis in democracies' (Hussain and Yunus, 2021: 250). When considering the challenges to populism, the ideas of educational thinkers such as John Dewey, Paulo Freire, Michael Apple, Basil Bernstein, Henry Giroux and bell hooks will be briefly considered.

First, this chapter will delve more into the phenomenon of populism, including its relationship with democracy and neoliberalism. It will then examine the various modes and characteristics of populism globally and in the UK, as well as considering the possible reasons for its increasing attraction for governments, including its relationship with democracy and neoliberalism. The chapter will define democracy and neoliberalism, explore the differences of left- and right-wing populism where appropriate, consider some of the characteristics of populism, and then look at examples of populist rhetoric, particularly the use of slogans. Second, the chapter will briefly reflect on the effect that topics and events has had, and is having, in the context of populism and education. Next, how populism has impacted on education policy and practice, including how ideology and the language used has been employed to appeal to 'the people' in opposition to 'the elite'. There will then be an overview of English education and its perceived links with populism. This will take into account education as a whole, including matters of initial teacher education (ITE) and the curriculum. Third, areas where populism in education can be challenged will be offered as possible ways to pursue an alternative and democratic path to learning and teaching, which will conclude with some ideas for practice.

POPULISM: CONCEPTS AND CHARACTERISTICS

To fully appreciate the context which follows, there is the need to consider the relationship of populism with two other concepts: democracy and neoliberalism. Similar to populism, democracy is a highly disputed notion, and it is further argued that there are at times close associations between the two concepts. The word 'democracy' originates from the Greek word *demos*, which translates as 'power to the people' (Mouffe, 2018: 14), while Mudde and Kaltwasser (2017: 80) define democracy 'as the combination of popular sovereignty and majority; nothing more, nothing less'; democracy is associated with selecting leaders by fair and free elections, where the people agree that the candidate with the majority of votes will govern them. Democracy is presented in a number of models, although it is not within the scope of this book to examine these in detail. The most pertinent term for this chapter would be '**liberal democracy**'. Mudde and Kaltwasser (2017: 80) explain liberal democracy as:

> A political regime, which not only respects popular sovereignty and majority rule, but also establishes independent institutions specialized in the protection of fundamental rights, such as the freedom of expression and the protection of minorities.

Mudde and Kaltwasser (2017) have created a very informative table which sets out the positive and negative effects of populism on liberal democracy.

Table 5.1   Positive and negative effects of populism on liberal democracy

Positive effects	*Negative effects*
Populism can give voice to groups that do not feel represented by the political elite.	Populism can use the notion and praxis of majority rule to circumvent minority rights.
Populism can mobilise excluded sectors of society, improving their integration into the political system.	Populism can use the notion and praxis of popular sovereignty to erode the institutions specialised in the protection of fundamental rights.
Populism can improve the responsiveness of the political system by fostering the implementation of policies preferred by excluded sectors of society.	Populism can promote the establishment of a new political cleavage which impedes the formation of stable political coalitions.
Populism can increase democratic accountability by making issues and policies part of the political realm.	Populism can lead to a moralisation of politics whereby reaching agreements becomes extremely difficult, if not impossible.

Source: Mudde and Kaltwasser (2017: 83).

In Europe, and particularly within the European Union (EU), populist activists are increasingly Eurosceptic and blame 'European elites of having created an all-powerful supranational organization that promotes (neo)liberalism at the expense and against the wishes of the people' (Mudde and Kaltwasser, 2017: 118). Neoliberalism is an important element of right-wing populism; it is a political undertaking which aims to make financial gains through influencing political decisions, particularly in privatising public sector institutions. This is usually promoted with the emphasis on common sense. In education, this has taken the form of removing many schools from democratic local authority control and into private profit-making companies which are charged, in some cases, with the provision of ITE, the curriculum and testing regimes (Hastings, 2019).

There are populist parties worldwide that may come from any point on the political continuum. On the left, for example, there was Venezuela's President Chavez, while in Europe there is the Podemos Party in Spain, the Syriza Party in Greece, the Die Linke in Germany, the Bloco de Esquerda in Portugal and in France La France Insoumise (Mouffe, 2018; Molloy, 2018). Mouffe (2018) also alludes to Jeremy Corbyn, the then leader of the UK Labour Party, and in the USA the one-time Democratic Party presidential candidate Bernie Sanders, as left-wing populists. Examples of right-wing populism include Jair Bolsonaro's Social Liberal Party in Brazil, Marine Le Pen's National Rally (previously the National Front) in France, Viktor Orban and the Fidesz Party in Hungary (which has recently been elected to a fourth term in office at a time of Putin's Russian invasion of Ukraine), and the previous president of the USA Donald Trump. It is argued that these populists have a commonality in that they merge their populist rhetoric with autocracy and a push against immigration (Molloy, 2018).

> The right-wing populists also pit the pure, innocent, always hardworking people against the corrupt elite who do not really work (other than to further their self-interest) and … also against the very bottom of society (those also do not really work and live like parasites off the work of others).
>
> (Muller, 2017: 23)

Mouffe (2018), cited in Hussain and Yunus (2021: 250) argues that right-wing populism can be found in the liberal democracies of the UK and Western Europe, and traced back to 'the neoliberal hegemonic formation that replaced the socio-democratic Keynesian welfare state'. It is the rise of the right and its populist agenda, as Muller (2017) has stressed, which poses the main danger to democracy, a danger that has been exasperated by changes in society such as globalism and multiculturalism (Molloy, 2018).

Although populism is presented in different political shades, there are certain characteristics that are common to all. Populists do not have an issue with representation if they are the representatives; also, they have no problem with elites if they are the elites governing the people (Muller, 2017). Furthermore, Muller (2017: 32) notes that conspiracy theories are not an 'addition to populist rhetoric; they are rooted in and emerge from the very logic of populism itself'. Another, contested, characteristic is that of the populist leader having a charismatic appeal. Charisma is a contested phenomenon because it is such an idiosyncratic and culturally defined term. Nevertheless, charisma is a trait frequently used to describe many populist leaders. Such charisma tends to serve them well, as it builds loyalty and enables them to have a strong bond with the people as well as enabling them to surmount internal differences within a broader alliance (Mudde and Kaltwasser, 2017). Molloy (2018) also adds 'bad manners' or behaving in a way that's not typical of politicians to the characteristic of right-wing populist leaders, citing Donald Trump as one example.

In her book *For a Left Populism* (2018: 23–4), Mouffe contrasts the difference between right- and left-wing populism:

> Right-wing populism claims it will bring back popular sovereignty and restore democracy, but this sovereignty is understood as 'national sovereignty' and reserved for those deemed to be true 'nationals'. Right-wing populists do not address the demand for equality and they construct a 'people' that excludes numerous categories, usually immigrants, seen as a threat to the identity and prosperity of the nation. ... Left populism, on the contrary, wants to recover democracy to deepen and extend it. A left populist strategy aims at federating the democratic demands into a collective will to construct a 'we', a 'people' confronting a common adversary: the oligarchy [oligarchy: a small group who have most of the power].

Other characteristics of right-wing populism include a call for common sense and simplistic remedies over empirical evidence, as well as appealing to the people on the principle of sovereignty to condemn institutions that try to defend the rights of liberal democracy: 'among those most targeted institutions are the judiciary and the media' (Mudde and Kaltwasser, 2017: 81). Populist targeting of the media when they perceive they are being critical, as well as targeting the judiciary when they have the power to overturn laws voted by government, has, it is argued, become more prevalent in recent times and hence weakens the fabric of representative liberal democracy. Another feature of right-wing populism is blaming the elite for imposing forms of political correctness in speech and in writing, which they say is limiting the independence of the people to express themselves without fear of causing an offence. Malik (2020a) calls this the political correctness myth which is spun by right-wing populists; she closely associates it with the myth of the free speech crisis. She argues that the purpose of the myth is not about safeguarding freedom of speech, which is the personal choice to declare a viewpoint without suppression, or the fear of breaking the law, but rather 'the purpose is to secure the licence to speak with impunity; not freedom of expression, but rather freedom from the consequences of that expression' (Malik, 2020a: 98).

A trait which is often cited with populism is the nature of rhetoric used, particularly in the use of simplistic slogans, to replace the complexity which is involved in implementing complicated policy and legislation (Laclau, 2018). Populist rhetoric focuses and persists with 'their representative claim no matter what; because their claim is of a moral and symbolic – not an empirical – nature, it cannot be disproven' (Muller, 2017: 39). Generally, populist rhetoric is mostly delivered in unsophisticated short phrases emphasising their close links with the people and accentuating their achievements. The tone of rhetoric towards any opposition is defamatory and often dismissive. Social media is increasingly used to vent such rhetoric. Muller (2017: 3) contests that populists, as well as being anti-elitist, are also '*antipluralist* ... [they] claim that they, and they alone, represent the people', citing the Turkish President Recep Tayyip Erdoğan, as an example, 'declaring at a party congress in defiance of his numerous domestic critics, "We are the people. Who are you?"' We offer just a few (there are many) examples of the brief phrases or slogans used, and often repeated, by populist leaders to connect with the people, mainly aimed at their political followers. In the USA, Donald Trump was a renowned user of slogans (especially on social media) such as 'drain the swamp', and in particular 'Make America Great Again'. Muller (2017: 38) contends that 'Make America Great Again' just means that the people have been let down by the elites 'and that anybody who opposes Trump must also somehow be against "American Greatness"'.

Nigel Farage, the one-time leader of the UKIP and Brexit parties, announced that the result of the 2016 referendum on leaving the EU was a 'victory for real people', indicating that populists think that only some people are real, as nearly half of the electorate voted to remain in the UK. Staying with the UK and Brexit, Boris Johnson, during his time as prime minister, frequently used the phrase 'get Brexit done' to garner support for finishing the Brexit process in order to 'take back control'. In France during the 1970s and 1980s, the National Front displayed posters that proclaimed 'Two million unemployed is two million immigrants too many!'. The message was simple and the resolution could be made by everyone with common sense (Muller, 2017). Whatever the topic or context, populist rhetoric is usually quite vacuous, simple, symbolic and panders to those who they consider to be the 'real people' (their followers). In summary, populist rhetoric is anti-elite and anti-intellectual (Malik, 2020a).

What has been noticeable in the UK, from about the time of the Brexit campaign, has been a determination of the government to embark on a culture war against what they term as a 'woke agenda'. This culture war declared by the increasingly right-wing UK government is evident in education policy, as well as in society as a whole. This is a populist strategy that is very reminiscent of Donald Trump's actions when he was president of the USA. Although in the UK 'woke' is a fairly recent term, it originates from Black slang in the 1960s USA, which means to be awake to forms of social injustice; woke is either taken as a compliment or, coming from the right-wing media, as an insult (Fenwick, 2021). It is a war waged by Conservative media against the woke agenda who, they claim, are anti-patriotic, anti- 'free speech', lacking in respect for what they perceive as British history and have a socialist or Marxist schedule.

The government itself, it is contended, is in the driving seat with this cultural war by playing to people's patriotic responsiveness with arguments over flags, statues, race and immigration. It has picked arguments with what they consider to be part of the 'elite', as we have seen, with the judiciary, the BBC, universities and lately, even with the Archbishop of Canterbury criticising the plan to process asylum seekers in Rwanda as part of the Nationality and Borders Act which passed through Parliament on 27 April 2022. The culture war has touched on the Black Lives Matter (BLM) movement, including the cool response from the prime minister and some government ministers regarding footballers taking the knee before games, and their lack of condemnation of elements of the crowd who booed the players for their action. This action 'that once depicted a solemn moment of silence and solidarity with the victims of racial injustice has become a symbol of censorship and reverse discrimination' (Malik, 2020b: 3). Some of these aspects of the culture war in education will become apparent in the next section.

POPULISM: EDUCATION POLICY, LANGUAGE AND IDEOLOGY

Prior to considering the relationship between populism and education, it is opportune to make a brief comment on some topics which are relevant to education in the UK. First, the narrative around Brexit and immigration, which, according to Mac an Ghaill and Haywood (2021: 276), has resulted in a rise in hate crimes, as well as a visible hardening of national borders, and the 'criminalisation of ethnic and religious differences'. Globally, the impact of populism on education has become more palpable due to the COVID-19 pandemic, and the widespread BLM demonstrations in reaction to the murder by white police officers of George Floyd in Minneapolis, USA. This reignited the 'racial fault lines in our democratic and educational institutions … leading to grassroots movements for change including calls for the decolonisation of education' (Hussain and Yunus, 2021: 253). It is argued that the BLM movement in the UK and the call for the **decolonisation of the curriculum** has acted as a catalyst for the **culture wars** being pursued by the populist Conservative government. There have also been moves from the DfE to guide teachers to teach some topics in a 'balanced manner', such as those relating to the British Empire or the reputations of British historic figures such as Sir Winston Churchill. Furthermore, teachers should not promote such groups as BLM or the views of environmental pressure groups – all of which hampers any effort by teachers to stimulate serious debate (Hazell, 2022).

Right-wing populists in the UK and elsewhere have ways of influencing education policy and practice which reflect their ideology, this is done through controlling the content of the curriculum and the selection of texts used in teaching. They also affect education through the repeated use of populist rhetoric and setting 'the people' (parents and teachers) against 'the elite' (the educational establishment), evidenced in some of the speeches and documents employed by Michael Gove, the Education

Secretary (in the Conservative-led coalition government) between 2010 and 2014. Gove's drive to reform education in England focused on his proposed populist policies being right for 'the people', while the present policies are against 'the people'. His reforms were positioned 'within a populist frame, which constituted ... [his] ... attempt to reorganise the social imagery of education' (Craske, 2021: 280). Furthermore, Craske emphasises the significance of Gove, as

> *the* key figure for understanding the type of conservatism that underpins the education reform (alongside his special advisor Dominic Cummings) had substantial control over content and strategy of the reforms in education ... [he] ... formed a tight grip on the content and strategy of the reforms to curriculum, pedagogy and teacher training.
>
> (Craske, 2021: 283–4)

Later, we will be taking into account some of Gove's ideas and policies, as well as those of some of his successors. Before looking into populist education policy and practice in the UK in more detail, the following offers a brief comparative activity about the populist impact on education in Brazil. Brazil is an interesting case when considering populism, since the country saw a spectacular reversal of voting choice which culminated in a right-wing populist government in 2018. Right-wing politicians were able to muster widespread electoral support for their socially conservative manifesto, including their traditional views on education, mainly due to an economic recession during 2015–2016 (Hussain and Yunus, 2021).

Jair Bolsonaro, a former military officer and far-right politician, became the president of Brazil in 2019. His presidential campaign speeches, and the rhetoric used, were filled with militarist, nationalist, racist and homophobic commentary. Bolsonaro's election was the result of over a decade of left-of-centre governments. During his election campaign, he took advantage of the poor economic state of Brazil and civil unrest, and vowed to deliver a series of neoliberal programmes to the country, including its education. One of Bolsonaro's promises was that he would place the military inside schools 'rather than teachers, who would be sole instructors of the mandated curriculum, using authoritarian and disciplinary methods to transform students into passive recipients' (Knijnik, 2021: 356). He was influenced by the radically inspired conservative groups who called for a traditional anti-Communist and Christian education system – more specifically, these groups wanted to eliminate any evidence of the philosophies of the Brazilian educator Paulo Freire (Alves et al., 2021). Freire was one of the leading critical educational thinkers of the late twentieth century. His strong belief was that democratic and dialogic education had a significant part to play in freeing people from oppression. Freire's ideas are significant in challenging the global inequality in education (Apple et al., 2001). Freire wrote extensively; his most renowned book is *Pedagogy of the Oppressed* (which was first published in 1970 and revised in 1996). The significance of Freire's writing is best summed up by Henry Giroux: 'Against the growing forces of authoritarian pedagogy … Freire's work offers both a resource for critique and a language of possibility' (2011: 165).

In the early twenty-first century, Brazil's education policies were based on promoting diversity and inclusion with the aim of 'racial equity, equal treatment of students based on gender and LGBTQ recognition' (Alves et al., 2021: 332). Since the Bolsonaro government took office, education policy and practice has been based upon an ultra-conservative ideology and all the promise of diversity and inclusion has vanished. The vanguard for these ultra-conservative, anti-Communist, traditionalist and anti-Freire mode of education groups was the influential *Escola sem Partido* (ESP), which is translated as 'School without a Party'. Apart from promoting their traditional, populist and authoritarian ideas, particularly in eradicating any Freirean thought, they have been instrumental in conducting a witch hunt of mainly online abuse against teachers and some parents who, despite the Bolsonaro government's education policies, continue to promote Freire's democratic and dialogic teaching. Nevertheless, many academics, parents and teachers have been challenging the tactics of ESP in their populist and authoritarian agenda (Knijnik, 2021). It is probably safe to say that the Bolsonaro government has a very overt right-wing populist agenda. This is exemplified, for example, in the emphasis on the promotion of traditional teaching and learning, and the vilification and attempts at eliminating the work of Freire and his progressive notions of critical and emancipatory education. Bolsonaro's term in office came to an end in December 2022 when he was replaced by Lula da Silva, the previous left-wing Brazilian president.

ENGLISH EDUCATION SINCE 2010 AND POPULISM

Turning our attention to the UK, or, more correctly, to English education since devolution, which occurred in 1997/1998. From that time, Wales, Scotland (although Scotland had a fair amoint of autonomy regarding education) and Northern Ireland were able to implement and manage their own ideas on education, including their own curriculum, education systems and language choices (Brighouse and Waters, 2021). Therefore, regarding the focus of populism and education, this chapter will limit its discussion to the English education system and mainly consider the period from 2010 when the Conservative-led coalition (with the Liberal Democrats) took over from the defeated New Labour government. Although limiting the timing of this chapter starting from 2010, it is argued that Margaret Thatcher, herself Secretary of State for Education from 1970 to 1974 and as Prime Minister from 1979 to 1990, employed a strategy that was

> clearly a populist one. It consisted in drawing a political frontier between, on one side, the 'forces of the establishment', identified with the oppressive state bureaucrats, trade unions and those who benefited from state handouts, and on the other, the industrious 'people' who were the victims of the various bureaucratic forces and their different allies.

> (Mouffe, 2018: 29)

The coalition government ended when the Conservative Party gained a majority which was enough to win the May 2015 general election. Since 2010, there have been five Conservative prime ministers: David Cameron, 2010–16; Theresa May, 2016–19; Boris Johnson, 2019–22; Liz Truss, 2022; Rishi Sunak, 2022– . During this same period there have been ten secretaries of state for education – all Conservatives: Michael Gove, 2010–14; Nicky Morgan, 2014–16; Justine Greening, 2016–18; Damian Hinds, 2018–19; Gavin Williamson, 2019–21; Nadim Zahawi, 2021–22; Michelle Donelan, 2022; James Cleverly, 2022; Kit Malthouse, 2022; Gillian Keegan, 2022– . The rapid changes in prime ministers and secretaries of state during 2022 were the chaotic outcome of Boris Johnson being forced to stand down, the fleeting premiership of Liz Truss and then the succession of Rishi Sunak voted into office by Conservative MPs.

Before delving into the education policy reforms that started with the coalition government, a short overview of the previous New Labour government will give context to the widespread changes made by Michael Gove. New Labour were in government between 1997 and 2010. The prime ministers were: Tony Blair, 1997–2007 and Gordon Brown, 2007–10; in that time, there were six secretaries of state for education. Although Blair and Brown's New Labour Party was an amalgamation of socialism and free market neoliberalism (termed the 'third way'), it mostly endeavoured to embrace the notions of social justice and inclusion in education and in society as a whole (Bartlett and Burton, 2020). New Labour's education policies and initiatives included the drive for lifelong learning, setting up of Sure Start centres for children up to four years of age and their families in areas of high deprivation, as well as Every Child Matters (ECM), a shared programme between education, health, social services and probation, to support families, children and their families. New Labour's policies also included specialist schools and academies, Building Schools for the Future (BSF) programme, and the expansion of higher education and the introduction of the Education Maintenance Allowance (EMA) for 16- to 18-year-olds. Given the drive by New Labour to align education with families, the Department for Education and Skills (DfES) was renamed the Department for Children, Schools and Families (DCSF). The 2010 general election was a time of international financial hardship, and in the UK a deepening recession and dissatisfaction with some Labour politicians involved in an expenses scandal (Bartlett and Burton, 2020).

With breathtaking zeal, Michael Gove, once the coalition government had formed, set about his ideologically driven education reforms. With an indication of the coalition's focus to solely concentrate on education, rather than combining schools with broader social aspects, Gove changed his department from the DCSF to the Department for Education (DfE), with an emphasis on subject-based learning and a return to traditional methods of teaching. The start of Gove's time in office was a period of considerable instability and rapid change (Brighouse and Waters, 2021); it could be argued that his whole tenure as Secretary of State was a time of instability and rapid change. During the coalition take-over, the UK was affected by economic difficulties.

Nevertheless, the neoliberal ideological thrust of the government and the DfE was evident, with cuts to the funding of socially based education initiatives such as the ECM, EMA, Sure Start and BSF being particularly impacted. This was made even more apparent with students having to pay considerably more for their university education, which signified a shift away from government support for some parts of education provision (Bartlett and Burton, 2020).

Whereas New Labour initiated the idea of creating academies as a way of resolving the issue of failing schools, Gove promoted academies for all schools and also advanced the creation of free schools, which were historic changes in English schooling. Both these changes are evidence of a move away from the bureaucratic, yet democratic, local government control and a push towards market forces. This in turn saw academies and free schools receiving funding directly from government, as well as giving autonomy to head teachers on how the funding should be spent. The results were to create more competition between schools and a shift away from democratic local government control (Bartlett and Burton, 2020). During the period of the coalition government, it was obvious that there was a robust neoconservative ideology underpinning the educational reforms, as well as the accompanying rhetoric. There was a strong emphasis on behaviour, a focus on school uniforms, streaming of students according to ability, the drive for a knowledge-based curriculum which included a more 'rigorous' focus on subject knowledge, the importance of exams over coursework and a prominence of British values (Bartlett and Burton, 2020). As already mentioned, Gove was the driving force behind these reforms. Brighouse and Waters (2021) suggested that he wanted to make a name for himself and drive the reforms with ideological vigour. At times he acted on a personal impulse – for example, when he sent a copy of the King James Bible to every school.

Craske (2021: 279) argues that between 2010 and 2014, Gove and his fellow education ministers in the DfE 'mobilised a deliberate populist strategy' to push through their education reforms. This populist strategy is evident in Gove's rhetoric, in both his writing and speeches. For the most part, apart from praising the benefits of cognitive science, little attempt is made to support these assertions with theoretical or empirical evidence. In true populist adversarial style, Gove wrote an article published in the *Daily Mail* on 23 March 2013 entitled: 'I refuse to surrender to the Marxist teachers hell-bent on destroying our schools: Education Secretary berates "the enemies of promise for opposing his plans"'. The piece was in response to education academics who challenged his reforms. He referred to these enemies of the people as 'The Blob', who were a 'network of educational gurus in and around our universities who praised each other's research, sat on committees that drafted politically correct curricula' (Gove, 2013a). Interestingly, this use of 'enemies' was also adopted by the *Daily Mail* again in 2016, when it called three judges 'the enemies of the people' who ruled against the government saying they would have to attain the consent of Parliament to give notice of Brexit. Speaking to the Independent Academies Trust in 2012, Gove re-emphasised his mistrust in intellectuals when he argued that 'the anti-intellectual strain in British life, and thinking, may have protected us from following the sort of ideological fashions that captured continental minds over the last century'. He also vented his criticisms of the teaching unions, whom he called a 'tiny, but vocal, group of militant activists' (Gove, 2013b).

Before looking beyond Gove's tenure as Education Secretary, there are two other aspects of his reforms which were important to him. First, curriculum reform, and second the provision of initial teacher education; both of these were underpinned again by traditionalist thinking that Gove argued for in a combative manner. His curriculum and exam reforms were to replace what he felt was a substandard curriculum that lacked depth and the acquisition of subject-based knowledge. The core subjects for the new curriculum were chosen for their academic rigour at the expense of the arts and vocational areas (Bartlett and Burton, 2020). His final curriculum framework was finished in 2014 and bolstered subject knowledge and with a focus on key skills. A new weight was given to exams over coursework. Exams were overhauled with a new GCSE grading system which replaced attainment levels. Furthermore, the Ebacc qualification was promoted and, without consultation, became part of the league tables for schools (Chitty, 2014; Bartlett and Burton, 2020). The second important aspect for Gove – initial teacher education – was driven, it is argued, by populist and anti-intellectual thinking. He encouraged increasing the number of teachers being trained in schools rather than those on university-based ITE programmes. Chitty (2014: 96) contests that for the coalition government, teacher education was 'primarily concerned with the acquisition of a certain set of rudimentary skills – and principally related to good behaviour management'. This focus on behaviour for teacher education is also reflected by Gove's Troops into Teaching initiative which attempted to interest those members of the armed forces to train as teachers, even if they did not have the required degree-level qualification (Chitty, 2014). This perceived attraction for the military in education was also linked with the pupils themselves when Gavin Williamson proclaimed government backing for the re-establishment of Cadet Forces in schools (Brighouse and Waters, 2021). Such alignment with the military, it is contended, is in keeping with other populist agendas worldwide.

Tim Brighouse and Mick Waters (2021) have interviewed fourteen UK secretaries of state as well as a number of well-known figures in education, the results of which have been documented in a detailed and thoroughly commended text on English state education since 1976: *About our Schools: Improving on Previous Best*. In the book, they gave an appraisal of Gove's tenure as Secretary of State for Education:

> Many of the people we interviewed for this book hold Gove responsible for some of the fundamental problems with schooling in England today: the mess created by the fractured system of academy and local authority schooling, the worrying rate of exclusions, the curriculum unsuited to a changing world, as well as professional disharmony over salaries, status and working conditions. His legacy has not been a positive one.
>
> (Brighouse and Waters, 2021: 163)

Many of the secretaries of state who followed Gove have ended up trying to complete the initiatives and policies he started. The academies and free schools policies were promoted as radical and market-driven solutions, but they appear now to be somewhat simplistically and ideologically adopted, and some of the untangling of these ideas have still not been resolved but remain Conservative educational policy, such as the core subject-based curriculum, traditional teaching methods and the reliance on examinations. Furthermore, some of these ideas are not in keeping with the educational thinking in the other UK home nations. Gavin Williamson had to pick up these ongoing issues, along with having to manage the effects of the COVID-19 pandemic, an event of huge consequences for social justice and educational development in all sectors of education. Issues such as the exams algorithm fiasco, the disparities of provision in home schooling, particularly with access to online learning materials, learners and staff being absent because they were isolating, and matters of social distancing in schools, were some of the problems that Williamson encountered. While doing this, he also endeavoured to continue with the push for wholesale academisation and the promotion of T-levels as alternatives to A-levels. Nevertheless, Williamson appeared not to consult with school leaders or the teaching unions during this period. Brighouse and Waters (2021: 78) noted that 'the impression given was that during the first lockdown Williamson and the various unions, individually or collectively, used the media to make their points rather than speaking directly to each other'. Nadim Zahawi who succeeded Williamson gained a reputation of efficiency as the minister for the COVID-19 vaccine distribution. He also had a huge task to drive through the polices initiated by Gove, as well as the catch-up programme for learners affected by the lapse in schooling; this was in addition to trying to change education to address the Conservative government's priorities, such as the Levelling Up agenda. These issues, some of which have been present since 2010, raise a number of challenges that need addressing.

CHALLENGING THE POPULIST EDUCATION AGENDA

It is appropriate to consider ways of challenging populism in general before exploring ways to challenge the populist education agenda since the solutions are similar. Furthermore, such challenges to populism require a nuanced and complex response. Mudde and Kaltwasser (2017: 109) argue that any 'overreacting to the populist challenge can do more harm than good'. They offer two ways in which populists could be confronted by the establishment: first, by depicting them as vile and irrational; second, by adopting the same rhetoric used by the populists. However, Mudde and Kaltwasser (2017: 116) warn that 'both approaches further intensify the moralization and polarization of politics and society; which fundamentally undermines the foundations of liberal democracy'. So, it is evident that challenging populism, which includes a populist education agenda, is a problematic undertaking, particularly while endeavouring to advance the notion of liberal democracy. Nevertheless, Mudde and Kaltwasser (2017: 118) offer a resolution:

> The best way to deal with populism is to engage – as difficult as it is – in an open dialogue with populist actors and supporters. The aim of the dialogue should be to better understand the claims and grievances of the populist elites and masses and to develop liberal democratic responses to them.

Jorge Knijnik's research regarding the anti-Freire pressure against teachers by the ESP movement in Brazil also found that dialogue could be a successful response to their populist right-wing antagonism. This, he argued, could be achieved by using the Freirean 'critical dialogue, teachers and school communities will be able to construct their own methods to counter the dictatorial demands of the ESP' (Knijnik, 2021: 368). Engagement and dialogue are also important methods promoted by the progressive critical educators.

A word of caution before considering ways in which populist educational ideas, practice and policy can be challenged: there are certain real constraints which are in place that will hamper attempts at successful challenge. Different education systems will have varying degrees of constraints; what we propose is relevant in the UK, but especially England. These constraints, it is argued, are a threat to democratic forms of education and include increasing elements of control and compliance such as Ofsted, league tables, the increasing marketisation of education, a restricted curriculum that gives less prominence to the arts and vocational subjects, the promotion of a traditional instructional type of teaching methods, opposition to most forms of educational research, the emphasis of formal examinations and a focus on behavioural issues. All the same, we take the view of Michael Apple who contests that teachers, where appropriate, 'will mediate, transform and attempt to generally set limits on what is being imposed from the outside' (Apple, 1988: 26). Addressing all the issues listed above would be outside the scope of this chapter. Therefore, we have limited them to which practitioners, in line with Apple (1988), can possibly make a difference in countering the populist education agenda, mainly by addressing the over-reliance on traditional teaching methods. Resolutions and ideas are offered in the spirit of dialogue and engagement.

Gove, and those who followed as secretaries of state, appear to be fixated with traditional teaching methods and the need to instil 'extensive factual knowledge' (Gove, 2012). The main evidence stated for this cognitive science is exemplified by Barak Rosenshine's 2012 paper, Principles of instruction: Research-based strategies that all teachers should know. Principles of instruction is gradually becoming a popular teaching method in English schools, possibly because it is a prescribed formula that meets the Ofsted requirements. It is also a shift from the more child-centred, discovery and experimental approaches of the constructivist and progressive educational thinkers

(Aubrey and Riley, 2022). Although principles of instruction can be an effective teaching method for some students, it is argued that this is a somewhat simplistic and nostalgic populist notion, and that learning and teaching is a more complex and multidimensional phenomenon. There is a broad range of educational theories that have evolved to take account of changing times. These ideas have emanated from the different psychological schools of thought, as well as some radical and progressive ideas that promote democratic and emancipatory education. They take into account the importance of reflection, dialogue and the praxis between theory and practice, all of which is 'not just knowing about what you do and how you do it. It is also about why you do it' (Williams, 2004: 5). With the increasing drive, stimulated by Gove, and still seemingly a priority for those who have succeeded him, to move ITE provision away from universities and into 'learning on the job', perhaps a deeper understanding and appreciation of alternative ways of teaching will diminish.

The leading progressive education thinker, John Dewey, whose work spanned the nineteenth and twentieth centuries, challenged the traditional education system and passive ways of learning. He championed a more democratic and participatory form of teaching and learning. For Dewey, democratic schools were learner-centred sites where children learned and contributed equally regardless of culture, ability or faith. His ideas on discovery, play and experimental learning are similar to many theorists, particularly the social constructivists. His thoughts on democracy in education have strong associations with social justice and ultimately fostering active participation in society when students leave school. Contemporary progressive educational thinkers, such as Basil Bernstein, Michael Apple, bell hooks and Henry Giroux, have been drawn to Dewey's democratic ideas.

Bernstein was a British educational sociologist of distinction and although he died in 2000, his work was of substance and significance, and will be of consequence in the years to come (Moore, 2006). His main concepts centred on social justice in education, with a focus on sociolinguistics and democratic pedagogy. He denounced what he considered the marketisation of education, which he thought created advantage and profit, as well as competition rather than cooperation. Democratic pedagogy for Bernstein was the opposite of traditional instructional teaching promoted by populists: it was about emancipation. Bernstein saw the learner 'as an active being, who is entitled to control over his or her destiny' (Kelly, 2009: 99). A central core to democratic pedagogy was the need to defend and maintain three interrelated rights for students: enhancement, inclusion and participation. First, enhancement is about 'experiencing boundaries, be they social, intellectual or personal ... it is the right to the means of critical understanding and new possibilities'. Second, inclusion 'is the right to be included socially, intellectually and personally'. Third, participation 'is the right to participate in construction, maintenance and transformation of order' (Bernstein, 2000: xx). These rights are outlined in Table 5.2.

Table 5.2 Students' democratic rights

Rights	Conditions	Levels
Enhancement	Confidence	Individual
Inclusion	Communities	Social
Participation	Civil discourse	Political

Source: Bernstein (2000: xxi).

The views on the importance of democracy by Michael Apple, the American critical educator, are similar to Dewey's. Both thought that democracy in education guided students towards democracy in society where they become active and questioning citizens. Apple particularly advanced the notion that democracy embraces social justice and in turn takes into account matters of race, class and gender equality. He also criticised the neoliberal policy-makers who, he argued, would lead to greater competition, as well as a business model of educational structures that incorporates methods of measurement and accountability. bell hooks, another American progressive and democratic educational thinker, was also critical of the passive teaching methods offered by traditionalists. Her concept of engaged pedagogy fosters and supports students' own experiences as a way of explaining the process of interaction learning and teaching, which she termed 'education as the practice of freedom' (hooks, 1994). hooks also emphasised the importance of spirituality in teaching and the importance of forgiveness, tolerance and kindness. Another critical educator was Henry Giroux, whose notion of **critical pedagogy** was to expose the inequities that are hidden in education and to emancipate students in their classrooms (Aubrey and Riley, 2021). He, too, is critical of the increasing neoliberalism in education, which has resulted in 'winning at all costs … ruthless competitiveness … [and a] … market-driven rationality' (Giroux, 2011: 9). These ideas from a few progressive educators offer democratic, yet radical, alternatives to those outlined in populist policies and practices.

OVERVIEW OF IDEAS FOR PRACTICE

Taking into account the necessary caution above, please accept these ideas for practice, which are offered as some possible ways to create democratic classroom environments and as a counter to practice promoted by the populist education agenda; many of these ideas are, of course, aspects of good practice.

- Promote active and cooperative learning experiences, which includes discovery and, if appropriate, play.

- Use methods that encourage students to employ reason and discussion to find things out.
- Concentrate mostly on process rather than product, and praise the stages of the learning development.
- Employ a dialogical approach to teaching and encourage students to question knowledge to stimulate critical thinking.
- Foster the use of group problem-solving project tasks which encourage discussion between students and between students and teachers.
- Use student experiences and real-life events to solve problems and to allow students to contextualise the situation.
- Adopt a flexible approach, where possible, if students raise a pertinent, but perhaps not a strictly relevant, point to seize the moment.
- Get to know the students, such as their culture and points of interest.
- Look for opportunities to encourage the student voice and student choice.
- Raise topics for discussion that are of cultural interest to students.
- Seek opportunities to make links between academic subjects to broaden their over-all understanding and, where possible, include aspects of democracy and social justice.

SUMMARY

Populism has become a common phenomenon over the recent past in the UK. It is a difficult term to define, but the core of populism is the idea of 'the pure people' versus 'the corrupt elite' (Mudde and Kaltwasser, 2017: 6). It is firmly connected to politics and can take the form of left- or right-wing ideology. Furthermore, populism is evident in many government policies and rhetoric throughout the world. There are close ties between populism and democracy; these ties are particularly promoted by populists eager to advance their legitimacy. Although there are positive effects of populism on liberal democracy, some scholars of populism caution that populism can have its sinister side and can, if not challenged, become authoritarian and an actual danger to liberal democracy (Mudde and Kaltwasser, 2017; Muller, 2017). With the context of populism and education, the focus in the chapter has been on right-wing populism with its emphasis on neoliberalism, traditional teaching methods, the reintroduction of examinations and a restricted academic subject-based curriculum – all evident in English education over the last twelve years.

Populist rhetoric in politics has been more noticeable in the UK during, and since, the Brexit referendum, with its characteristic anti-immigration and nationalistic calls for sovereignty, as well as the waging of culture wars. The culture wars, stoked by the right-wing media, rile against the woke agenda, take aim at those who they label as anti-patriotic, anti-'free speech' and with a lack of respect for British history, who they consider have a socialist or Marxist agenda. Unfortunately, such feelings and rhetoric are mirrored to some extent with the drive to reform English education since 2010, when Michael Grove became Secretary of State for Education as part of the Conservative-led coalition government. Gove's actions on taking over as Secretary of State were rapid and extensive. He either cancelled or reduced the funding of social justice initiatives connected with education such as ECM and Sure Start centres. Furthermore, he set about transforming the English curriculum by focusing mainly on academic subjects at the expense of the arts and vocational subjects. There was a return to formal exams, traditional teaching methods, a focus on behaviour and in-school ITE. He promoted the expansion of academies and the formation of free schools.

Challenging such a populist educational agenda is a problematic undertaking. However, Mudde and Kaltwasser (2017) argue that the best method is to engage the populists with dialogue, a method that has also been used effectively in Brazil to counter the populist education activists. One way of engaging with the populist agenda in English education is to draw upon the work of progressive democratic educators such as Dewey, Freire, Bernstein, Apple, hooks and Giroux, all of whom take a stance against the traditional instructional and didactic teaching methods, and call for a more engaged and emancipatory approach to learning and teaching. This approach fosters questioning and critical students who are actively involved in the learning process, which can then be replicated in society as a whole, rather than passive recipients of knowledge.

GLOSSARY OF TERMS

Critical pedagogy

The term is used by critical educators such as Michael Apple and Henry Giroux as the practice of encouraging students to challenge the knowledge which they encounter to understand its source and social composition. It endeavours to assist students in uncovering inequalities which they come across in the curriculum and in the education system with the purpose of creating a democratic learning situation that fosters social justice through critical dialogue.

Culture wars

The term surfaced in the USA some thirty years ago. Culture wars happen when there is a high level of disagreement and conflict between two distinct and deeply held views of what is right and what is wrong. For example, it is particularly evident in right-wing populism which tends to emphasise the significance of the importance of patriotism and the positive aspects of history and empire (Duffy and Hewlett, 2021; Fenwick, 2021).

Decolonisation of the curriculum

Decolonisation of the curriculum is not just diversifying the curriculum. 'Diversifying is simply adding different content. Decolonising goes deeper than that: it requires an awareness of "white privilege" and an appreciation that mindsets have created institutional structures that favour the white majority' (Moncrieffe and Harris, 2020: 14).

Democratic education

For Dewey and many other progressive thinkers, democratic education and democracy in society are naturally linked. It is about offering students choices about what they learn and, by using their experiences, helps them develop into questioning and active members of a democratic society. Moreover, for Apple, democracy also includes social justice, and encompasses aspects of social justice, class and gender equality (Aubrey and Riley, 2021).

Ideology

Generally, ideology is a collection of ideas and philosophies that can be aligned with a particular political viewpoint, such as socialism, conservatism, fascism or liberalism.

Liberal democracy

'A political regime, which not only respects popular sovereignty and majority rule, but also establishes independent institutions specialized in the protection of fundamental rights, such as the freedom of expression and the protection of minorities' (Mudde and Kaltwasser, 2017: 80).

Neoliberalism

Neoliberalism is an important element of right-wing populism and a political undertaking that aims to make financial gains through influencing political decisions particularly in the privatising of public sector institutions. It is promoted with the emphasis on common sense. In education, this has taken the form of removing many schools from democratic local authority control and into private profit-making companies which are charged, in some cases, with the provision of ITE, the curriculum and testing regimes (Hastings, 2019).

The people; the elite

These are the two antagonistic elements of the populist cause. Populists pit one against the other to meet their own agenda. For example, in the UK the elite are those establishments that could thwart the government agenda such as the judiciary, trade unions and some elements of the media, such as the BBC, which are perceived to have, in some cases, anti-government intentions; the people are the voting public. In education, the elite are the academics in university schools of education; the people are the parents and, according to the current UK government, an element of the teaching profession.

Populism

Populism is a term that is difficult to define, yet in the context of this book, Mudde and Kaltwasser (2017: 6) explain populism as 'a thin-centred ideology' that considers society to be ultimately separated into two homogeneous and antagonistic camps, 'the pure people' versus 'the corrupt elite', and which argues that politics should be an expression of the ... (general will) ... of the people. They refer to populism as a 'thin-centred' ideology, which is not like the 'thick-centred' or 'full' ideologies (e.g., fascism, liberalism, socialism); populism tends to attach itself to one of the thick-centred ideologies to bolster its appeal to the public (Mudde and Kaltwasser, 2017: 6).

Rhetoric

In politics, rhetoric is the use of written or verbal communication to create a convincing argument. Much of populist rhetoric is formed in simple short phrase slogans, which are often repeated for effect. The rhetoric is also usually used to appeal to supporters of their own political ideology.

FURTHER READING

Brown, A. and Wisby, E. (eds) (2020) *Knowledge, Policy and Practice in Education and the Struggle for Social Justice: Essays Inspired by the work of Geoff Whitty*. London: University College London Press.

A compilation of essays by a number of progressive educators, including Michael Apple, Alan Cribb, and Sharon Gewirtz. The essays explore and celebrate the work of the education sociologist Geoff Whitty, including aspects of social justice, democracy, the nature of knowledge, policy and practice.

Protzer, E. and Sommerville, P. (2021) *Reclaiming Populism: How Economic Fairness Can Win Back Disenchanted Voters*. Cambridge: Polity Press.

A review of populism, including the rise of Donald Trump and an analysis of the conflict between populism and inequality. It also includes ideas for solving social and economic differences.

Sullivan, D. (2019) *Education. Liberal Democracy and Populism: Arguments from Plato, Locke, Rousseau and Mill* (Routledge Research in Education Policy and Politics). London: Routledge.

An in-depth and informative critical overview of the significance of the early philosophers on the debates between populists and liberals on education.

Zembylas, M. (2021) *Affect and the Rise of Right-Wing Populism: Pedagogies for the Renewal of Democratic Education.* Cambridge: Cambridge University Press.

Contemporary view of populism based on the rise of Donald Trump and the clash with the search for a democratic form of education, including a practical guide to creating a democratic learning environment in the classroom.

REFERENCES

Alves, M., Segatto, C. and Pinda, A. (2021) Changes in Brazilian education policy and the rise of right-wing populism. Populist logic in the Conservative reforms to English schooling. *British Educational Research Journal,* 47(2): 332–54.

Apple, M. (1988) *Teachers and Texts: A Political Economy of Class and Gender Relations in Education.* London: Routledge.

Apple, M., Gandin. L. and Hypolito, A. (2001) Paulo Freire, 1921–97. In: J. Palmer (ed.) *Fifty Modern Thinkers on Education.* Abingdon: Routledge.

Aubrey, K. and Riley, A. (2021) *Understanding and Using Challenging Educational Theories* (2nd edn). London: Sage.

Aubrey, K. and Riley, A. (2022) *Understanding and Using Educational Theories* (3rd edn). London: Sage.

Bartlett, S. and Burton, D. (2020) *Introduction to Education Studies* (5th edn). London: Sage.

Bernstein, B. (2000) *Pedagogy, Symbolic Control, and Identity: Theory, Research, and Critique* (revised edn). London: Taylor & Francis.

Brighouse, T. and Waters, M. (2021) *About Our Schools: Improving on Previous Best.* Carmarthen: Crown House Publishing.

Chitty, C. (2014) *Education Policy in Britain* (3rd edn). Basingstoke: Palgrave Macmillan.

Craske, J. (2021) Logics, rhetoric and 'the blob': Populist logic in the Conservative reforms to English schooling. *British Educational Research Journal,* 47(2): 279–98.

Duffy, B. and Hewlett, K. (2021) How culture wars start. Available at: www.kcl.ac.uk/news/how-culture-wars-start (accessed 13 March 2023).

Fenwick, J. (2021) Woke: Compliment or criticism, it is now fuelling the culture wars. Available at: www.bbc.co.uk/news/uk-politics-58281576 (accessed 13 March 2023).

Freire, P. ([1970] 1996) *Pedagogy of the Oppressed.* London: Penguin.

Giroux, H. (2011) *On Critical Pedagogy.* New York: Continuum.

Gove, M. (2012) Secretary of State for Education Michael Gove gives speech to IAA. Speech at Independent Academies Trust, 14 November. Available at: www.gov.uk/government/speeches/secretary-of-state-for-education-michael-gove-gives-speech-to-iaa (accessed 13 March 2023).

Gove, M. (2013a) I refuse to surrender to the Marxist teachers hell-bent on destroying our schools: Education Secretary berates 'the new enemies of promise' for opposing his plans (*Daily Mail,* 23 March). Available at: www.dailymail.co.uk/debate/article-2298146/I-refuse-surrender-Marxist-teachers-hell-bent-destroying-schools-Education-Secretary-berates-new-enemies-promise-opposing-plans.html (accessed 13 March 2023).

Gove, M. (2013b) Michael Gove speech to teachers and headteachers at the National College for Teaching and Leadership, 25 April. Available at: www.gov.uk/government/speeches/michael-gove-speech-to-teachers-and-headteachers-at-the-national-college-for-teaching-and-leadership (accessed 13 March 2023).

Hastings, M. (2019) *Neoliberalism and Education: Oxford Education Research*. Oxford University Press. Available at: https://doi.org/10.1093/acrefore/9780190264093.013.404 (accessed 13 March 2023).

Hazell, W. (2022) Political impartiality rules 'silencing classes'. *The I*, 12 April.

hooks, b. (1994) *Teaching to Transgress: Education as the Practice of Freedom*. London: Routledge.

Hussain, S. and Yunus, R. (2021) Right-wing populism and education: Introduction to the special issue. *British Educational Research Journal*, 47(2), 247–63.

Kelly, A. (2009) *The Curriculum: Theory and Practice* (6th edn). London: Sage.

Knijnik, J. (2021) To Freire or not to Freire: Educational freedom and the populist right-wing 'Escola sem Partido' movement in Brazil. *British Educational Research Journal*, 47(2): 355–71.

Laclau, E. (2018) *On Populist Reason*. London: Verso.

Mac an Ghaill, M. and Haywood, C. (2021) The British state's production of the Muslim school: A simultaneity of categories of difference analysis. *British Educational Research Journal*, 47(2): 262–78.

Malik, N. (2020a) *We Need New Stories: Challenging the Toxic Myths Behind Our Age of Discontent*. London: Weidenfeld & Nicolson.

Malik, N. (2020b) Rightwing media slurs will not halt Black Lives Matter. *The Guardian Journal*, 21 September.

Molloy, D. (2018) What is populism, and what does it actually mean? *BBC News online, 6 March*. Available at: www.bbc.co.uk/news/world-43301423 (accessed 13 March 2023).

Moncrieffe, M. and Harris, R. (2020) Repositioning curriculum teaching and learning through Black British history. *Research Intelligence* (BERA), Autumn, 144, 14–15.

Moore, A. (2006) The structure of pedagogic discourse. In: H. Lauder, P. Brown, J.-A. Dillabough and A. Halsey (eds) *Education, Globalization and Social Change*. Oxford: Oxford University Press.

Mouffe, C. (2018) *For a Left Populism*. London: Verso.

Mudde, C. and Kaltwasser, R. (2017) *Populism: A Very Short Introduction*. Oxford: Oxford University Press.

Muller, J.-W. (2017) *What Is Populism?* London: Penguin Random House.

Rosenshine, B. (2012) Principles of instruction: Research-based strategies that all teachers should know. *American Educator*, Spring, 12–39.

Sant, E. and Brown, T. (2021) The fantasy of the populist disease and the educational cure. *British Educational Research Journal*, 47(2): 409–26.

Williams, J. (2004) *Great Minds: Education's Most Influential Philosophers* (A Times Education Supplement Essential Guide).

6

BLACK LIVES MATTER

LEARNING OUTCOMES

Having read this chapter, you should be able to:

- understand and appreciate the foundations of the Black Lives Matter movement;
- recognise the place of education as a vehicle for social justice;
- identify and apply some of the theories relating to social justice for a more equitable educational experience for all.

> ### KEY WORDS
>
> cultural capital; decolonisation of the curriculum; funds of knowledge; marginalisation; stratification; symbolic violence; systemic oppression; white gaze.

INTRODUCTION

The social media campaign #BlackLivesMatter is an ideology intended to counter the 'historical and contemporary framing of African Americans that strips them of social value' (Langford and Speight, 2015: 78). While it had its roots in American politics as a means by which to raise awareness of the habitual violence targeted against Black

Americans, with a view to promoting a positive message about the individual and collective worth of Black lives, arguably a number of high-profile cases has resulted in #BlackLivesMatter becoming a global phenomenon.

The inception of the Black Lives Matter movement was in direct response to the death of Trayvon Martin in 2013, and the subsequent acquittal of his shooter George Zimmerman. Following the acquittal, Alice Garza, co-founder of the Black Lives Matter movement, posted on her Facebook status: 'Black people. I love you. I love us. Our lives matter' (2013), a sentiment that was reposted by her friend Patrisse Cullors and consequently resulted in the social media campaign that later included Opal Tometi and resulted in the sharing of stories through Twitter and Tumblr accounts. Within a two-year period, what began as a social media campaign, #Black Lives Matter had become a movement in its own right.

Nevertheless, while it was the death of Trayvon Martin which prompted the movement, it could be argued that the death of George Floyd in 2020 at the hands of police officers, raised prominence of the movement globally. Silverstein (2021: para. 1) writes:

> George Floyd's murder in Minneapolis in May 2020 sparked the largest racial justice protests in the United States since the Civil Rights Movement. But the movement went far beyond this nation's borders – it inspired a global reckoning with racism.

Silverstein (2021) goes on to observe that what followed was some of the largest Black Lives Matters protests across the globe, inspired by the videos seen across the world of Floyd's death while in police custody. Moreover, Black activists related to Floyd's death, recognising it as 'a symbol of the intolerance and injustice they felt at home' (Silverstein, 2021, para. 2).

The immediate aftermath of Floyd's death resulted in protests in countries across the world, including in England, which saw protestors demonstrating by tearing down and vandalising statues of slave traders and political leaders, including that of Sir Winston Churchill and Edward Colston. Protests and demonstrations were seen across the country, which led to debates about shortcomings in UK policy relating to tackling racism against Black people. The aftermath of the protests and demonstrations has necessitated a reflection on policy and practice in the UK. Imarn Ayton, one of the organisers of the BLM protests in the UK, observes that while England may not be an overtly racist country, covert racism does exist, with racism seen in a much more polite and subtle way than is seen in other countries (Silverstein, 2021). Nevertheless, any existence of racism must be acknowledged and addressed, with education serving as one vehicle by which racism and inequality might be tackled. This chapter therefore aims to view Black Lives Matter through the lens of education policy and practice, with a view to understanding how theories of education might be applied to addressing some of the issues identified in the chapter.

BLACK LIVES MATTER: LESSONS FROM HISTORY?

From its inception in 2013 as a Twitter hashtag (Rickford, 2016; Castillo-Montoya et al., 2019; Lebron, 2019) #Black Lives Matter (BLM) has become firmly established as a Black liberation movement, serving as a platform to aggregate and document the daily violence and **systemic oppression** experienced by Black people (Langford and Speight, 2015) and as expressed by Lebron (2019) it 'has now become a force demanding change in America' and one that is likely to 'define our generation' (2019: p. xi).

The BLM movement was founded by three women – Alicia Garza, Patrice Cullors and Opal Tometi – in direct response to the trial of the young Black man Trayvon Martin, who, as expressed by Alicia Garza, 'was posthumously placed on trial for his own murder' (2016, cited in Lebron, 2019: xi), while the killer George Zimmerman, a neighbourhood-watch volunteer, walked free. While it was the death of Trayvon Martin that triggered the movement, Garza, Cullors and Tometi saw this as a protest against the pervasive killing of a significant number of Black men, including Eric Garner, Derek Williams, Leslie Prater, Michael Brown and Ahmaud Arbery, all of whom seemingly committed a similar crime as Trayvon Martin – that of being a young Black man. Indeed, in Martin's case, his only crime appeared to be walking through a Florida community, wearing a hoodie and holding a soft drink and candy, actions that George Zimmerman considered to be suspicious, leading him to make a 911 call to the police. Despite being advised to await the police arrival, Zimmerman initiated a confrontation with the young man, resulting in a scuffle that led to the shooting and subsequent death of Martin – he was 17 years of age. Although initially charged with Martin's death, Zimmerman was later acquitted on the grounds that his actions were in self-defence, a claim that the police chief investigating the case stated was irrefutable. Moreover, the police chief stated that Zimmerman had the right to defend himself with lethal force under state law.

Lebron (2019) observes that it was this lack of accountability and the failure of the justice system to account for the unnecessary death of a young Black American that prompted the women to offer the three basic and urgent words to American people, with Alicia Garza posting: 'Black people. I love you. I love us. Our lives matter', and urging friends to share stories on why #Black Lives Matter (King, 2015: para. 2). From its inception, #Black Lives Matter steadily grew, with the death in 2014 of 18-year-old Michael Brown at the hands of police officer Michael Wilson marking a turning point for the movement. The slogan suddenly became synonymous with protests across the country with calls to end police violence against young Black men and the negative media portrayal of African Americans, thus galvanising what can best be described as a civic justice movement (Langford and Speight, 2015). Obiakor (2021: 84) observes that 'Black Lives Matter' has subsequently grown into an 'organisation that agitates for myriad socio-economic, political, and educational freedoms of Blacks in the United States'.

Nevertheless, the needless death of George Floyd in May 2020, which once again highlighted the existence and works of the movement, only serves to remind us how much more needs to be done to realise socioeconomic, racial, political and educational equanimities. Floyd, a 46-year-old Black man, lost his life to Derek Chauvin, a 44-year-old white police officer, who knelt on Floyd's neck for nine minutes while he was pinned to the ground (BBC.co.uk, 2020). Floyd had reportedly paid for a packet of cigarettes with a fake $20 bill which led to police presence at the grocery store in Minneapolis. Floyd was subsequently arrested, pinned to the floor and, according to witness accounts, despite crying out numerous times that he was struggling to breathe, continued to be restrained by Chauvin. Floyd was pronounced dead one hour after the arrest.

Obiakor (2021) observes that Black people have been historically vulnerable at all levels of society, and it could be argued that the Black Lives Matter movement and the mass following it has established is an indication of the pain and frustration brought about by racial injustice. Cases such as Martin, Brown and Floyd illustrate what Lebron (2019: xii) refers to as the 'nation's [America] murderous racial history', which he describes as one that 'spans and reaches like a weed across centuries' (ibid.). Lebron (2019) maintains that Black people's struggle for human acknowledgement can be traced back through history and urges that ideas about the struggle should be informed by lessons from the past. Such lessons can arguably be traced back to the introduction of the Jim Crow laws, following the legal abolition of slavery in 1865, which Lebron argues was a 'virulent form of white supremacy moved to fill the void emancipation had left in America's racial power struggle' (2019: xv).

Up until 1865, slavery was considered the backbone of America's social order and economic logic (Lebron, 2019). However, abolitionists argued that slavery was dissonant to America's democratic ideal, subsequently leading to its abolition. However, the freedom that abolitionists sought was not forthcoming and while Black people were unshackled from their role as slaves, white people sought to maintain their control through the introduction of laws that legalised racial segregation in public places, such as waiting rooms in train and bus stations, rest rooms and water fountains. These laws, which endured until 1968, sought to marginalise African Americans further through measures such as denying them the right to vote and preventing them from benefitting from opportunities to better themselves, such as gaining an education and holding down jobs. African Americans were forbidden from living in white neighbourhoods, while in Southern states marriage and cohabitation between white and Black people was strictly forbidden (History.com, 2022).

The introduction of the Jim Crow laws quickly became a means by which to control African Americans as they were forced into indentured servitude through laws detailing where and when they could work. Furthermore, the state controlled Black people's right to travel and where they lived, alongside seizing children for labour purposes.

Moreover, anyone defying these laws faced harsh punishments, including arrests, fines, prison sentences and, in some cases, death. Inequality was further exacerbated by a legal system that was stacked against African Americans, making it difficult for justice to be sought. Lebron (2019: 3) describes this as a 'form of racial resentment and terror masquerading as justice'.

Despite a number of civil rights activists who sought to abolish the Jim Crow laws, including Ida B. Wells, a journalist who advocated for the arming of Black people and who published her investigations into the lynching of African Americans, the laws only officially came to an end in 1968. This in itself was a protracted process, and while in the period following the Second World War the civil rights movement allowed opportunities for the African American community to vote, it was not until 1964 that President Lyndon B. Johnson signed the civil rights act which legally ended segregation. Nevertheless, as illustrated by the need for such movements as Black Lives Matter, it seems that the abolition of the Jim Crow laws has failed to guarantee the full integration to anti-racism laws throughout the United States. As observed by journalist Hannah Jones, co-founder of the Ida B. Wells Society for Investigative Reporting, when asked 'What if Wells were alive today?', her response was:

> 'I think she would be very unsurprised by the America of 2018,' she says. 'In many ways, it would look very familiar to her. As long as she was able, she would be one of the sharpest critics of this country right now.'

> (Jones, cited in Smith, 2018)

It should be noted at this juncture that while the context for the Black Lives Movement has its origins in the politics of America, it could be argued that lessons learned can be similarly applied in the context of England in which disparities are also seen to exist. For example, statistics from GOV.UK (2019) revealed that young Black people were 9.6 times more likely to be stopped and searched as white British people; furthermore, they were 3.8 times as likely to be arrested than white British people. Moreover, the aforementioned protests in the UK following the death of George Floyd saw protestors sparking debates about the shortcoming of the UK in tackling racism against Black people.

From the perspective of education, which will form the remainder of this chapter, school exclusions for Black pupils were higher than that of white British students, with Black Caribbean pupils particularly being twice as likely to be temporarily excluded from school as their white British peers, and being almost three times as likely to be permanently excluded (GOV.UK, 2019). As we have alluded to earlier in this text (see Chapter 4), education can be used as an effective vehicle to address areas of social injustice. In view of this, what follows will be an examination of some of these educational inequalities and consideration of the practical application of education policy and provision as a means to address some of these issues.

WHITE GAZE AND THE EDUCATION EXPERIENCE FOR BLACK LEARNERS

Gale de Saxe reminds us that in reflecting on the distinctions between achievement and the opportunity gap and education debt, it is necessary to acknowledge that there exists 'multiple circumstances that lead to educational differences and disparities, as well as pronounced inequities within education' (2021: 66). Drawing from Ladson-Billing's 2006 work, Gale de Saxe (2021) explains that when considering the persistent inequalities in education, emphasis is most commonly placed on the attainment gap. However, Ladson-Billings (2006) calls into question the wisdom of focusing on this, arguing that by concentrating solely on the attainment gap, short term solutions to the problems will only ever be achieved. Instead, she advocates an emphasis on the long-term underlying problems, or education debt, which she sees as the juxtaposition between historical, economic, sociopolitical and moral issues, which work together to suppress opportunities in education, which at the same time perpetuate and system-ise inequality, **stratification** and **marginalisation** (Gale de Saxe, 2021). Moreover, Ladson-Billings expresses that inequity exists from primary through to university education, arguing that the deep-rooted, systemic and predetermined nature of education should be of concern from the start of formal education.

Traditionally, education has been seen as a marker for social stratification and this is no different in the case of equity between racial groups. As seen earlier in the chapter, the Jim Crow laws saw segregation between Black and white pupils in school settings, with many students of colour being denied any form of education. Where schooling did exist for Black students, inequality existed through, for example, second-hand or separate textbooks and shorter school terms, leading to an inequitable and oppressive form of education (Gale de Saxe, 2021). Moreover, schools for African American pupils were frequently in a state of disrepair, with large class sizes and mixed grades in one classroom, taught by just one teacher (Brooker, 2022). The curriculum accessible to Black students was limited too, since white school leaders wanted to restrict Black pupils from ideas related to equality and freedom. This included books that contained information on the Declaration of Independence or US constitution, which clearly state that the government's power came from those it governed. Exposure to such informa-tion would surely lead African Americans to confirm that they were being denied their rights as American citizens (Brooker, 2022).

Mercifully, such extremes of inequality seen through historic debt no longer exist in the education system. However, as observed by Gale de Saxe (2021), the economic debt that sits alongside the historic debt remains one of concern. Gale de Saxe (2021) observes that the funding disparities that exist across education systems highlight the value placed on education for minority groups and emphasises the stark difference in funding between inner city, urban and rural settings. In the American context, Ladson-Billings expresses that while it cannot be proven that schools are poorly funded as a result of the cultural background of the students they serve, it can be demonstrated that 'the amount of funding rises with the rise in White students' (2006: 6). Moreover, she postulates that this has its foundation in history whereby 'Whites were not prepared to invest their fiscal resources in these strange "others."' (ibid.).

Ladson-Billings (2006) observes a correlation between years of schooling and earning ratios, stating that more schooling results in higher earnings. The effect of this is cumulative, where gaps in wealth hold implications for social positioning. Moreover, wealth frequently acts as a source of political and social power. This has implications when the evidence suggests a disparity in attainment between pupils from different cultural backgrounds (Haynes et al., 2006; DfE, 2015; Kirby and Cullinane, 2016). In the UK context, a study undertaken by Haynes et al. (2006) reported that both Black Caribbean and white/Black Caribbean pupils had below-average achievement levels and were more likely to be permanently excluded from school than any other minority group in English schools. They determined that this was a result of socioeconomic disadvantage and low teacher expectations. Furthermore, in the case of those from mixed white/Black Caribbean backgrounds, there was evidence of misunderstandings relating to individual identities, with behavioural issues and attitudes towards learning evidently linked to peer group pressure. Haynes et al. (2006) concluded that even in cases where young people from Black Caribbean backgrounds demonstrated academic aspirations or the desire for a school education, this was frequently negated by teacher expectations and negative perceptions, leading to disengagement from certain subjects or from school itself.

Nevertheless, a 2015 research study undertaken by the DfE suggests that the attainment gap between young people from different ethnic groups narrowed over the past two decades when compared with white British pupils. However, while this was particularly noticeable for Black African pupils, pupils from Black Caribbean and mixed white and Black Caribbean communities continued to be less likely to reach the attainment levels of their white British peers, which the report suggests may well be attributed to different school practices that impact on outcomes for Black Caribbean or Black other students (DfE, 2015).

Obiakor, writing in the context of the American education system, observes that across all levels of education, Black children are taught by 'culturally insensitive teachers who lack the knowledge-base and skill-sets to teach them' (2021: 83). He goes on to suggest that Black pupils are disproportionally represented in classes for pupils with emotional and behavioural needs, while few Black students are placed in gifted programmes. Obiakor (2021) proposes that within education systems and institutions there is a prevalence of biological determinism that assumes that Black students are mentally incapable of tackling quality and challenging educational tasks. Moreover, given a lack of Black role models in teaching and leadership roles, multiculturalism is rarely seen in these settings. Obiakor (2021) observes that Black students frequently drop out of school, resulting in poor life outcomes.

Obiakor (2021) posits that the disproportionate representation of Black pupils identified as having special needs may be a result of test instruments that lack reliability and validity, and that disadvantage pupils from Black backgrounds. As observed by Skiba et al., the disproportionate identification of Black pupils with special educational needs (SEN) is 'among the most critical and enduring problems in the field of special education' (2008: 264), which they suggest has its 'roots in a long history of educational segregation and discrimination' (ibid.)

Similarly, studies undertaken in England over the past 25 years (Strand and Lindsay, 2009; Strand 2012) have revealed findings that reflect those in America. For example, the studies showed that Black Caribbean pupils were 1.5 times more likely to be identified with moderate learning difficulties (MLD) than white pupils, while Black Caribbean and mixed white and Black Caribbean pupils were almost twice as likely to be identified with social, emotional and mental health (SEMH) needs than white British pupils. Strand and Lindorff observe that possible negative outcomes linked to a diagnosis of MLD and SEMH include 'an inappropriate or narrowed curriculum, restriction of opportunities because of lowered expectations, or feelings of stigmatisation/labelling on the part of identified pupils' (2018: 1). Long-term implications might equally lead to the perpetuation of unequal outcomes in the future, leading to a cycle of reproduction. Perhaps a more disquieting observation made by Strand and Lindorff (2018) is that the over-representation of Black pupils with MLD/SEMH may be explained through the inappropriate interpretation of ethnic and cultural differences, seen through teacher racism, low expectations and a failure to provide quality instruction or effective classroom management. This, too, has echoes with the observation made earlier regarding a lack of Black role models in teaching and management positions since a 2020 study undertaken by UCL Institute of Education (IoE) revealed that '46% of all schools in England have no Black, Asian and minority ethnic (BAME) teachers … even in ethnically diverse schools BAME teachers are underrepresented in senior leadership teams' (Tereschenko et al., 2020). Consequently, minority ethnic pupils are unable to see themselves represented in their teachers and risk missing out on 'the diversity of experiences and understanding, and potentially socially just and race-conscious teaching' (2018: 3).

It could then be argued that the disproportionate identification of SEMD/MLD may be a result of misdiagnosis, potentially from practitioners who lack understanding of the specific needs of pupils from Black backgrounds or through flawed testing systems that disadvantage these pupils. Similar to the aforementioned observation made by Obiakor (2021), Coutinho and Oswald (2000) determine that the instruments and processes used to determine special education referral are often culturally and linguistically loaded; furthermore, ability, achievement and the behaviour of students are measured differently across ethnic groups (p. 147). Knotec (2003) observes that there exists an ethnic bias in identification and assessment for SEN's leading to disproportionate referrals for provision for students from socioeconomically disadvantaged backgrounds or minority ethnic groups.

It is not just through the identification of special educational needs that sees Black pupils disadvantaged in school settings, since, as observed by Stewart and Gachago (2020), white privilege is unintentionally promoted through hidden curricula in settings, suggesting that the 'whiteness' of those delivering learning puts them in a privileged position that negatively impact praxis. Stewart and Gachago (2020) draw from the work of Massei (2008) in exploring how white teachers see themselves as 'other', suggesting that they skirt around race dialogues, ignoring issues surrounding race and fail to acknowledge any pain felt by students of colour. Moreover, there remains a tendency to ignore their own whiteness in a bid to discount the issue of the relationship between white supremacy and Black pain. Kinloch et al. (2020) posit that education systems can promote a culture in which people of colour are negatively positioned by discourses that favour mainstream linguistic and cultural practices or dominant academic English (DAE). Kinloch et al. (2020) cite the work of Toni Morrison, who refers to this as the **'white gaze'** in which the white oppressor or literary imagination 'renders the lives, cultural practices, and intellectual tradition of People of Colour invisible if they are not aligned to whiteness' (2020: 383).

In a classroom, this culture of whiteness, or 'white gaze', can be seen through the actions of practitioners, the curriculum they deliver and through messages given by way of the hidden curriculum. Stewart and Gachago propose that practitioners consider how the classroom culture 'might work to reify outside-of-classroom cultural and heritage status' (2020: 3) and remind us of the power that teachers hold in deciding whose narratives to embrace. They see the hidden curriculum as the existence of 'us' and 'them' within a classroom, or whiteness versus blackness.

An emphasis on white over Black culture reflects Bourdieu's theory of **cultural capital**, in which the dominant culture comprises the group whose members are in the majority and who wield the most power. Since the dominant culture in England is arguably that of a white, middle-class society, this intensifies the potential of the hidden curriculum to maintain the position of white pupils over Black pupils, which would reflect a form of **symbolic violence**. Bourdieu and Passeron define symbolic violence as 'power which manages to impose meanings and to impose them as legitimate by concealing the power relations which are the basis of its force' (1990: 4). Ergin et al. (2019) suggest that symbolic power can be seen when both dominant and subordinate groups accept the inequitable distribution of power, forging a link between culturally reinforced beliefs and socially distributed rewards. Thus, education is more accessible to those in possession of cultural capital, which is subsequently rewarded through educational attainment. Yosso proposes that there is an assumption that 'People of Color lack the social and cultural capital required for social mobility' (2006: 70) and thus to counter the potential impact of symbolic violence argues that schools should work from this assumption in promoting a curriculum that addressed the disadvantages experienced by students whose race and culture might render them deficient in knowledge, social skills, abilities and cultural capital.

It could be argued that the drive to promote a more equitable educational system has been seen in recent years through a focus on the **decolonisation of the curriculum**, which Arshad (2021) proposes emerged as a result of the 2015 'Rhodes Must Fall' campaign in Cape Town. Targeting the Cecil John Rhodes statue at the University of Cape Town, students demanded immediate decolonisation of the university, arguing for cognitive justice, changes to the curriculum and a decommissioning of offensive/colonial symbols. Moreover, students demanded the right to free, quality and relevant education, offering a cultural freedom and changing the Western focus of the university to an 'African University' (Ndlovu-Gatsheni, 2022). Arshad (2021) observes that during colonial times 'knowledge became a commodity in colonial exploitation' (para. 2), which subsequently resulted in curricula that ignored cultural world views or that antagonised those knowledge systems that sit outside those of the colonisers (ibid., para. 3). Nevertheless, Arshad presents that decolonising the curriculum is not intended as a means by which to dismiss or delete what has been before as feared by some, but rather to 'situate the histories and knowledges that do not originate from the West in the context of imperialism, colonialism and power and to consider why these have been marginalised and decentred' (2021, para. 4). The next section will examine further the concept of decolonisation of the curriculum as it applies to the UK context.

DECOLONISING THE CURRICULUM AS A RESPONSE TO BLACK LIVES MATTER

Decolonisation of the curriculum is justifiably defended as a positive force for social equality, which extends further than internationalisation and diversity. Moreover, decolonisation gives learners the chance to 'appreciate the role of power and privilege in terms of what gets taught by whom' (Wilson et al., 2021: 142). Nevertheless, it is a complex, and at times contested, perspective with even the devolved UK nations having a differing approach. There has been an increasing call to decolonise what is considered a predominantly Eurocentric curriculum. This call has been intensified following the aforementioned killing of African American George Floyd in 2020 by a white police officer in Minneapolis, which resulted in widespread demonstrations throughout the world, a cause which, as discussed previously, was taken up by the Black Lives Matter movement. Such demonstrations in the UK have:

thrown a critical focus on how the narrative of British history is represented publicly. Concerns over a historical narrative that portrays black history in terms of slavery and colonisation have seen black and white protesters tearing down statues of those seen to have benefitted from the exploitation and oppression of black people.

(Moncrieffe and Harris, 2020: 14)

Cole and Blair (2006) stress that cultural, social and religious diversity is not a new event in the UK, evidenced by the discrete differences in Scotland, England, Wales and Northern Ireland, as well as migration from Ireland and the rest of Europe. Furthermore, there are established connections between Britain and Africa where Africans served with the Roman imperial army; there are also strong links with India. People from the African and Asian continents have lived in Britain from the sixteenth century (Cole and Blair, 2006). Yet it is the era of Britain's empire that lasted some 500 years, and involved the governance and administration of millions of peoples worldwide, that attracts a defensive response regarding the history curriculum, particularly in England. The curriculum content prefers to paint a weighted picture of the empire as a glorious commercial and military success, with little mention of the horrors of slavery. 'This cherry-picking, this confining of history committed by Britain outside its borders as belonging to the countries which it colonised, leaves us with a heavily editorialised and truncated history – it leaves us with Henrys and Hitler' (Malik, 2020: 176–7). Furthermore, Nesrine Malik (2020) argues that British history is even today limited to the British Isles, with little regard for those British subjects whose rights have diminished over time. This resulted in the Windrush scandal of 2018, in which Caribbean British subjects were regarded as illegal immigrants and, in some cases, deported from the UK.

In response to increasing criticism that not enough was being done to address the Eurocentric curriculum and the lack of Black histories, the DfE Black history in schools blog of the 9 June 2020, and in the aftermath of the death of George Floyd, offered some ideas for how Black history could be taught in schools. The blog suggested that the flexibility of the English national curriculum provided ample opportunity for teachers to incorporate black voices and history as a seamless part of any subject. It went further by suggesting that teachers could call upon the resources available from a number of associated bodies such as the Runnymede Trust and the Historical Association. The blog also indicated a number of key areas of the curriculum where Black history could be included – for example:

- Key Stage 2: non-European society which contrasts with British history.
- Key Stage 3: the impact of migration from within the British Isles, as well as from the end of the British Empire and from Indian independence.
- Key Stage 4: as part of Citizenship, learners are taught about the diversity of national, regional and ethnic identities in the UK, and the need for shared understanding and respect.

The summary of the DfE blog emphasises the abhorrence of racism, which has no part in society, and the importance of Black history as a topic which could be taught at every stage of the history curriculum (DfE, 2020).

In reaction, Stamou et al. (2020) pointed out that the above government response falls short of their endorsement of 'British values', in that it was not left to the teachers and schools to decide areas where they could include Black history in the key stages. Unlike the suggestions from the DfE above, the British values were precisely, explicitly and formally indicated for teachers in the curriculum, as well as being part of the initial teacher education standards. The different weighting placed on Black histories and British values show distinct primacies that 'indicate the dominant approach to "diversity management"'. By doing so, they feed into the emerging forms of neo-nationalism' (Stamou et al., 2020). The government appears to be entrenched in a state of cultural traditionalism and persistent in promoting a one-sided sense of British culture, one that is epitomised and promoted by the populist government as part of the culture wars. Revealing illustrations from the English national curriculum are:

- The over-representation of Romantic literature, pre-1914 texts and Shakespeare's plays in the English curriculum at the expense of contemporary multicultural literature.
- Religious education guidelines that emphasise the study of Christianity in connection to British heritage and identity.
- History curricula featuring Eurocentrism, dominated by normative state-orientated perspectives on the national past and which sideline in-depth examination of Britain's imperial and colonial past, black histories and the contributions of ethnic minorities to the making of modern Britain.

Stamou et al. (2020) conclude by implying that teachers are left to make decisions regarding the decolonising of the curriculum because the government is disinclined to act. The relationship between decolonisation of the curriculum and the culture wars being waged by the UK government in connection with the English national curriculum, and in particular with the subject of history, is best summed up by Professor Andrew Moran:

> Decolonising the curriculum is about telling a more complete picture, ensuring that everyone sees themselves reflected in a classroom and that we do not hide from the past. Spoiler alert: the empire was brutal, cruel and exploitative. It involved slavery, murder, and the stealing of land and resources from other people.
>
> (Moran, 2022: 9)

The aspiration to decolonise the curriculum is a worldwide phenomenon, and much of the thinking underpinning this has originated from American critical and engaged pedagogy educationalists such as Paulo Freire, Michael Apple, Henry Giroux and bell hooks. For Freire, decolonisation is the first stage of liberation from the dominant international viewpoint which fails to recognise the culture and dynamics of oppressed peoples (Schugurensky, 2014). Freire coined the term 'culture of silence' to describe how some in society did not fulfil their true potential and became dispossessed. He strongly felt that the education system was the reason for the continuation of this culture of silence (Freire, [1970] 1996: 120). His philosophy of education includes the three interlinking features of praxis, dialogue and conscientisation. Each of these features are rooted in the cultural, social and political lives of both students and teachers. Praxis is the practice of education which is informed by, and based upon, their cultural values. The promotion of dialogue which is critical, but based on mutual respect, is also important. Also of significance is the cultivation conscientisation, which inspires people to transform their lives and the world around them in the cause of social justice (Aubrey and Riley, 2022). hooks, a close associate of Freire, struggled with the colonising education process and her thinking was very much influenced by her own experience as a Black female growing up in the South of the United States. She particularly links the process of decolonisation with Freire's notion of conscientisation mentioned above, 'particularly as it affects African Americans living within white supremacist culture of the United States' (hooks, 2010: 46–7). Her idea of engaged pedagogy aims to empower students to think critically, take risks and challenge conventional educational thinking to promote the full promise of anti-racist and democratic integration (hooks, 2003).

Giroux's praxis curriculum model, as we have already considered in Chapter 3 of this text, advanced the idea of social transformation and acknowledged that knowledge is conditional and open to challenge. His notion of corporate public pedagogy argued that neoliberalism functioned as a competitive tool for economic gain at the expense of addressing problems of social injustice. Instead, with corporate public pedagogy, matters of social injustices, race and social class are undervalued for the greater good of economic advantage. For Giroux, the hidden curriculum is about the promotion of 'social control, one that functions to provide differential forms of schooling for different classes of children' (Giroux, 1983: 47). Neoliberalism and the New Right perspective are very much focused on competition and economic gain, rather than overcoming the difficulties of social injustice. Giroux especially advocates that features of social justice include race, class and gender equality.

Dutta observes that

> Decolonizing the curriculum is not only about disrupting and dismantling normativity of the Euro-American vantage point; it is also about nurturing capacities to imagine alternatives.

(2018: 273)

This would suggest that while decolonising the curriculum is a much-needed course of action in the promotion of a more equitable curriculum, it should certainly not be seen in isolation, and more work is needed to address the inequities, as previously observed. Shajahan et al. (2022), through their review of literature around decolonising the curriculum, propose that room should be made for decolonising alternatives and identify key vocabulary from the literature to promote an alternative approach that includes assertion, liberation, empowerment, self-determination and transforming. The next section will examine further strategies that might be applied following or in accordance with decolonisation of the curriculum.

BEYOND DECOLONISING THE CURRICULUM

Castillo-Montoya et al. (2019) propose that racially minoritised students are disadvantaged through the American higher education system as a result of teaching and learning policies and practices that serve to protect whiteness and heteronormative patriarchy. They go on to argue that Black and other racially minoritised students are expected to sacrifice their own cultural ways of knowing and being through the promotion of culturally neutral teaching (Quaye and Harper, 2007; Perdomo, 2014). Such practices can significantly hinder opportunities for Black students, especially when set in the toxic racial environments that prevail at predominantly white institutions (Castillo-Montoya et al., 2019). To counter this, and in accordance with the Black Lives Matter movement, it is suggested that Black students should be exposed to a pedagogy that reflects their own cultural identity and lived realities. Thus, far from merely decolonising the curriculum, curricula should actively promote practices and philosophies that 'center students' emancipation from racist ideologies and engagement in resistance of racial domination and oppression' (Castillo-Montoya et al., 2019: 1126).

In advance of the Black Lives Matter agenda, Ladson-Billings (1995) had already proposed a culturally relevant theory of education, arguing for a culturally relevant pedagogy that 'not only addresses student achievement but also helps students to accept and affirm their cultural identity while developing critical perspectives that challenge inequities that schools (and other institutions) perpetuate' (1995: 469). Through such a pedagogy, Ladson-Billings suggests that students would not only achieve academically, but also demonstrate cultural competence and would understand and critique the existing social order. Reviewing practices of practitioners who experienced success with pupils from diverse backgrounds, situated in middle-class settings, Ladson-Billings (1995) observed that success frequently came at the expense of their cultural and psychosocial well-being, with these students 'acting white' (Fordham and Ogbu (1986), cited in Ladson-Billings (1995)) and finding themselves ostracised from their peers. Moreover, these students also found themselves to be social isolates, having neither African American or white friends. To counteract this, Ladson-Billings (1995) proposed that a culturally relevant pedagogy should enable academic success, but without the need to sacrifice cultural integrity. She observed that rather than trying to determine what was wrong with African American learners, educators should ask themselves what was right with them. Examining good practice where success had been achieved, Ladson-Billings observed practices such as employing the lyrics of rap songs to teach poetry and utilising students' potential for leadership by drawing from their cultural competence in applying for school leadership roles such as grade president. Far from inhibiting cultural practices, these were embraced in a way that enabled pupils to see how they could be directed to further themselves.

Revisiting her work some twenty years later, Ladson-Billings (2014) acknowledges that while much of her original work has been adopted and amended, there remains a need for further revisions to address what she sees as a more dynamic view of culture. Ladson-Billings (2014) observes that research and practice are constantly evolving, most especially in the arena of youth culture which has increased in prominence and which is arguably more influential than the more traditional view of culture – that of being part of a nation-state, ethnic or religious group. Moreover, Ladson-Billings (2014) posits that constant revisions to a culturally relevant pedagogy will be required to reflect the ever-changing nature of culture, arguing that should practice stop evolving, this could potentially result in a situation whereby growth stops and subsequently lead to a form of 'classroom death' (2014: 77). Drawing from Apple's (1993) work, she explains that 'death in the classroom refers to teachers who stop trying to teach each and every student or teachers who succumb to rules and regulations that are dehumanizing and result in deskilling' (2014: 77).

Drawing from her work on the First Wave programme, an innovative spoken word and hip-hop arts programme at the University of Wisconsin-Madison, Ladson-Billings (2014) proposes that an investment in such youth culture might change the way that people think, learn, perceive and perform in the world. Much like athletes who are supported in higher education through scholarship programmes, talented artists were scouted through poetry slams and festivals, and provided with opportunities to pursue these interests while accessing existing undergraduate majors, allowing them to subsequently seek roles in education or policy-making.

While Ladson-Billing's work is very much set in the context of the American higher education system, the underlying message and drive for a culturally relevant pedagogy can very much be translated to other spheres of education and within the UK context, this being to learn about the cultural diversity which is unique to educational settings and to capitalise on this in curriculum delivery. This requires moving away from the white gaze as defined by Morrison and seeing the world through the eyes of the student cohort. Of note here is Obiakor's (2021) observation that Black students are frequently taught by culturally and linguistically insensitive teachers, which leads to the conclusion that the drive towards developing a culturally relevant pedagogy can be harnessed through teacher training programmes that embrace cultural diversity. Castillo-Montoya et al. (2019) observe that:

> At the center of a racially liberatory pedagogy is a focus on students' cultural knowledge and lived experiences as valuable assets to further their personal cultural development, aid in their navigation of white, dominant culture, and support academic learning.

(2019: 1128)

However, it stands to reason that this focus can only truly be realised through culturally informed and sensitive practitioners, who are able to draw on the students' **funds of knowledge** in developing and delivering a culturally sensitive curriculum.

SUMMARY

It is without question that Black Lives Matter has raised awareness of the inequalities that exist for Black people worldwide and has been influential in revisiting some long overdue debates into why such inequalities exist. Furthermore, the global reach of Black Lives Matter has arguably facilitated discussion around the need for those in a position of power to act towards the creation of a more equal and fair society for all. While the inception of Black Lives Matter was in the American context, where it could be argued that more overt racism exists, the agenda has forced countries such as the UK to reflect on their own position on racism, particularly in view of the observation made by Imarn Ayton that racism in the UK exists covertly (Silverstein, 2021). The concern that this racism may exist in the subtle and polite way as identified by Ayton is of note, since this potentially results in a situation where racism is undetected or even disregarded, leading to a cycle of reproduction, as noted in this chapter. It should also be noted that following the protests in the UK, a government-commissioned report into race and ethnic disparities concluded that the system in Britain was no longer deliberately rigged against ethnic minorities, and suggested that racism was often used as a catch-all explanation, which was implicitly accepted rather than explicitly examined, a view that Ayton suggests is taking one step forward and five steps back in the bid to tackle racism (Silverstein, 2021).

While it could be argued that the UK government's response to the Black Lives Matter agenda is a tentative one, which appears to reflect an unwillingness to recognise or acknowledge the existence of racism, more encouraging are the steps that can be taken from an education perspective to address this. As noted by Obiakor, the vulnerability of Black youngsters in education 'poses the greatest threat to their sacred existence in our nation and world' (2021: 86), which he goes on to argue puts them at risk from a social, economic and political position. It is, then, imperative that those in education seek to find ways of addressing the inequalities that exist between ethnic minority groups, as highlighted in this chapter.

The drive to decolonise the curriculum can be seen as a positive start to acknowledging and addressing some of the past social injustices. However, it could be argued that this is just one step and in order to fully realise equality, more needs to be done to raise awareness of culture and to ensure that the curriculum is responsive to all pupils. Drawing from the work of Ladson-Billings (2006, 2014), teachers should be aware of the cultural heritage of all pupils and should endeavour to draw on this respectfully in planning opportunities for pupils. Moreover, this should not be viewed as a perfunctory nod to equality, but firmly embedded into practice, with a view to updating and amending to reflect the changing nature of culture. Obiakor (2021) proposes that this can be best achieved through the recruitment and retention of teachers from minority groups, serving as role models to Black pupils; alternatively, teacher education and CPD should promote cultural awareness as part of training programmes in order that practitioners might reflect on their own position and the potential impact of teaching from a position of whiteness (Mayorger and Picower, 2018; Stewart and Gacahgo, 2020).

As we have seen in previous chapters, education can serve as a powerful vehicle in addressing areas of inequality and striving towards equal opportunities. Moreover, the role of education in this should start as early as possible, with the very youngest in society being encouraged to embrace and show pride in their cultural heritage. As observed by Obiakor (2021: 87), 'Early childhood education has the power to groom young minds and build their self-concepts'. Building on this, subsequent programmes should be culturally and linguistically sensitive and should embrace the power of the community in showing Black pupils what can be achieved and ensuring that their voices which have so long been silenced might finally be heard. Obiakor states that 'the future of Black people does not rest solely on White people's shoulders. We have to play proactive and positive roles in projecting good images about Black people and the Black race' (2021: 94). However, it is imperative that all those involved in education are aware of their own role in promoting equality and are equipped with the tools to play their own part in facilitating this.

GLOSSARY OF TERMS

Cultural capital

Traditionally, cultural capital refers to a familiarity with the dominant culture in society. Families pass on cultural capital through exposing their children to cultural activities such as theatre visits and meals in restaurants. A more current application of cultural capital, however, refers to the ability of an individual to respond to a given situation in an appropriate manner. Moreover, knowledge of culture captures more than just that which is seen as traditional and reflects an ability to embrace a wide range of cultures.

Decolonisation of the curriculum

Decolonising the curriculum requires a reflection on where a viewpoint might have originated from, with a view to questioning the currency and appropriateness of this. By opening a dialogue regarding what is taught through any one curriculum, it is intended that consideration is given to how far all cultures and knowledge systems are reflected through what is taught.

Funds of knowledge

Funds of knowledge capture the knowledge, skills and understanding that individuals draw from their homes and communities, and that educational practitioners should utilise when planning experiences to support learning.

Marginalisation

Marginalisation sees certain individuals or groups relegated to inferior positions in society. In the context of this work, marginalisation occurs as a result of race and skin colour, leading to unequal power relationships.

Stratification

A system of inequality whereby an individual's position in society is ranked according to certain characteristics. Racial stratification can result in unequal outcomes and socioeconomic disadvantage.

Symbolic violence

This term coined by Bourdieu is used to explain the non-physical violence that results from the power differential between social groups. Those in possession of the legitimate culture automatically assume power over those lacking cultural capital. Bourdieu suggested that this was perpetuated by the victims of symbolic violence since they consented to it through their acceptance of the status quo.

Systemic oppression

Systemic oppression is rooted in history and refers to the way in which certain groups, such as Black Americans, are disadvantaged as a result of their identity. Moreover, in systemic oppression those dominating gain advantage over those they oppress.

White gaze

This term, coined by writer Toni Morrison, assumes that those receiving information are doing so from the perspective of being white, and in so doing does not account for any differences in culture. The white gaze reflects how a culture of whiteness dominates in society, with an adherence to white standards and norms, and a failure to acknowledge the existence or viewpoints of alternative cultures.

FURTHER READING

Choudry, S. (2021) *Equitable Education: What Everyone Working in Education Should Know About Closing the Attainment Gap for All Pupils*. St Albans: Critical Publishing.

Chapter 5 looks at minority ethnic achievement. The text examines some of the complex issues relating to the attainment of diverse student groups and provides practical suggestions as to how this might be addressed.

Hillstrom, L. (2018) *Black Lives Matter: From a Moment to a Movement*. Santa Barbara, CA: Greenwood.

A history of the Black Lives Matter movement from its inception to its current position as a force for racial justice. Detailed information is given relating to the specific topics that led to its emergence, as well as biographical snapshots of those involved with the movement.

Luttrell, J.C. (2019) *White People and Black Lives Matter: Ignorance, Empathy and Justice*. Switzerland: Springer Nature.

A white response to the Black Lives Matter movement, with a reflection on the positionality and reaction of white people to the issues raised through the movement. Luttrell raises some of the challenges experienced by white people in showing empathy towards the movement and encourages readers to engage in critical engagement and self-reflection.

Olusoga, D. (2021) *Black and British: A Forgotten History*. London: Picador.

An historical account of the relationship between the British Isles and people from Africa and the Caribbean, including chapters on the Windrush scandal and Black Lives Matter from the British perspective.

REFERENCES

Apple, M. (1993). The politics of official knowledge: Does a national curriculum make sense? *Teachers College Record*, 95(2): 222–241.

Arshad, R. (2021) *Decolonising the curriculum – how do I get started?* Available at: www.timeshighereducation.com/campus/decolonising-curriculum-how-do-i-get-started (accessed 15 March 2023).

Aubrey, K. and Riley, A. (2022) *Understanding and Using Educational Theories* (3rd edn). London: Sage.

BBC.co.uk, (2020) George Floyd: What happened in the final moments of his life? Available at: www.bbc.co.uk/news/world-us-canada-52861726 (accessed 27 March 2023).

Bourdieu, P. and J.C. Passeron (1990) *Reproduction in Education, Society, and Culture*. London: Sage.

Brooker, R. (2022) *The Education of Black Children in the Jim Crow South*. Available at: www.abhmuseum.org/education-for-blacks-in-the-jim-crow-south/ (accessed 15 March 2023).

Castillo-Montoya, M., Abreu, J. and Abad, A. (2019) Racially liberatory pedagogy: A Black Lives Matter approach to education. *International Journal of Qualitative Studies in Education*. 32(9): 1125–45.

Cole, M. and Blair, M. (2006) Racism and education: From Empire to New Labour. In: M. Cole (ed.) *Education, Equality and Human Rights: Issues of Gender, 'Race', Sexuality, Disability and Social Class* (2nd edn). Abingdon: Routledge.

Coutinho, M.J. and Oswald, D.P. (2000) Disproportionate representation in special education: A synthesis and recommendations. *Journal of Child and Family Studies*, 9: 135–56.

Department for Education (DfE) (2015) *Ethnicity, Deprivation and Educational Achievement at Age 16 in England: Trends over Time*. London: Crown copyright.

Department for Education (DfE) (2020) *Black history in schools* (Blog: The Education Hub). Available at: https://educationhub.blog.gov.uk/2020/06/09/black-history-in-schools/ (accessed: 15 March 2023).

Dutta, U. (2018) Decolonizing 'community' in community psychology. *American Journal of Community Psychology*, 62(3–4): 272–82. Available at: https://doi.org/10.1002/ajcp.12281 (accessed 14 March 2023).

Ergin, M., Rankin, B. and Gökşen, F. (2019) Education and symbolic violence in contemporary Turkey. *British Journal of Sociology of Education*, 40(1): 128–42.

Gale de Saxe, J. (2021). Unpacking and interrogating White supremacy educating for critical consciousness and praxis. *Whiteness and Education*, 6(1): 60–74.

Giroux, H. (1983) *Theory and Resistance in Education: A Pedagogy for the Opposition*. London: Heinemann Educational.

GOV.UK (2019) *Black Caribbean Ethnic Group: Facts and Figure*.

Haynes, J., Tikly, L. and Caballero, C. (2006) The Barriers to achievement for White/Black Caribbean pupils in English schools. http://lst-iiep.iiep-unesco.org/cgi-bin/wwwi32.exe/[in=epidoc1.in]/?t2000=025449/(100). 27. 10.1080/01425690600958766.

History.com (2022) Jim Crow Laws. Available at: www.history.com/topics/early-20th-century-us/jim-crow-laws (accessed 15 March 2023).

hooks, b. (2003) *Teaching Community: A Pedagogy of Hope*. Available at: www.ethnicity-facts-figures.service.gov.uk/summaries/black-caribbean-ethnic-group#stop-and-search (accessed 15 March 2023).

hooks, b. (2010) *Teaching Critical Thinking: Practical Wisdom*. London: Routledge.

King, J. (2015) *#BlackLivesMatter: The evolution of an iconic hashtag*. Available at: www.occupy.com/article/blacklivesmatter-evolution-iconic-hashtag#sthash.OAKbi833.dpbs. (accessed 15 March 2023).

Kinloch, V., Penn, C. and Burkhard, T. (2020) Black Lives Matter: Storying, identities, and counternarratives. *Journal of Literacy Research*, 52(4): 382–405.

Kirby, P. and Cullinane, C. (2016) *Class differences: Ethnicity and disadvantage. Research Brief*, Edition 14. The Sutton Trust. Available at: www.suttontrust.com/wp-content/uploads/2016/11/Class-differences-report_References-available-online.pdf (accessed 15 March 2023).

Knotec, S. (2003) Bias in problem solving and the social process of student study teams: A qualitative investigation. *Journal of Special Education*, 37: 2–14.

Ladson-Billings, G. (1995) Toward a theory of culturally relevant pedagogy. *American Educational Research Journal*, 32(3): 465–91.

Ladson-Billings, G. (2006) 2006 Presidential address: From the achievement gap to the education debt: Understanding achievement in U.S. schools. *Educational Researcher*, 35(7): 3–12.

Ladson-Billings, G. (2014) Culturally relevant pedagogy 2.0: Aka the remix. *Harvard Educational Review*, 84(1): 74–135.

Langford, C.L. and Speight, M. (2015) #BlackLivesMatter: Epistemic positioning, challenges, and possibilities. *Journal of Contemporary Rhetoric*, 5(3/4): 78–89.

Lebron, C.J. (2019) *The Making of Black Lives Matter: A Brief History of an Idea*. New York: Oxford University Press.

Malik, N. (2020) *We Need New Stories: Challenging the Toxic Myths Behind Our Age of Discontent*. London: Weidenfield & Nicolson.

Mayorger, E. and Picower, B. (2018) Active solidarity: Centering the demands and vision of the Black Lives Matter movement in teacher education. *Urban Education*, 53(2): 212–30.

Mazzei, L. (2008) Silence speaks: Whiteness revealed in the absence of voice. *Teaching and Teacher Education*, 5 (24): 1125–1136. doi:10.1016/j.tate.2007.02.00.

Moncrieffe, M. and Harris, R. (2020) Repositioning curriculum teaching and learning through Black-British history. *Research Intelligence* (BERA), Autumn, 144: 14–15.

Moran, A. (2022) Letters. *The Guardian Journal*, 22 Feburary, p. 9.

Ndlovu-Gatsheni, S.J. (2022) *'Rhodes Must Fall:' South African Universities as Site of Struggle*. Available at: www.revistatabularasa.org/en/issue25/rhodes-must-fall-south-african-universities-as-site-of-struggle/ (accessed 15 March 2023).

Obiakor, F.E. (2021) Black Lives Matter in education and society. *Multicultural Learning and Teaching,* 16(1): 81–96.

Perdomo, S. (2014) Raw tongue: How Black women and Latinas bring their multiple identities into collegiate classrooms. In: D. Mitchell, Jr (ed.) *Intersectionality & Higher Education: Theory, Research, & Praxis*. New York: Lang, pp. 123–34.

Quaye, S.J. and Harper, S.R. (2007) Shifting the onus from racial/ethnic minority students to faculty: Accountability for culturally inclusive pedagogy and curricula. *Liberal Education*, 92(3): 19–24.

Rickford, R. (2016) Black Lives Matter: Towards a modern practice of mass struggle. *New Labor Forum,* 25(1): 31–42.

Schugurensky, D. (2014) *Paulo Freire*. London: Bloomsbury.

Silverstein, J. (2021) *The global impact of George Floyd: How Black Lives Matter protests shaped movements around the world*. Available at: www.cbsnews.com/news/george-floyd-black-lives-matter-impact/ (accessed 15 March 2023).

Skiba, R.J., Simmons, A.B., Ritter, S., Gibb, A.C., Karega Rausch, M., Cuadrado, J. and Chung, C. (2008) Achieving equity in special education: History, status, and current challenges. *Council for Exceptional Children*, 74(3): 264–88.

Smith, D. (2018) *Ida B. Wells: The unsung hero of the civil rights movement*. Available at: www.theguardian.com/world/2018/apr/27/ida-b-wells-civil-rights-movement-reporter

Stamou, E., Popov, A. and Soytemel, E. (2020) *Decolonisation of the curriculum from sidelines? Responsibility transfer and neo-nationalism* (BERA Blog). Available at: www.bera.ac.uk/blog/decolonisation-of-the-curriculum-from-the-sidelines-responsibility-transfer-and-neo-nationalism (accessed: 15 March 2023).

Stewart, K.D. and Gachago, D. (2020) Step into the discomfort: (Re)orienting the white gaze and strategies to disrupt whiteness in educational spaces. *Whiteness and Education*. DOI: 10.1080/23793406.2020.1803760

Strand, S. (2012) The White British–Black Caribbean achievement gap: Tests, tiers and teacher expectations. *British Educational Research Journal, 38(1): 75–101*.

Strand, S. and Lindorff, A. (2018) Ethnic disproportionality in the identification of Special Educational Needs (SEN) in England: Extent, causes and consequences. University of Oxford: Department of Education. Available at www.education.ox.ac.uk/wp-content/uploads/2018/08/Executive-Summary_2018-12-20.pdf (Accessed 27 March 2023).

Strand, S. and Lindsay, G. (2009) Evidence of ethnic disproportionality in special education in an English population. *Journal of Special Education*, 43(3): 174–90.

Tereshchenko, A., Mills, M. and Bradbury, A. (2020) *Making Progress? Employment and Retention of BAME Teachers in England*. London: UCL Institute of Education.

Wilson, C., Broughan, C. and Daly, G. (2021) *Case Study: Decolonising the Curriculum: An Exemplification*. Cambridge University Press online. Available at: www.cambridge.org/core/journals/social-policy-and-society/article/case-study-decolonising-the-curriculum-an-exemplification/E050D532A0E75ED25FD7AB1BC83AF24F (accessed 14 March 2023).

Yosso, T.J. (2006) Whose culture has capital? A critical race theory discussion of community wealth. *Race, Ethnicity and Education*, 8(1): 69–91.

7

EDUCATION AND THE COVID-19 PANDEMIC

LEARNING OUTCOMES

Having read this chapter, you should be able to:

- understand the different provisions to maintain education provision for the pandemic;
- critically appraise the social and educational inequalities evident during the pandemic;
- appraise the learning and teaching methods which were employed and evaluate their effectiveness;
- identify possible ways to manage education for events which cause disruption and turbulence.

KEY WORDS

algorithm; blended learning; COVID-19 pandemic; digital divide; home schooling; learning webs.

INTRODUCTION

The **COVID-19 pandemic** was a colossal and unique test for education structures, systems and practices for over 1.5 billion students in over 200 countries, and has brought about widespread transformation for how we conduct our lives (Pokhrel and Chhetri, 2021). Dr Rowan Williams (2022), the former Archbishop of Canterbury (2002–12), argued that the pandemic has revealed the extent of the inequalities in certain sections of society. These inequalities have damaged the learning opportunities for students, as well as their well-being, and currently there is no way of measuring the level of harm or how it will shape the lives of young people. Moreover, Billington et al. (2022: 110) emphasise that 'we are all in unknown territory in respect of the eventual implications for the lives of young people, members of staff and schools in the years ahead'. Despite the creativity of teachers, the innovative use of technology and the incredible efforts of practitioners and education leaders in coping with the impact of the pandemic as events unfolded, a more sustainable level of planning and guidance from governments is required. Williams (2022: xxvi–xxvii) contests that:

> What seems to be lacking is the political will to turn this situation around. It should be obvious that challenges to educational justice and effectiveness cannot be dealt with by hastily improvised strategies, switching tacks without warning or training in ways that are damaging to teachers and students alike … it is essential that what we have learned in the period of the pandemic about problems that have largely gone unnoticed should be a driver of prompt and creative action by governments and professional bodies.

In early 2020, the pandemic had taken hold, and schools and other centres for learning were being closed in many countries. Prior to this, in 2009 the World Health Organization (WHO) published guidance on reducing the transmission of pandemics in schools based upon the experiences of those countries that managed the H1N1 (influenza) pandemics, which included the closure of schools. This guidance had emphasised the need for pre-planning for such events, including the importance of local and national authorities leading and coordinating planning, the need to plan for processes that allow for the continuity of learning, and the significance of clear communication strategies. Although some countries made plans to align with the World Health Organization 2009 guidance, many did not (WHO, 2009; Fotheringham et al., 2022; Leask and Younie, 2022).

In May 2021, following increasing pressure, the then Prime Minister Boris Johnson promised to launch a UK national public inquiry into handling of the pandemic. That inquiry opened in July 2022 and encompasses the impact of the pandemic across society as a whole, including education. Overall, the number who have died with COVID-19 on their death certificates is over 198,000 (BBC, 2022a). The chair of the inquiry is Baroness Hallett, a former High Court judge. Areas of focus for the inquiry include: how well prepared the UK had been, the response when the pandemic hit, and the decision to introduce lockdown and other restrictions on the public (BBC, 2022a). Although the impact, and the resultant lessons learned, for education will be explicitly highlighted as part of the Hallett Inquiry, education practitioners, researchers and writers have been proactive in collecting data during and in the closing stages (hopefully) of the pandemic. There are many international journal articles, particularly the articles and blogs of the *British Educational Research Journal*. Texts are also emerging that consider the impact of the pandemic on education. There are two timely and comprehensive texts on the matter, both of which are based upon research from practice and which also offer ideas for the future: Tony Breslin's (2021) *Lessons from Lockdown: The Educational Legacy of COVID-19*, and Marilyn Leask and Sarah Younie's (2022) *Education for All in Times of Crisis: Lessons from Covid-19*.

The chapter will explore the impact of the COVID-19 pandemic on education provision generally, but particularly its effect on statutory schooling in the UK. The scope of the chapter limits in-depth detail of the impact of the pandemic on the learning experience of students and indeed staff; we are sure that this impact will be explored in detail in the future – it certainly merits such investigation. Where appropriate, it will consider the efficacy, or otherwise, of education policies and initiatives implemented to tackle the pandemic. First, aspects of lockdown, the closure of educational establishments, as well as matters of leadership, particularly from a national level, will be reviewed. Second, there will also be a reflection on the new innovative practices that have emerged, including schools with vulnerable pupils and the children of key workers, home learning and the use of technology. Third, the rise in marginalisation and social inequality for learners is considered. The chapter will then go on to explore how inspections, the curriculum and examinations were managed. Lastly, we take a critical look at 'catching-up', the term used by government to recover academic learning; more crucially, we offer ideas and possibilities for the future, including the well-being of students and practitioners alike.

LOCKDOWN, CLOSURES AND LEADERSHIP

On 18 March 2020, the prime minister announced that children would not be able to attend nurseries, schools and colleges with effect from Friday, 20 March, apart from those who were vulnerable and those belonging to designated key workers (Timmins, 2021). On 23 March, Boris Johnson announced the first UK lockdown, which ordered all people to stay at home (Timmins, 2021). After the announcement of the closure of schools, the Department for Education (DfE) issued guidance to local authorities and to schools. Fotheringham et al. (2022) argued that changing, at such short notice, the process of schooling from face-to-face learning to remote learning was a challenging process for practitioners and their leaders. What followed the closure of schools 'was easily the most disruptive period in children's education since at least the start of the Second World War ... at times it felt as though the school system was in chaos' (Timmins, 2021: 4). Other problems emerged as time elapsed following the initial closures. There was uncertainty as schools were opened, closed and then reopened once more. There were other troubles as the 2020 and 2021 formal summer examinations such as A-levels, GCSEs and BTECs were cancelled, which in turn had a knock-on effect on admissions to higher education. There were issues including access to laptops for **home schooling**, COVID-19 testing for staff and pupils, political arguments on free school meals, and the '**algorithm**' (Timmins, 2021). These issues will be considered as part of this chapter.

An analysis of the government's response to the management of education during the pandemic was published in a report by the Institute for Government in 2021 and written by Nicholas Timmins: *Schools and Coronavirus: The Government's Handling of Education during the Pandemic*. The DfE refuted the claims made in the report regarding the lack of contingency planning, particularly regarding qualifications (Adams, 2021). Nevertheless, it is argued that the report offers a worthwhile challenge to the over-optimistic claims made by government leaders, including the Prime Minister and the then Secretary of State for Education, Gavin Williamson (Adams, 2021). As such, the report poses a counter, and critical, view of the government's handling of the pandemic from an educational viewpoint. Leask and Younie (2022) discovered that once the closure of schools began, what was needed was coherent and dynamic leadership and guidance on education from the government. However, when this was not forthcoming at the outset, school leaders and practitioners, along with teaching unions, became proactive in creating their own contingency plans for overseeing schooling in the COVID-19 crisis. However, this put an extra burden on school staff, and particularly on leaders who were left to quickly draft local contingency plans and accept responsibility to manage the learning when schools were abruptly closed. As a result, 'teachers reported a sense of abandonment and neglect when government advice was not forthcoming, timely or reliable' (Leask and Younie, 2022: 53).

Brighouse and Waters (2021) report a decline in the relationship between secretaries of state, local authorities and schools themselves. They cite an example of this decline during the pandemic when, during the latter half of 2020, schools had reopened for the first time and increasing numbers of young people were testing positive for COVID-19 or isolating. This was particularly the case in London and the South East. Teachers and teaching unions were becoming increasingly worried about the safety of staff and students in keeping schools open. Then Greenwich in South East London ordered its schools to close, which in turn provoked Gavin Williamson to employ the newly legislated pandemic emergency powers to legally enforce the local authority to keep their schools open. This resulted in an awkward and public disagreement between the DfE, the local authority and the schools. Williamson's 'absolutist position at the end of a long period of stress for all concerned played out as a war of words in the media. Just a few working days later, the entire country went into another lockdown' (Brighouse and Waters, 2021: 109). Other examples of the national response by government will be considered when exploring specific aspects of the pandemic.

The challenges faced by leadership at national, local authority and school levels were real and complex. To some extent, particularly at the start of the pandemic, the DfE was making decisions in a time of uncertainty, and any plans that the government did have were for an influenza pandemic. Decisions about the designation of who were key workers, and the resolve to keep schools open for vulnerable children and the children of key workers were made swiftly by the DfE. Also, many other countries were unprepared for the pandemic and also implemented comparable methods to the DfE. However, there were many troubling aspects of the government's managing of schools during the pandemic, such as overly centralised processes of working with schools; poor communication; a lack of trust in local authorities; recurrent announcements of the closure or opening of schools, or that examinations would be held despite uncertainties. All of this brought about U-turns, and caused confusion and bafflement for school staff, parents and students (Timmins, 2021).

Aligned with, and comparable to, these troubling aspects of the DfE's management of the pandemic are the findings of Leask and Younie's (2022) research which drew from the experiences and data from around the world on how education responded to the COVID-19 crisis. They found that countries who faired well were those that had clear communication between national, regional and local government, as well as those countries that encouraged flexible responses to local sensitivities. However, they did find that in matters of communication between levels of government:

> England was an extreme outlier in the research. The application of free market philosophies had been applied to education, leading to the breakup of the national/regional/local channels of communication, and this seemed to create, at the local level, a lack of effective co-ordination and resource sharing, exacerbated by local competition between schools for prestige and pupils.
>
> (Leask and Younie, 2022: 87)

Aspects and examples of leadership at local level will be integrated within the following sections of the chapter.

NEW PEDAGOGIES: SCHOOL, HOME AND THE ROLE OF TECHNOLOGY

The COVID-19 pandemic has produced a devastating jolt to the systems and processes of all sectors of education and training. This shock of the pandemic did not only mean that teachers and school leaders had to adapt their pedagogies accordingly, but they also had to cope with practical infection control matters, such as placing students into bubbles, staggering start and finish times, and the testing process – all aspects that worsened when schools started to reopen. The experience of the pandemic has brought about new and innovative pedagogies in aspects such as 'assessment, home learning and online and **blended learning** … [which] … offer pointers to the education and training strategies and facilities of tomorrow' (Breslin, 2021: xvi). Although these innovative pedagogies have been implemented creatively, they are, as a whole, no substitute for the relationships and social contact offered by school attendance (Muller, 2022). Without this social interaction in learning, students can feel detached and demotivated due to a lack of stimulation. Nevertheless, apart from the children of key workers and vulnerable pupils, lockdown and closures necessitated original thinking which incorporated, where possible, a degree of social learning and contact. Despite the best efforts of leaders and practitioners in schools, social learning and contact was not always possible.

Before delving into the pedagogies during the pandemic, it is perhaps fitting that we briefly consider the ideas of several progressive educationalists aligned with these practices. These ideas were not the result of an international crisis, such as the pandemic; rather, they resulted from their quest for social justice in education. Long before the school closures and following their reopening, some children were (and still are) schooled at home as long as their parents abide by a set of legal obligations. Home schooling as a concept was championed by John Holt who felt that schools inhibited children's creativity and curiosity. He also considered that children learned and developed differently, and therefore should not be constrained by the set stages of compulsory education. Holt advocated personalised learning (Meighan, 2007). His ideas of home schooling were popular, particularly in the USA, at the time of the publication of his books: *How Children Fail* (1964) and *How Children Learn* (1967). Another progressive educator with similar ideas as Holt was Ivan Illich whose critical views of schools and traditional education were outlined in his seminal and radical text *Deschooling Society* (1971). His argument about why schools fail originates from poverty and not the inherent abilities of the child (Thomas, 2013). A key aspect of his idea of deschooling pertinent to the pandemic with its reliance on technology is his concept of **learning webs,** which provides access to learning resources and the sharing of knowledge, ideas and skills. In learning webs, Illich 'had seen social networking and its promise 30 years ahead of its actual appearance' (Thomas, 2013: 113).

Many schools set up a virtual school programme that facilitated parity of access with those students in school and those at home. Just one example from one school among many, in Jemima Rhys-Evans's primary school in London those pupils actually in school were split into groups and were taught by staff who might, or might not be teaching their own year groups or in their area of expertise. In the frantic period just before closure, the school's web designer created a user-friendly portal by which all children could access lessons appropriate to year groups. It became evident that children engaged very well with video. Teachers spent their mornings planning and recording lessons and in the afternoons answering children's emails. Group feedback and celebrations were held weekly and were designed to be motivating. Assessment in her school was developed to include online interactive worksheets, which allowed children to get prompt feedback and for teachers to pinpoint any misconceptions. Processes were also augmented to ensure engagement, inclusion and pastoral support, which included sending families daily emails giving them details of the learning for the day; calling families to check on their well-being and to see if further support was required, such as loans of laptops, as well as to explain tasks and offer emotional support (Rhys-Evans, 2020).

In what they termed 'crisis-resilient creative pedagogies', the findings of Leask and Younie's (2022) worldwide research echoed many of the strategies employed by Rhys-Evans above. This was also evident in the need for teachers across low-, middle- and high-income countries to upskill and adapt, and to work creatively. In turn, this 'has produced a pedagogic revolution' (Leask and Younie, 2022: 119). They also reported the positive outcome of knowledge-sharing between teachers and schools, including educators with different viewpoints and expertise. Knowledge-sharing involved peer discussions, and collaborative problem solving further helped develop ideas for innovative practice. Furthermore, internationally, knowledge-sharing was championed by non-governmental organisations (NGOs) and the UN via online events.

Among the issues raised across the range was the difficulty in planning teaching to cater for both synchronous and asynchronous learning (Leask and Younie, 2022). Wallace (2008) explains the difference: synchronous learning is found in conventional learning where all learners are participating and taking part at the same time, whereas asynchronous learning is normally aligned with online or other forms of distance learning where students are following the same programme of study but they interact with their teachers and access learning resources at different times (Wallace, 2008). The difference between these terms is significant. There is a notion that synchronous learning, which is aligned with face-to-face teaching is more effective; in the pandemic this equated to teaching the curriculum to all students through live online lessons. Although this approach might be favourable to some students and impress parents, it is by no means a solution because of the problems with technology and difficulties for some learners in accessing the internet and/or devices, as well as its unsustainability. Even though asynchronous learning may appear less effective, it does include learning in many forms, including real-time teaching and interaction. Furthermore, asynchronous learning helps overcome the barriers of out-of-school learning, such as access and motivation, especially if students have to manage responsibilities at home (Leask and Younie, 2022). Blended learning is a combination of synchronous and asynchronous learning (Wallace, 2008).

During lockdown periods, there have been many illustrations of effective engagement and the forming of positive partnerships between parents and schools. This has resulted in most cases in a more transparent communications relationship between home and school, greatly enhanced by the flexible use of technology. The choice of online meetings with teachers is better suited for parents to fit in with their home and work responsibilities (Breslin, 2021). Many parents struggled with supporting their children's learning at home for a number of reasons, including their commitments to other family members and work, as well as acquainting themselves with different subjects and learning processes. For many parents, this led to a newly discovered respect for teachers and perhaps a degree of relief when children returned to school in person. There were some very positive experiences of home schooling, particularly for many the flexibility and openness of communication and a renewed joint regard between school and parents (Breslin, 2021). However, there were certainly difficulties with home schooling, especially with regard to access to technology, which will be discussed in the next section.

The use of online learning can be a positive step for some learners who may find face-to-face teaching in schools a difficult proposition. Muller (2022) suggests that many students with special educational needs (SEND) gained from online learning because they could modify their learning to better suit their requirements. This included using accessible software where students could revisit content which they found to be an advantage 'as it allowed the students to rewatch lessons and even use them to revise content with parents, guardians or siblings' (Muller, 2022: 18). Yet, learning through the medium of digital technology was not a matter of preference for the vast majority of students during lockdown. Breslin (2021) emphasises that when using digital technology for learning

> *access* is *everything*; access for teachers to the best available equipment; access to comparable equipment in the home for both pupils and their parents or carers; access to universal, high-quality internet connectivity; access to training for all parties, coupled with the ability to affirmatively target this training at those in the greatest need.
>
> (p. 166)

Despite the great efforts of teachers in adopting their practice to provide opportunities for virtual learning, these opportunities were imposed upon them by the pandemic and virtual pedagogical methods were needed to be planned at speed once the closures of schools were announced. The further onus of improving their skills using technology together with the short time-scale available in preparing for school closures added to the strains of the profession (Leask and Younie, 2022). The strains experienced by the teachers due to the use and access of digital technology were replicated and magnified by many students, families and carers in society when school closures began.

MARGINALISATION AND SOCIAL INEQUALITIES

Although digital technology has created learning opportunities during lockdown, these opportunities were not equally shared across society; in reality, the pandemic has extended the **digital divide**. Devices, for example, such as laptops, computers, phones, gaming consoles and tablets, as well as radio and television could give students access to remote learning. Access to technology for children from wealthy homes, particularly if the parents are skilled in using devices and able to work from home, have an advantage in making the most of technology as a learning resource. Conversely, children from less well-off homes with little space and where access to a laptop and internet connection is limited, or even non-existent, are at a distinct disadvantage. 'Technology, against the background of such inequality of opportunity, is a double-edged sword – great if you have access to it but part of the problem if you do not' (Breslin, 2021: 168). This digital divide is also a social divide that worsened during lockdown. As well as missed opportunities in learning for those with no, or limited, access to the internet, they also lost their sense of belonging without connections with their teachers and friends. Furthermore, as pupils were not physically in front of teachers, it became difficult to judge whether they were becoming disengaged and, as such, there was the possibility that they were '"at risk" of becoming marginalised with remote learning' (Leask and Younie, 2022: 3). Although a new virtual academy was launched and the BBC provided educational resources, as well as the DfE promising to provide devices to some disadvantaged young people at the start of school closures, this was small comfort for those with little or no access to technology (Coughlan, 2020).

Apart from the points raised above regarding the areas that amplified the digital divide and led to increased marginalisation, other areas were also apparent, such as poor reliability of internet connectivity, particularly in rural settings; some religious groups were reluctant to allow children to use technology; and when synchronous teaching was used, it was difficult for some families with limited devices to allow children to access the teaching at the same time (Leask and Younie, 2022). Other possible issues faced by students which further impaired their learning was the lack of parental guidance because of their unfamiliarity with the curriculum or having poor skills in using technology. If parents or carers were working, some students themselves may also have had caring responsibilities to look after family members (Pokhrel and Chherti, 2021). Breslin (2021) identifies three types of learners in how they managed school closures, although he stresses that learners may have moved between the categories during lockdown:

1 *Lockdown thrivers*: these are the students who have something that has worked more effectively than school, which they experienced before lockdown. Perhaps they struggled with the structure of school. Lockdown thrivers may include students who come from comfortable homes with good internet access and with families who take a positive viewpoint of home with the cultural capital resources to support home schooling.

2 *Lockdown survivors*: these are students who have just about got through the lockdown who have gained some new skills and experiences but rather missed the social aspects of school. They would look forward to returning to school.

3 *Lockdown strugglers*: these students may have found, for a number of reasons, lockdown very difficult. For example they could have experienced abuse, family conflict and even violence and possibly lived in poor socio-economic conditions, and faced loneliness and anxiety which could have an effect on their self-esteem. A number would have had little opportunity to make the most of internet access.

(Adapted from Breslin, 2021: 112–13)

Concerns were raised as the school closures were being discussed that vulnerable pupils and those from deprived areas would suffer the heaviest burden in their learning by not being in schools. The DfE announced a plan to provide free laptops for remote learning to those most in need a month after lockdown. Yet the plan experienced delays, which in turn led to complaints from teachers that the laptops were being delivered slowly and in insufficient numbers. The DfE policy from September 2020 to June 2021 included those disadvantaged children with no digital devices in their household and whose only available device was a smart phone; those with a single device in the household shared with more than one other family member; and those with no access to the internet at home. Plans were made to extend the provision of devices and 4G routers to many other disadvantaged young people such as care leavers and their social workers (DfE, 2020a). Although 220,000 laptops were distributed by August 2020, the children's commissioner cautioned that this only benefitted just over a third of those in need of the devices (Savage, 2020). Problems with the supply of laptops was always going to be a challenge for the DfE, mainly due to the increased global demand. Interestingly, Wales appeared to have had a more forward-looking plan for the supply of devices, delivering in May as many laptops per head as England managed by the end of term in July 2020. Criticism of the supply lingered on until January 2021. However, in March 2021 there were 1.3 million devices and 4G routers had been supplied to those in need in the UK, which compared favourably with many other European countries. The magnitude of this supply will probably have enduring and helpful effects on the pupils who received these devices (Timmins, 2021).

However, when lockdown and school closures began, it extended and made more transparent marginalisation and a range of inequalities. Breslin (2021) argues, referring to research undertaken by health and education sociologists over the last ten years, that their work shows:

> Illness, well-being and educational outcomes are closely intertwined with socio-economic status, gender, ethnicity, age, disability and a range of sometimes less visible patterns of stratification and differentiation. The differential impact of COVID-19 on those already in poor health (who are overrepresented in the most disadvantaged groups), those who work in lower-paid jobs, those from black and other minority ethnic communities and the elderly underlines just how discriminatory illness is.
>
> (pp. 30–1)

Breslin (2021: 39) contests that 'the loneliness of modern poverty' underpins many of these inequalities and marginalisation. Brighouse and Waters (2021) raise the concerns of the extent and the different ways that the pandemic has impacted on children's development. These concerns are coupled with the omnipresent effects 'of social media, well-being, mental health issues, social withdrawal, aspects of poor physical health, learning delays and difficult family relationships' (Brighouse and Waters, 2021: 586).

Inequality and marginalisation during the pandemic affected different people in different ways and in different sectors of education. Leask and Younie (2022) found that some groups were in danger of being forgotten and isolated, particularly those who needed additional support, such as SEND and English as an additional language (EAL) students, as well as those living in remote coastal and rural settings. Early years education research has uncovered examples of areas of inequality and marginalisation. Findings by Walton and Darkes-Sutcliffe (2021: 6) into the impact of COVID-19 on the mental health and learning of young children revealed the absence of the key person in the setting significantly disrupted the 'triangle of trust' between the parent, child and practitioner, which in turn diminished the stability of emotional support available. They also found that SEND children were especially impacted, and that assumptions about children's resilience did not always take into account the awareness of the emotional and psychological affect of the pandemic on the young learners (Walton and Darkes-Sutcliffe, 2021). BBC (2022b) reported an increased number of speech and language referrals recorded of young children as they had not spent time in each other's company, which impacted on their communication skills. This has particularly affected poorer pupils in Wales, and the Welsh government has now launched the Talk With Me campaign which offers speech and language training to parents and carers.

There are further examples of inequality and marginalisation which have been exacerbated by the pandemic, two of which merit additional comment as they indicate a possible warning for future inequity, particularly in the UK: hunger poverty and chronic school absences. Hunger poverty is not a new phenomenon, yet it possibly became more evident in the UK with the period of austerity that began in earnest with the 2010 Conservative-led coalition government. Those families who were poor at the time became poorer and more isolated; they became the 'left behind', a state that was made worse by the pandemic (Breslin, 2021: 42). It took Marcus Rashford, a 22-year-old Manchester United footballer, to make a difference in persuading the government to give meal vouchers during the school holidays to families with children receiving free school meals. In an open letter to the government and using his own childhood experiences, he stressed the importance of food security. During a BBC interview in 15 June 2020, he spoke from the heart about the impact of poverty on families who struggle financially. A day after the interview, the government made their first U-turn of the pandemic when Boris Johnson promised to expand the voucher scheme for the summer holiday (Breslin, 2021). Using information provided by the DfE, the BBC reported that the impact of the COVID-19 pandemic had resulted in 'unprecedented' numbers of children categorised as being chronically absent, which meant that the children had missed classes for more than 10 per cent of the year. Furthermore, and more worryingly, concern by the children's commissioner for England is that 'some children never fully returned to school after lockdown' (Meredith, 2022).

INSPECTIONS, CURRICULUM AND EXAMINATIONS

The normal processes of education such as inspections, the curriculum and examinations during lockdown were modified and, in some instances, suspended because of the school closures. The effect of these modifications varied from being beneficial to the children, to adding to the inequalities considered above. One process that was welcomed by school leaders and staff was the postponement of Ofsted inspections, which was made known very shortly after lockdown started. Part of the relief from school staff in England was that they were working towards a new inspection framework which, for those schools not involved in the pilot, had only come into operation months before. Ofsted's initial decision to postpone inspections was followed by an announcement that it would focus its energies in the autumn of 2020 in carrying out a series of non-judgemental 'visits' to schools and colleges. Visits were non-graded, but would report on the discussions that Ofsted 'visitors' had with school and college leaders, especially on their plans to help students return to full-time schooling (Breslin, 2021). It is strongly suggested that the decision to suspend inspections and start visits enabled teachers to be more creative in their teaching, both the face-to-face teaching with vulnerable children and the children of key workers, as well in their use of technology for remote learning and teaching. From a progressive viewpoint, the shift from inspections to visits, albeit temporary, is an idea to consider for the future.

The suspensions of Ofsted inspections and following the cancellation of all written examinations in the UK in 2020, and then again in 2021, was an ideal opportunity to have a rethink on the purpose and content of the curriculum, and what should and should not be assessed (Breslin, 2021). Numerous teachers felt a sense of freedom because they were not constrained by examinations, while many took the opportunity to take part in thoughtful and detailed collaboration about the curriculum (Hyman, 2020). However, it is argued that freedom and collaboration to instigate change is particularly difficult regarding the English national curriculum in its current form with its increasingly academic and grade-orientated focus together with the subordination of vocational subjects. Overall, different schools, colleges and individual teachers varied in their adherence to following the set or national curriculum. We have considered how teachers took a very flexible personalised learning approach to learning and teaching: some closely followed the set curriculum, while others took a more personal development pathway, allowing students to pursue their interests (Zhao and Watterston, 2021). Daniel (2020) suggested a middle ground adopted by most teachers, to keep their practice positioned towards the set curriculum and associated assessments, but to maintain student interest through providing 'varied assignments – not least, perhaps, by work that sets the present COVID-19 crisis in a wider global and historical context' (p. 94).

It is contested that the matter of solving the problems of written examinations during the pandemic in schools and colleges in the UK was poorly managed by the government. When it was considered that there was a strong possibility that GCSEs, A-levels and BTEC exams would be cancelled, the DfE entered discussions with the Office of Qualifications and Examinations Regulation (Ofqual) to consider the various options, including carrying on regardless within the constraints of COVID-19 regulations, delaying the exams or scrapping the exams altogether, and using teacher assessment and other evidence for grading. At this early stage, it was evident that the prime minister, the government and those in the DfE did not want to cancel formal exams. The mishandling caused anxiety, and even anger for students, parents and the teachers trying to cope with the resulting U-turns, short-notice communications from the DfE, and the chaos of algorithms in calculating grades. The anxiety and anger were quite understandable, as it affected student entry to university and their aspirations for the future. What unfolded from these early stages of looking for a solution was disappointing, and it is argued lacked forethought and continency planning for what was to follow. Kelly (2021) in his research into the calculated grades systems in England and Ireland went as far as stating that 'the system in England suffered what was probably its greatest policy failure of modern times' (p. 725).

The unfolding of the events relating to the cancellation of exams and the calculations of grades is probably best outlined by summarising Timmins's analysis of the handling of exams in *Schools and Coronavirus: The Government's Handling of Education During the Pandemic* (2021).

Table 7.1   Unfolding the use of algorithms and processes for grade calculations during the pandemic

Date	Event/decision	Commentary
31 March 2020	Gavin Williamson stated that exams would be cancelled and calculated grades would be used.	Announced without consultation with Ofqual. DfE emphasised from the outset that it was sacrosanct that whatever system was chosen to award exam grades, it should prevent or at the very least restrict grade inflation.
3 April 2020	Ofqual announced an outline guide for how exam grades would be awarded.	Grades to be decided by a combination of teacher assessment and adjustment, with teachers positioning their students within their class, as well as taking into account the school's previous performance; those results would then go through a standardisation process termed the 'algorithm'. (All devolved nations also decided to use an algorithm but the formula used varied.)
May 2020	Criticism intensified of the unfairness in the way that grades were to be awarded by schools and students.	Criticisms were varied, but were mainly concerned about how improving schools would be at a disadvantage, as well as very bright students in badly performing schools. There was also uncertainty at this stage of the appeal process.
4 August 2020	Results came out in Scotland and 124,000 teacher assessments seemed to have been downgraded; university places were in doubt.	Scotland ditched its algorithm on 11 August and used teacher-only assessments.
12 August 2020	The day before the announcement of the A-level results in England, and possibly feeling there might be trouble ahead, Williamson promised a triple lock to students prior to the A-level and GCSE results. Students were offered three options: accept their calculated grade, appeal to receive a valid mock result, or sit exams to ensure their achievements are recognised (DfE and Williams, 2020b).	

13 August 2020	Although the A-level results showed a record high of A and A* grades, nearly 40 per cent of predicted grades were downgraded – a much greater percentage than in Scotland.	There was widespread disquiet in the media, with many students distraught at their results. Williamson gave a categorical denial that he would not perform a U-turn as happened in Scotland.
17 August 2020	The foreseeable happened: students were given their predicted or their calculated grades.	Williamson appeared to put the blame on Ofqual. In contrast to Scotland, which ditched their algorithm, the Scottish Education Minister, and not the Scottish Qualifications Authority, took full responsibility. A week after, the Chief Executive of Ofqual resigned.
4 January 2021	The closure of schools was announced again.	The prime minister recognised that it was impossible for fair exams to take place in the summer. No contingency plans had taken place following the situation regarding exams since the previous summer.
6 January 2021	Williamson was not able to state how GCSEs, A-Levels and BTECs would be assessed.	A two-week consultation took place between the DfE and Ofqual on how the assessment system would operate.
February 2021	A wide range of information was outlined which could go towards calculating grades, including mock exams, in-class tests, tests provided by exam boards (although these would not be compulsory), completed work by students.	
9 March 2021	Schools were promised plenty of guidance on how to grade student work. This was just as schools were returning.	The government was adamant that they did not want to be suspected of using an algorithm, or that they would be using assessment in traditional examination conditions. It became evident that schools would use different methods.
August 2021	Results at A-level were generally higher than in 2020, particularly at A*–B. Results for GCSEs were higher at Grade 7, but generally stable in other grades (GOV.UK, 2021).	Williamson was replaced as Secretary of State for Education on 15 September 2021 by Nadhim Zahawi. At the time of writing, there have been two other Secretaries of State, with further changes possible.

Adapted from Timmins (2021).

The top grades in the 2022 A-level exam grades for England, Wales and Northern Ireland had not matched the teacher assessments of 2020 and 2021 (BBC, 2022c). There was a similar drop in the top grades for Highers and Advanced Highers in Scotland (Scottish Qualifications Authority, 2022). Yet UK top grades of 2022 were slightly up on those of the last formal exams in 2019 (BBC, 2022c). Given the differences of grading processes, it is difficult to make a meaningful comparison between the pandemic and formal exam grades.

'CATCHING-UP', ENDINGS AND POSSIBILITIES

There is no doubt that lockdown had a huge impact, affecting the lives of children, parents, carers and school staff, and there was a longing for schools to reopen so that things could 'get back to normal', to continue as before. However, Peter Hyman, writing just three months into lockdown (2020), made a strong argument against getting back to 'normal':

> Normal for schools had become unbalanced, at times unhinged. Tunnel vision. A pressure that was unhealthy, often toxic; Ofsted inspections, high-stakes exams, the crowding out of creativity. Normal was vindictive: 30% labelled as failures each year, after 12 years of education. Normal meant too many committed and creative teachers battling against the odds: 40% leaving the profession within five years. Normal could be dispiriting, with growing mental health problems in young people. Normal was scarred by deep inequalities.

Hyman was one of many educators hoping that from the experiences, both negative and positive, of lockdown a new progressive, fair and child-centred education would emerge for all. However, at the time of writing, which coincides with chaotic changes in the UK government (three different prime ministers and five different education secretaries in the space of three months), apart from some positive initiatives locally and research findings regarding COVID-19, little has changed from the 'normal'. Perhaps more time is needed since the reopening of schools, as well as the political will to debate what is required to make the transition from 'normal' education to one that addresses Hyman's argument above.

Nevertheless, not long after lockdown, the government announced that the National Tutoring Programme (NTP), a major initiative created chiefly by the Education Endowment Foundation (EEF), would help schools tackle the 'catch-up' of lost learning caused by the pandemic. The NTP has two strands. First, the Tuition Partners programme which could draw on substantial government funding to support schools and teachers to supplement classroom teaching with 'high quality tutoring … from an approved list of Tuition Partners'. Second, Academic Mentors who were 'embedded in schools, providing frequent and intensive support to pupils … [and] … led by Teach First' to improve learning attainment (Education Endowment Foundation, 2021). However, the effectiveness of the NTP has attracted criticism, particularly from the parliamentary Education Select Committee which called on 'the government to "refocus" its efforts on a "fragmented and bureaucratic" catch-up programme' (Jeffreys, 2022). There were also problems in employing sufficient quality practitioners to the NTP; some schools used the funding to support their own staff instead of using tutoring agencies (or Tuition Partners) as 'money can be better spent by those of us who know our children better' (Jeffreys, 2022).

Although he acknowledges that children have lost a considerable amount of formal learning and there will be gaps to tackle, Breslin (2021) is critical of the language of 'catch-up' and 'recovery'. 'Catch-up' discounts the different types of learning that children have benefitted from. The use of 'recovery' aligns with the deficit notion of education that depicts 'schooling as merely the "filling of empty vessels" with "knowledge"; policy makers and systems leaders need to address this austerity of curricular and pedagogic thinking' (Breslin, 2021: 99). There is a clear association between the 'filling of empty vessels' and Paulo Freire's banking concept of education where students submissively accumulate knowledge to memorise and recite, where 'knowledge is a gift bestowed by those who consider themselves knowledgeable upon those they consider to know nothing' (Freire, [1970] 1996: 53). It is argued that the concern raised by Breslin (2021) of the paucity of 'pedagogic thinking' and the lack of educational research-informed policy-making is evident in much of the government's response to its 'catch-up' programme, which is a matter for the future.

Much of the 'catch-up' focuses on curriculum and knowledge, which is important; it is also quantifiable and making headway can be assessed against knowledge acquisition. However, tackling the many and varied issues of well-being caused by the pandemic and the closure of schools is a much more problematic proposition. For example, in attempting to create a safe environment in schools – 'masks, bubbles, spacing, sanitiser, staggered start and finishing times … insufficient time is given to the diagnosis of what will be highly individualised well-being related needs' (Breslin, 2021: 119). Yet he emphasises the importance of prioritising well-being in post-lockdown schooling: 'securing well-being is a prerequisite for curriculum catch-up, not its poor relation' (Breslin, 2021: 114). Many schools' staff and governors had taken the lead with ensuring students' well-being during lockdown by engaging with families through regular communications, such as telephone calls and emails with parents. As a result, they got to know each other much better and were able to give support to both children and their families where needed (Rhys-Evans, 2020). The well-being of teachers and school staff was also an important concern during and following the uncertainties, staff absences and the turmoil of the pandemic. Some staff will have coped, while others will have found the situation difficult, but it is imperative that all staff have access to help and advice, and the time to feel comfortable to teach again. Leask and Younie

(2022) suggested that school staff should make use of their communities of practice to offer mutual support with each other's well-being.

It is reasonable to say that future pandemics, including those that caused COVID-19, will reoccur in the future, and this will probably result in the closure of schools. Measures that address the closure of schools should obviously be planned; it should be best suited to the needs of students and staff, taking into account the lessons learned. The reopening of schools also needs scrutiny, given the consequences of attempting to reopen schools in the UK in September 2020. Although there was a general consensus that schools should reopen as long as it was safe to do so, there was considerable anxiety and a degree of mistrust of the government by some parents, especially those with a number of children at the same school, which they felt negated the bubble system, and from those with elderly and clinically vulnerable people in the household. Unlike the devolved nations, Gavin Williamson threatened to fine parents in England who did not let their children return to school at the start of the 2020 autumn term, with head teachers responsible for activating the fines – a decision that was met with disbelief by parents and teachers. A letter to *The Times* on 4 July 2020 emphasised the disbelief:

> It is a sobering thought that the education secretary (Gavin Williamson MP) appears so devoid of persuasive or constructive ideas that he considers one of the best ways of ensuring a full return to school life in September is to fine those parents who may choose to keep their children at home for perfectly understandable reasons.
>
> (Claughton, 2020, cited in Breslin, 2021: 107)

The reopening of schools at that time was too soon and was prompted at best by opaque reasons rather than consensus with concerned parties. Many schools still lacked ventilation units and there were insufficient virus tests for schools (Timmins, 2021). Furthermore, the COVID-19 virus was still evident and school closures were needed again by the end of the year and into 2021, causing further unsettling periods of disruption. When outlining the lessons learned about reopening schools, Leask and Younie (2022) found that learning was more disrupted on the reopening of schools than if remote teaching had continued due to teachers and students being busy in school, and as such they had less time to focus on the remote teaching for those isolating or at home for other reasons.

Finally, Breslin (2021: 176) argues that because schooling has changed so much and so quickly during the pandemic, it has made the task of recommendations for the future a challenging task. Instead, he offers the following six themes to work with, which he maintains will probably prevail in the years ahead:

1 Putting well-being first.
2 Closing the achievement gap.
3 Rethinking the curriculum and its assessment.

4   Growing digital connectivity and digital literacy.
5   Building a new relationship between schools, families and communities.
6   Creating a teaching profession and schooling system prepared for tomorrow, and for a world as yet unknown.

To sum up the possibilities for a post-pandemic education, it is fitting that this section concludes with a quotation from Brighouse and Waters (2021: 34) which looks forward to

> a new educational age – a time of hope, ambition and collaborative partnership … [with] … the changes that will lead us to that world in what follows as we seek to improve the previous best.

SUMMARY

The COVID-19 pandemic caused untold disruption to education throughout the world; it also revealed the magnitude of inequalities in some sections of society. These inequalities have impaired the learning opportunities and well-being for many students, and these inequalities will persist for some time. Different countries managed the pandemic from an educational perspective differently; this difference was evident within the devolved nations of the UK. There were some errors in the decision-making at government level. Leading up to the school closures and lockdown, there was a lack of specific guidance from the DfE on processes to adopt at local level, although head teachers, staff, governors as well as teaching unions became proactive in preparing for closures and managing the situation themselves once lockdown began. The swift actions by teaching staff included innovative planning for teaching and learning, both for the children in schools and the majority who were learning remotely at home. The use of digital technology for teaching and learning became a very well-used medium, with many creative ideas explored. Teachers, freed from the constraints of Ofsted inspections and adapting flexibly to the needs of the curriculum, were able to try learner-centred ideas of teaching, some aligned to the more progressive educators such as John Holt (home schooling) and Ivan Illich (learning webs).

  The benefits of digital technology were in some degree offset by the inequality that it caused. Not all children had unfettered access to devices or indeed the internet. Although the DfE promised to distribute devices and improve internet connectivity for those disadvantaged learners, this was slow to come. Students reacted differently to lockdown. For the lockdown strugglers, it was a period of difficulty for a number of reasons, and they struggled with their learning and well-being (Breslin, 2021). The summer examinations for both 2020 and 2021 were cancelled amid confusion and

U-turns; the DfE was subject to criticism in the way they managed the alternative ways of grading students for A-levels and GCSEs. First, regarding the aborted use of the algorithm and then its method of teacher assessment, the DfE put together a programme for 'catch-up' using the NTP with varying degrees of success. However, the 'catch-up' programme was focused on academic success and not on children's well-being. There have been many innovative ideas that teaching professionals can take forward for the future, not only in relation to pedagogy, but also about collaboration and partnerships, and working without too many constraints on inspection, the curriculum and assessment.

GLOSSARY OF TERMS

Algorithm

A series of steps used to calculate outcomes, or grades in this instance, using a computer. The calculation of grades for students' summer 2020 written exams would have included previous internal work and assessments and their weighting, which were passed on to examination boards and administered by Ofqual and the Scottish Qualifications Authority (Breslin, 2021).

Blended learning

This is a mixture of different types of learning, such as distance learning, home learning, face-to-face with teacher and pupil/s (in person or via Zoom), supported by online and hard-copy learning and assessment resources.

COVID-19

'A mild to severe respiratory illness that is caused by a coronavirus ... transmitted chiefly by contact with infectious material (such as respiratory droplets) or with objects or surfaces contaminated by the causative virus, and is characterized especially by fever, cough, and shortness of breath and may progress to pneumonia and respiratory failure' (*Merriam-Webster Dictionary*, n.d.).

Digital divide

This is the disparity between access to digital technology for remote learning. Some students have unfettered access to devices and internet connectivity, while others struggle to gain access for a number of reasons, including poverty, students who are in households with other learners also trying to access learning, and those lacking digital literacy.

Home-schooling

Home-schooling as a practice has been used for a considerable time, and before school closures and after reopening, some children were schooled at home as long as their parents abided by set legal obligations. Home-schooling as a concept was championed by the progressive educational thinker, John Holt, who believed that schools inhibited children's creativity and curiosity. He further argued that children learned and developed differently and therefore should not be constrained by the set stages of compulsory education. He advocated personalised learning as an alternative (Meighan, 2007).

Learning webs

The idea of learning webs came from Ivan Illich, a progressive educator who was also critical of schools and traditional learning. For Illich, the reason why schools fail originates from poverty and not the inherent abilities of the child (Thomas, 2013). One of his major ideas pertinent to the pandemic with its reliance on technology is his concept of learning webs which provide access to learning resources and the sharing of knowledge, ideas and skills.

Pandemic

An outbreak of a disease which is widespread over a number of countries and which affects a large number of the population.

FURTHER READING

Kaplan, A. (2021) *Higher Education at the Crossroads of Disruption: The University of the 21st Century*. Bingley: Emerald Publishing.

A review of the way that higher education has, and can, adapt to the disruption of the COVID-19 pandemic, taking into account distance learning, on-site vs. off-site learning and teaching, artificial intelligence and the rise of digital innovation.

Reimers, F. (ed.) (2021) *Primary and Secondary Education during Covid-19: Disruptions to Educational Opportunity During a Pandemic*. Cham, Switzerland: Singer Publishing.

An open access comparative text which explores international efforts to manage primary and secondary education from the views of teachers, students and education systems from Brazil, Finland, Japan, Mexico, Norway, Portugal, Russia, Singapore, Spain, South Africa, the UK and the USA.

Shoffner, M. and Webb, A. (eds) (2022) *Reconstructing Care in Teacher Education after COVID-19: Caring Enough to Change*. London: Routledge.

This text considers the meaning of care in teacher education following the COVID-19 pandemic, taking the views from over fifty international teacher educators. The book emphasises the importance of research and reflection as being the core to teacher education, with ideas to consider for the future.

Zepeda, S. and Lanoue, P. (2021) *A Leadership Guide to Navigating the Unknown in Education: New Narratives amid COVID-19*. London: Routledge.

This book by two North American authors explores how schools can effectively adapt in the face of disruption and turbulence caused by the pandemic, using the narratives from expert leaders from different education systems.

REFERENCES

Adams, R. (2021) Government is criticised for 'unforgivable' refusal to make Covid plan for English schools. *The Guardian*, 4 August.

BBC (2022a) Covid inquiry: Lessons will be learned before next pandemic (22 July). Available at: www.bbc.co.uk/news/health-62250899 (accessed 16 March 2023).

BBC (2022b) Covid: Parents urged to get help as speech referrals rise (8 August). Available at: www.bbc.co.uk/news/uk-wales-62465141 (accessed 16 March 2023).

BBC (2022c) Top A-level results fall but university admissions near record, 18 August. Available at: www.bbc.co.uk/news/live/education-62550119 (accessed 16 March 2023).

Billington, T., Gibson, S., Fogg, P., Lahmar, J. and Cameron, H. (2022) Conditions for mental health in education. Towards relational practice. *British Educational Research Journal*. 48(1): 95–119.

Breslin, T. (2021) *Lessons from Lockdown: The Educational Legacy of COVID-19*. London: Routledge.

Brighouse, T. and Waters, M. (2021) *About Our Schools: Improving on Previous Best*. Carmarthen: Crown House Publishing.

Coughlan, S. (2020) 'Digital poverty' in schools where few have laptops (24 April). Available at: www.bbc.co.uk/news/education-52399589 (accessed 16 March 2023).

Daniel, D. (2020) Education and the COVID-19 pandemic. *Prospects*, 49: 91–6. Available at: https://doi.org/10.1007/s11125-020-09464-3 (accessed 16 March 2023).

Department for Education (DfE) (2020a) Guidance: Get help with technology during coronavirus (COVID-19) (19 April). Available at: https://get-help-with-tech.education.gov.uk/devices/about-the-offer (accessed 16 March 2023).

DfE and Williams, G. (2020b) Press release: Triple lock for students ahead of A level and GCSE results (12 August). Available at: www.gov.uk/government/news/triple-lock-for-students-ahead-of-a-level-and-gcse-results (accessed 16 March 2023).

Education Endowment Foundation (2021) Evaluation of the impact of tutoring, as a response to COVID-19 learning loss. Available at: https://educationendowmentfoundation.org.uk/ (16 March 2023).

Fotheringham, P., Thomas, H., Healy, G., Arenge, G. and Wilson, E. (2022) Pressures and influences on school leaders navigating policy development during the COVID-19 pandemic. *British Educational Research Journal*, 48(2): 201–27.

Holt, J. (1964) *How Children Fail*. London: Penguin Books.

Holt, J. (1967) *How Children Learn*. London: Peguin Books.

Hyman, P. (2020) Our schools system is broken. Let's grab this opportunity to remake it. *The Observer*, 5 July.

Illich, I. (1971) *Deschooling Society*. London: Marion Boyars Publishers.

Jeffreys, B. (2022) Covid panic fuels deepening education inequalities in England, says MPs (10 March). Available at: www.bbc.co.uk/news/education-60683839 (accessed 16 March 2023).

Kelly, A. (2021) A tale of two algorithms: The appeal and repeal of calculated grades system in England and Ireland in 2020. *British Educational Research Journal,* 47(3): 725–41.

Leask, M. and Younie, S. (2022) *Education for All in Times of Crisis: Lessons from Covid-19.* London: Routledge.

Meighan, R. (2007) *John Holt.* London: Bloomsbury.

Meredith, R. (2022) Covid-19: Unprecedented levels of chronic absence in schools (4 August). Available at: www.bbc.co.uk/news/uk-northern-ireland-62412975 (accessed 16 March 2023).

Merriam-Webster Dictionary (n.d.) COVID-19. Available at: www.merriam-webster.com/dictionary/COVID-19 (accessed 16 March 2023).

Muller, L.-M. (2022) Education refocus in times of crisis: Teachers' experiences during the Covid-19 pandemic. *BERA Research Intelligence,* 151: 18–19 spring/summer.

Pokhrel, S. and Chhetri, R. (2021) A literature review on impact of COVID-19 pandemic on teaching and learning. *Higher Education for the Future,* 8(1): 133–41. Available at: https://journals.sagepub.com/doi/full/10.1177/2347631120983481 (accessed 16 March 2023).

Rhys-Evans, J. (2020) Supporting academic learning or wellbeing: A false dichotomy? *BERA Research Intelligence,* 144: 34–5, autumn.

Savage, M. (2020) How ministers made a shambles of our schools. *The Observer,* 20 December.

Scottish Qualifications Authority (2022) SQA publishes 2022 results (9 August). Available at: www.sqa.org.uk/sqa/102227.html (accessed 16 March 2023).

Thomas, G. (2013) *Education: A Very Short History.* Oxford: Oxford University Press.

Timmins, N. (2021) *Schools and Coronavirus: The Government's Handling of Education during the Pandemic.* Institute for Government. Available at: www.instituteforgovernment.org.uk/sites/default/files/publications/schools-and-coronavirus.pdf (accessed 16 March 2023).

Wallace, S. (2008) *Oxford Dictionary of Education.* Oxford: Oxford University Press.

Walton, J. and Darkes-Sutcliffe, J. (2021) The impact of Covid-19 on the mental health and learning of young children (Education & Covid-19 series). *British Educational Research Association.* Available at: www.bera.ac.uk/publication/new-teachers-responses-to-covid-19-building-on-initial-teacher-education-for-professional-learning (accessed 16 March 2023).

Williams, R. (2022) Foreword. In: M. Leask and S. Younie, *Education for All in Times of Crisis: Lessons from Covid-19.* London: Routledge.

World Health Organization (WHO) (2009) Reducing transmission of pandemic (H1N1) 2009 in school settings. Available at: www.who.int/publications/i/item/reducing-transmission-of-pandemic-(h1n1)-2009-in-school-settings (accessed 16 March 2023).

Zhao, Y. and Watterston, J. (2021) The changes we need: Education post COVID-19. *Journal of Educational Change,* 22: 3–12. Available at: https://link.springer.com/article/10.1007/s10833-021-09417-3 (accessed 16 March 2023).

8
TAKING PRIDE: THE LGBTQ+ EXPERIENCE IN SCHOOL

LEARNING OUTCOMES

Having read this chapter, you should be able to:

- understand the history behind the LGBT movement;
- recognise some of the challenges experienced by young people who identify as LGBT;
- reflect on the role of educational settings in supporting diversity;
- understand the importance of creating safe spaces for young people.

KEY WORDS

cisgendered; conversion therapy; heteronormative; heterosexual; homophobia; protected characteristics; Section 28; transgendered; transsexual.

INTRODUCTION

In the early hours of 28 June 1969, New York City police raided the Stonewall Inn, a gay night club that was located in Greenwich Village, New York city (History.com editors, 2022). Emerging as a gay bar in March 1967, at a time when such bars were illegal, the Stonewall Inn quickly gained a large clientele. Todd (2021) proposes that the success of the Stonewall Inn was its diversity, given that the management allowed people of the same gender to dance together, an act that at that time was illegal. Furthermore, as a large venue, not hidden away on a side street as many other such bars were, and with a cheap admission fee, the venue attracted many young men who had been ostracised by their families. While the Stonewall Inn attracted the typical clientele of gay bars at the time, white men dressing in a traditional masculine way, Todd expressed that there was also an edginess to the clientele, men in drag and make-up, effeminate men and butch lesbians – people living 'at the margins of an already marginalised community' (2021: 59).

Raids at the Stonewall Inn were then not unusual. However, due to its popularity, the management could afford to pay off the police, making the almost monthly raids a cursory act to placate the complaints of local neighbours. Moreover, the police often informed management before raids were carried out, conducting them early in the evening and making perfunctory arrests before the night continued in earnest. However, on the night of 27 June, one such raid was conducted without advance warning, and much later than normal, which Todd (2021) observes was a response to a growing intolerance of the police of the Stonewall Inn and the gay community in general. The situation was further inflamed by those inside the inn, who rather than the usual passive acceptance of the police raid, showed resistance to authorities, subsequently resulting in violent clashes between police and patrons. What followed were six days of protests outside the Stonewall Inn and in neighbouring streets, marking a major shift in advocacy for lesbian, gay, bisexual and transgender (LGBT)[1] people, and acting as a catalyst for the gay rights movement across the world (Belmonte, 2021; History.com editors, 2022).

In the two decades following the Stonewall riots, a growth in the gay liberation movement was seen worldwide, a social and political movement that encouraged lesbians and gay men to use radical direct actions as a means by which to counter the societal shame they had experienced with gay pride. In the UK, the first meeting of the Gay Liberation Freedom (GLF) was held in 1970, one year after Stonewall, and

---

[1]Traditionally, LGBT was the commonly used acronym to describe people who identify as lesbian, gay, bisexual and transsexual. However, as sexuality is evolving, the acronym has had several iterations, the most recent being LGBTIQAPD – lesbian, gay, bisexual, transgender, intersex, queer and/or questioning, asexual and/or ally, pansexual and demi-sexual. For the purpose of this text, LGBT/LGBTQ+ has been used interchangeably depending on the context.

while this was disbanded in 1973, the cause was subsequently taken up by the Campaign for Homosexual Equality (CHE) located in Manchester. In commemoration of the Stonewall riots, gay pride marches and festivals became a regular occurrence as a commemoration to the riots, and continue to this day, with global events occurring annually during the month of June (Dryden, n.d.).

Nevertheless, acceptance of gay rights has been slow to gather pace outside the gay community, a situation that was aggravated by the development of the Acquired Immune Deficiency Syndrome (AIDS) pandemic in the 1980s, which arguably revitalised contemporary **homophobia**, since AIDS was portrayed as a 'gay disease' in media propaganda, thereby reinforcing beliefs that 'homosexuality is morally deviant' (Forrest, 2018b: 168). In education particularly, the AIDS epidemic arguably resulted in the implementation of **Section 28** of the Education Act, which sought to prohibit the promotion of homosexuality in schools and led to further repression of those young people who identified as LGBT.

A repeal of Section 28 and the introduction of a revised Sex and Relationship Education (SRE) curriculum in September 2021 has, however, increased awareness of the needs of pupils who identify as LGBT, and has opened up much-needed debate on the need to direct attention away from the traditional **heteronormative** perspective of sexuality, and consider how education might promote and celebrate the diversity of pupils in our schools today.

This chapter seeks to briefly explore the history of the LGBT movement before considering the experiences of LGBT pupils in educational settings. Finally, the chapter will examine how education might build on the progress made since the repeal of Section 28 and set out some practical suggestions for school practice.

HISTORICAL CONTEXT

In 1988, an amendment to the 1986 Local Government Act was made which stated that local authorities should not

- intentionally promote homosexuality or publish material with the intention of promoting homosexuality;
- promote the teaching in any maintained school of the acceptability of homosexuality as a pretended family relationship.

(legislation.gov.uk, 1988, Section 28: 2a)

Enacted in May 1988 under Margaret Thatcher's government, the amendment, referred to as Section or Clause 28, was in part a response to the emerging HIV epidemic. Moreover, following the publication of the storybook *Jenny Lives with Eric and Martin* (Bosche, 1983), which sought to raise awareness in children of different types of families, tabloid newspapers made claims that young people were at risk of being corrupted through sex and relationships education in schools (Forrest, 2018a). Despite the fact that the book was promoted solely in an Inner London Education authority, predominantly for teachers who wanted to learn more about lesbian and gay parents, a headline in *The Sun Magazine* declaring 'Vile book in school: Pupils see picture of gay lovers' (LGBT Lawyers, 2021) provided the impetus for this legislation which would impact on LGBT rights for the next 15 years.

A quote from *The Independent* (1988) stated that:

> Section 28 marked a disturbing backwards step for tolerance and inclusivity after the strides made by the British LGBT+ movement.
>
> (Cited in LGBT lawyers, 2021, para. 3)

Nevertheless, then Prime Minister Margaret Thatcher declared:

> Children who need to be taught to respect traditional moral values are being taught that they have an inalienable right to be gay. All of those children are being cheated of a sound start in life.
>
> (1987, para. 46)

Nicholls (2021) proposed that the introduction of Section 28 in educational settings resulted in expunging any mention of being gay, past or present, with educators fearing losing their jobs should they make mention of this forbidden subject. Moreover, while up to this point the gay rights movement had been gathering momentum in the two decades since Stonewall, the HIV/AIDS epidemic saw a marked increase in anti-gay sentiment in the UK, with only 11 per cent of people surveyed believing that being gay was never wrong (Nicholls, 2021). AIDS became viewed as a gay disease and was seen as a punishment for immoral and inhuman behaviour (Nicholls, 2021), ultimately resulting in homophobia and anti-LGBT sentiment becoming both acceptable and a moral standpoint, arguably setting the cause back by decades.

Section 28 offers a lens into the complicated history of the LGBTQ+ community and while it is not possible to document this fully in a chapter of this length, it is, however, important to provide some context leading up to Section 28 and what has followed since its repeal in 2003. Todd (2021) observes that a disapproval of homosexual behaviour has existed in most cultures, even where that behaviour was tolerated or permitted, a view supported by Forrest (2018b) who explains that throughout the nineteenth century attempts were made to pathologise such sexual behaviour, with homosexuality being categorised as a mental disorder. Furthermore, psychologists began to categorise homosexuals as 'antisocial and incapable of love' (Belmonte, 2021: 78), with psychologist Edward Bergler, a student of Freud, declaring that homosexuals were a threat to others being intent on seducing unsuspecting youth. Arguably, such views led to the introduction of **conversion therapy** in a bid to treat this deviant behaviour, which Forrest describes as the 'institutional abuse of countless homosexuals, transvestites, **transgendered** and **transsexual** people' (2018b: 132).

Nevertheless, evidence of homosexual behaviour exists through time, with Ancient Greece and Rome being held up as examples of an enlightened ancient world due to their seemingly social acceptance of sexual relationships between older and younger men (Todd, 2021). Furthermore, Todd (2021) posits that Native Americans made reference to the existence of 'two-spirit people', a term encompassing a wide range of gender and sexual identities. However, Forrest (2018b) suggests that while acceptance of homosexual behaviour was evident, there was also evidence that this is not in the traditional sense that homosexuality would be viewed today, since in Ancient Greece particularly, rather than the act being performed as a mutual engagement between two people, it was an action performed by social superior on a social inferior (Halperin, 1989, cited in Forrest, 2018b).

Forrest (2018b) proposes that the shifting attitudes towards homosexuality can be understood through exploring the differences between sex and sexuality, and the teachings of the Church in respect of this. Drawing from Halperin's work, Forrest observes that sex refers to a natural fact, grounded in the functioning of the human body, while sexuality is more commonly associated with 'appropriation of the human body and of its physiological capacities by an ideological discourse' (Halperin, 1989: 146, cited in Forrest, 2018b: 141). In the eyes of the Christian Church, traditionally sexuality is viewed through a **heterosexual** lens, with the nuclear family being seen as the building blocks of society. Moreover, strict views of the Church on sex, both inside and outside of marriage, saw no place for activity between members of the same sex. Indeed, in the writings of St Paul, homosexual sex was viewed as a serious sin, ranked alongside incest, adultery and bestiality. The view of the Church, in which homosexuality was described as 'deviant unnatural and ungodly' (Forrest, 2018b: 144) resulted in death being seen as a suitable punishment for those convicted of homosexual acts. In the UK, this law of illegality endured for 700 years.

Nevertheless, Todd (2021) observes that attempts were made globally to sanction homophobia – for example, through the Buggery Act in Britain (1533), followed by a reduction in the penalty for gay sex from death to imprisonment in 1861. This was underpinned by the Criminal Law Amendment Act, pushed forward by British MP Henry Labouchere, which stated that any sexual act between two men was to be punishable with two years' imprisonment. Sanctioning homosexual behaviour arguably resulted in many gay people denying their sexuality or behaviour going underground, leading to a special police forced being established with the sole purpose of catching those involved in acts of 'gross indecency' (Todd, 2021: 14). While the late nineteenth century did see an increased visibility of homosexuality, especially at the fringes of artistic society, and during both world wars which saw a spread of sexual liberalism, a restoration of sexual morals were restored in the postwar years when Home Secretary

Maxwell-Fyfe ordered a crackdown, determined to 'rid England of this plague' (Forrest, 2018b; Todd, 2021: 16).

However, a subtle shift was seen in the years following the Second World War, particularly in light of the work of American sex researcher Alfred Kinsey, whose work revealed a much higher prevalence of homosexual behaviour than was originally thought. Furthermore, within the heterosexual community, it was also notable that there were surprisingly high incidences of premarital sex and masturbation (Belmonte, 2021). The knowledge that same-sex activity was not uncommon led to an empowerment among American gays and lesbians. In England, too, pressure was mounting for a review of the laws relating to punishment for homosexual activity, with activists questioning why the sins of adultery and fornication did not attract legal censure in the same way as homosexuality. This subsequently led to the recommendation that homosexual behaviour which was conducted in private between two consenting adults over the age of 21 should no longer be penalised. Head of the decision-making committee, John Wolfenden, concluded that it is not the business of the law to interfere with the private lives of citizens, and only where public decency is offended should criminal proceedings be instigated (Forrest, 2018b).

Although this would appear to paint a more promising picture of equality for the LGBT community, it should be noted that it took nine years before Wolfenden's recommendations were fully adopted. Furthermore, as can be seen from the introduction of the aforementioned Section 28, it is evident that policy-makers appear quick to bow down to external pressure over LGBT issues. Forrest proposes that authority continued to 'corral sexual acts into an identity that contains implications of ungodliness, unnaturalness and even potential sedition' (2018b: 146). This he sees as illustrated through the acceptance of the media portrayal of HIV/AIDs as a gay plague.

As noted earlier, the introduction of Section 28 in education saw a return to some of the earlier dogmas, in which relationships between gay and lesbian couples were no longer perceived to be valid. A return to the traditional heterosexual norms was promoted, subsequently resulting in a marginalisation of lesbian, gay and bisexual young people. Furthermore, in schools, some teachers saw this as an opportunity to make moral judgements about their pupils (Forrest, 2018b). While a Labour government came to power in 1997, traditionally holding more liberal views than the outgoing Conservative government, it took another six years before Section 28 was repealed, and only then following a protracted and bitter struggle with the House of Lords. As noted by Forrest (2018b), any further debates on the repeal of Section 28 were deflected through a passage in the Education Act stating that pupils at state-maintained schools should

- learn the nature of marriage and its importance for family life and the bringing up of children, and

- are protected from teaching materials which are inappropriate having regard to the age and the religious and cultural background of the pupils concerned.

(Act of Parliament, 2000, Section 148)

Forrest (2018b) proposes that this sent a clear message to teachers that any teaching related to sexuality would be subject to regulation and provides assurance to parents that any activities relating to sex education could be challenged if they proved to be offensive. Arguably, this reinforces the notion that heterosexuality is the norm, resulting in a guarded approach to exploring sexuality outside of this.

Nevertheless, the repeal of Section 28, and in the light of the Labour leader Tony Blair showing support for the LGBTQ cause, some positive moves towards equality were seen following the election of New Labour in 1997. Significantly, teenagers Euan Sutherland and Chris Morris took their case to reduce the age of consent for sexual activity between males to 16 to the European Court of Human Rights, leading to a change in the law in 2000. Following this, the ban on openly LGBT people serving in the armed forces was lifted, and adoption became legal for gay couples in 2003. Todd (2021) observes that within a decade of New Labour coming to power, the legal landscape for Britain's LGBTQ people had been transformed, with among further reforms, transgender people were able to change their legal gender and civil partnerships were legalised.

Following the defeat of the Labour Party in 2010, and in the dawn of a newly formed Conservative–Liberal Democrat coalition, there was understandably some apprehension that the advances made by the Labour government might be undermined given the Conservative Party's previous attitude towards LGBTQ people. However, Conservative leader David Cameron appeared to show a shift in his previous position regarding same-sex relationships and lifestyles, which was reflected in a public apology made for his support of Section 28 and subsequent government legislation. Cameron's stance towards equality did, however, appear to be incongruous, especially given his voting record on issues around the rights for homosexual couples to adopt and his opposition to giving lesbians the right to in-vitro fertilisation treatment, and it could then be argued that his change of heart was merely for political ends. Nevertheless, it should not be overlooked that under the coalition government the Equality Act 2010 was introduced, which can arguably be seen as a landmark piece of legislation replacing previous anti-discriminatory laws with one single act. The Act sought to 'protect people from discrimination in the workplace and in wider society' (2010, para. 1), with a particular emphasis on the protection of those who have, or are perceived to have, one or more of nine identified **protected characteristics** (GOV.UK, 2015). Protected characteristics directly relating to the LGBT+ community include gender reassignment, marriage and civil partnerships, and sexual orientation. Moreover, guidance sought to protect from discrimination those associated with someone with a protected classification, such as family member or friend.

For those individuals identifying as LGBTQ+, this act should surely be seen as a positive step forward, and with the introduction of a mandatory Sex and Relationships Education curriculum in English schools in 2021[2], a more equal future for children and young people must surely be on the horizon. The next section will examine the experience of LGBT+ pupils in educational settings, with a reflection on the roles that schools might take in promoting a more equitable landscape for pupils who identify as LGBT+.

LGBTQ+ AND THE EDUCATIONAL CONTEXT/RSE IN SCHOOLS

A 2017 report undertaken by Stonewall, a team dedicated to 'fighting for the freedom, equity and potential of LGBTQ+ people everywhere' (Stonewall, 2022), revealed some positive trends since the repeal of Section 28, with a fall in the number of lesbian, gay and bisexual pupils experiencing bullying as a result of their sexual orientation. Moreover, the number of schools recognising that this type of bullying is wrong had nearly trebled, suggesting that schools are taking reports of homophobic bullying far more seriously than they had in the past. The report observes that such actions and acknowledgement from school staff mean that more LGBT young people than ever are able to be themselves at school (2017: 4).

Nevertheless, while this would suggest a positive move forward, Stonewall (2022) acknowledges that there is still more left to do, and report that despite the fall in incidences bullying is still common for LGBT pupils, with trans pupils experiencing the highest levels of bullying. According to Stonewall (2022), nearly two in three trans pupils report being bullied for being LGBT in school, with one in ten receiving death threats. Homophobic bullying reported includes both verbal and physical abuse, with name calling being the most prevalent; pupils also report feelings of isolation, being gossiped about or being subjected to intimidating looks.

Not surprisingly, LGBT pupils experience poor levels of mental health and have little confidence that their concerns will be addressed, particularly for those who are exposed to offensive online content. Stonewall (2022) suggests that while some schools are taking steps to support LGBT pupils, many are not fully equipped to do so, lacking the policies and expertise to fully support these pupils. Furthermore, pupils report the school's failure to intervene where instances of homophobic bullying and language is reported, suggesting that teachers and other pupils act as passive bystanders. Formby (2015) reports that in some cases homophobic bullying from staff can

---

[2]The statutory guidance for relationships education, relationships and sex education and health education was first published in 2019 with a view to the regulations becoming mandatory in 2020; however, due to the disruption caused by the COVID-19 pandemic, settings were allowed to delay the introduction until Summer 2021 if they were not ready to deliver the new materials.

be just as problematic as from peers, with teachers using inappropriate, derogatory language to describe transgender pupils, or addressing pupils with the incorrect use of pronouns or names, leading to stress and anxiety.

More recently, Just Like Us, a registered LGBT+ young people's charity, stated that schools and colleges should be safe places in which LGBT+ students are accepted and celebrated. They advise that to achieve this, LGBT+ inclusive education is key, with a specific focus on tackling all forms of homophobic bullying, and through reviewing and changing policy to ensure that the needs of LGBT+ pupils are met, while at the same time ensuring that these pupils have a voice. Moreover, they outline the importance of a school culture that embraces diversity and in which annual LGBT+ events and days are freely celebrated (Just Like Us, 2021).

However, in their 2021 study of the well-being and mental health of pupils in the 11–18 age range, 39 per cent of whom identified as LGBT+, the Just Like Us report revealed that just under half of pupils (48 per cent) did not recall seeing positive messaging about being LGBT+, while visual signs of support for LGBT+ was minimal, with 33 per cent of pupils revealing that no such signage was evident. Despite Ofsted requirements for schools to take action to prevent homophobic, lesbophobic, biphobic and transphobic bullying, pupils surveyed were unaware of policies and initiatives in place to support LGBT+ pupils. This was further reflected by school staff surveyed, with 55 per cent of staff stating that while policies supporting LGBT+ were in place, in their settings such policies do not always appear to be supported by a LGBT+ inclusive curriculum or support for specific LGBT+ events such as Pride. Furthermore, 31 per cent of staff revealed that their schools did not run staff training on LGBT+ inclusion, although training would be welcomed (Just Like Us, 2021). This lack of training may help to understand why some homophobic bullying goes unnoticed, since, as observed by DePalma and Jennett (2010), some confusion exists around the use of the term 'gay' which has frequently been used as a slang term to describe something as rubbish and as such may not necessarily be seen as homophobic bullying.

Ostensibly, the reports from both Stonewall (2017) and Just Like Us (2021) suggest that while some progress has been made towards providing a more equitable educational experience for LGBT+ pupils, there appears to be inconsistencies both between and within settings, suggesting that there is still clearly much more that needs to be done for equality to be fully realised. It is pertinent, therefore, when considering the experiences of LGBT+ pupils in educational settings, to reflect on some of the underlying reasons why a full acceptance for LGBT+ pupils appears to be so challenging to achieve.

Forrest (2018a) supports the assertions of Just Like Us (2021) in that schools are at the front line in some of the popular debates around policies surrounding teaching and learning about gender, sex and sexualities, yet he proposes that schools have let down young LGBT+ pupils, particularly in respect of affirming the identities of those who present as LGBT+. Forrest argues that one of the reasons behind this may still be attributed to the legacy of Section 28, in which teaching beyond the norms of hetero-sexuality might be perceived as 'transgressive, subversive and inappropriate' (2018a: 158). This notion is supported by DePalma and Jennett (2010) whose interviews with teachers revealed that teachers feared reprisals from parents if they were to address LGBT equality in the classroom. Furthermore, teachers who identified as LGBT showed a reluctance to come out to colleagues, children or parents, and suggested there was a similar reticence from parents who identified as LGBT.

Sex education, or sex and relationships education (SRE) as it is more commonly known, has always been a contentious issue, particularly in primary education in England (Forrest, 2018b). Until recently, there has been very little change or develop-ments in the approach to the teaching of SRE, with the main focus of SRE teaching traditionally having a narrow focus, centred around heterosexuality and the traditional gender roles of men and women, and raising families (Forrest, 2018b). As expressed by Forrest, any exploration of the reality of modern-day relationships reflecting the 'complex, dynamic and diverse nature of human experiences of expression of gender, sex and sexuality is going to be troubling' (2018b: 159). DePalma and Jennett (2010) propose that in primary schools particularly, there is an assumed naivety and inno-cence of the child, especially around the issues of same-sex relationships, and some may argue that this should be protected. However, they go on to argue that such assumptions have been challenged by research, with many young people identifying as gay between the ages of 6 and 12, thus presenting a strong case for addressing LGBT identifies through SRE.

DePalma and Atkinson (2009) draw from Donelson and Rogers's 2004 research, which presented heteronormativity as organisational structures that exist in a school, supporting heterosexuality as the norm and anything else as deviant. They argue that in this case, homophobia becomes 'grounded in the normalising discourse of het-eronormativity' (2009: 838). Furthermore, homophobia becomes legitimised through such stereotypes as boys who show feelings being referred to as 'poofs' or girls, while girls who are tomboyish are referred to as dykes or lesbians (Forrest, 2018b).

Through their research with primary school teachers, DePalma and Atkinson (2009) observed that where teachers viewed sexual behaviour through a heterosexual lens, homosexuality was seen purely through a sexual lens, with a failure to acknowledge that this might also exist in a traditional sense – for example, through loving rela-tionships and family values. DePalma and Atkinson (2009) go on to suggest that the heteronormative lens that underpins policy and practice might lead to silence and invisibility, especially in view of the threat of bullying and exclusion associated with homosexuality. To counter this and to raise awareness of the needs of LGBT+ students, DePalma and Atkinson (2009) propose that primary school teachers take a more pro-active stance rather than adopting the passive and disingenuous tolerance of LGBT+ people which seems to exist.

However, Forrest (2018b) does present the argument that SRE in schools is a complicated issue, which has been exacerbated by a number of policies and the ongoing development of political and social movements. As seen earlier in the chapter, the repeal of Section 28 did not provide any additional guidance and came at a time of considerable change. There was growing recognition of the diversity in relationships, and third-wave feminism and LGBT rights were high on the agenda. As Forrest expresses:

> the irresistible emergence and visibility of new sexualities and identities, practices and relationship possibilities mean that the terrain feels ever shifting.
>
> (2018b: 160)

It is unsurprising, then, that teachers report a lack of confidence in teaching SRE in schools, which is subsequently reflected in pupils' suggestions that SRE in schools is too little, too late and too biological, with LGBT pupils reporting that LGBT issues were never taught in schools, including those lessons about sex and relationships (Stonewall, 2017; Forrest, 2018b).

In a report published by the Terrence Higgins Trust (THT) (2016), which surveyed young people from the age of 11–16 regarding provision of SRE in their settings, it was identified that SRE was not consistently taught. This was not surprising given that SRE was not made compulsory in both primary and secondary school settings in England until 2021. Prior to that, and at the time of the study, SRE was only compulsory in maintained secondary schools (40 per cent of schools) and not at all in primary settings. Moreover, the DfE guidance regarding SRE was deemed to be outdated, dating from 2000, and not reflective of an increasingly diverse society (THT, 2016). Indeed, SRE guidance, while not prescriptive, has an undercurrent of heteronormativity, since while a section on sexual orientation and sexual identity is included, the document clearly states that the promotion of sexual orientation or sexual activity would be inappropriate to teaching.

A survey of respondents' experience of SRE delivery indicated a somewhat clinical approach to the subject, consisting of 'reproduction, safe sex and body parts' (THT, 2016: 8), with only 5 per cent of pupils reporting that they were taught about LGBT sex and relationships. The focus on the biological aspects of SRE is unsurprising given that compulsory SRE was delivered predominantly through the science national curriculum, which has an emphasis on the biology of reproduction. Nevertheless, findings from the study revealed that age-appropriate SRE would be welcomed, with respondents suggesting that benefits of such teaching would include an improved understanding of other people, a reduction in bullying and a mechanism for safeguarding (THT, 2016). Furthermore, 97 per cent of respondents believed that SRE should be LGBT inclusive, with 91 per cent suggesting that trans awareness should also be taught in schools (THT, 2016).

The THT (2016) argues that in order to be fully effective, SRE should be embedded into the school curriculum rather than being delivered as one lesson a year, which appeared to be the experience of many of the young people surveyed. They suggest that young people would benefit from more frequent SRE lessons, affording them the opportunity to develop a better understanding and building on knowledge in order to equip them to make sensible and appropriate choices. According to the THT (2016), if young people are enabled to make positive choices regarding sexual health and relationships, they are more likely to be reassured of the validity of feelings which are not hetero-normative or **cisgendered**.

It is reassuring, therefore, that from 2019, statutory guidance for Relationships Education, Relationships and Sex Education (RSE), and Health Education was introduced, making Relationship Education compulsory in primary schools, and Relationships and Sex Education compulsory in secondary schools; Health Education became compulsory in all state-maintained schools. The document draws from the Equality Act 2010 in respect of the protected characteristics related to sexual orientation and gender reassignment, and requires that settings meet the needs of all pupils and ensure that pupils understand the importance of equality and respect (DfE, 2019). In response to some of the criticisms levelled at previous delivery of RSE, schools are required to teach pupils about LGBT at a time deemed appropriate to the children, and this should be fully integrated into the curriculum rather than teaching it as a stand-alone, one-off subject. Of note, the document also expresses that when teaching about families, children should be taught that these exist in a range of forms, including LGBT families, and that no stigma should be attached to children based on home circumstances (DfE, 2019). This is a significant development on the previous approach to both SRE and in respect of attitudes towards the LGBT community. Further, it could be argued that by integrating this into the curriculum, it becomes the norm rather than viewing it as a subject to be differentiated. This in turn should lead to an acceptance of all pupils, regardless of their sexual orientation.

SAFE SPACES

As previously noted, educational settings should be safe places in which LGBT+ pupils are accepted and celebrated (Just Like Us, 2021). This is supported by the 1994 Salamanca Statement which states that:

> Schools should accommodate all children regardless of their physical, intellectual, social, emotional, linguistic or other conditions. This should include disabled and gifted children, street and working children, children from remote or nomadic populations, children from linguistic, ethnic or cultural minorities and children from other disadvantaged or marginalized areas or groups.

(UNESCO, 1994: 5)

Nevertheless, in the Just Like Us (2021) survey, only 58 per cent of LGBT+ pupils reported that they felt safe at school every day; this is in comparison to 73 per cent of non-LGBT+ young people. As discussed earlier in the chapter, research indicates that LGBT+ pupils experience significant levels of homophobia, which is a key contributing factor in why schools are not seen as safe places, especially when this homophobia is linked to violence or threats of violence (Monk, 2011; Rivers, 2011; Hall, 2020; Just Like Us, 2021). Hope and Hall (2018) argue that in the light of such research, there exists a powerful justification for the need to create a safe space for young people who identify as LGBT+. Drawing from the work of French philosopher Michael Foucault, Hope and Hall (2018) suggest that one way of creating safe spaces for LGBT+ young people is through Foucault's notion of heterotopias. In his 1986 text, *Of Other Spaces,* Foucault presents the idea that while utopias, defined as 'an imagined place or state of things in which everything exists' (Dictionary.com), are fundamentally unreal places (Foucault and Miskowiec, 1986: 24), his definition of a heterotopia is one of an enacted utopia. In this sense, he suggests that

> all the other real sites that can be found within the culture, are simultaneously represented, contested, and inverted. Places of this kind are outside of all places, even though it may be possible to indicate their location in reality. Because these places are absolutely different from all the sites that they reflect and speak about, I shall call them, by way of contrast to utopias, heterotopias.
>
> (1986: 24)

Foucault identified two types of heterotopia. The first he referred to as crisis heterotopias, which he saw as places in which individuals lived while in a state of crisis. These he saw as disappearing environments that had traditionally been used to support certain groups of society – for example, military service for young men was designed to support the first manifestations of sexual virility away from the home environment, while up until the middle of the twentieth century, girls would traditionally go on a 'honeymoon trip' in which deflowering could take place (Foucault and Miskowiec, 1986). While heterotopias of crisis have disappeared over time, Foucault suggests that these have now been replaced with heterotopias of deviation, seen as spaces for those whose behaviour is considered to be deviant in relation to the mean or norm. Foucault presents rest homes, psychiatric homes and prisons as heterotopias of deviation. However, he also argues that as history unfolds, the nature and function of heterotopias of deviation might shift, since 'each heterotopia has a precise and determined function within a society and the same heterotopia can, according to the synchrony of the culture in which it occurs, have one function or another' (Foucault and Miskowiec, 1986: 25).

Foucault sees heterotopias as 'other spaces' which are separate from the norm, or a 'real space, as perfect, as meticulous, as well arranged as ours is messy, ill constructed, and jumbled. This latter type would be the heterotopia, not of illusion, but of compensation … ' (Foucault and Miskowiec, 1986: 27). Drawing from Foucault's work, Hope and Hall suggest that LGBT+ affirming schools might exist as heterotopias as 'sites of resistance and protest' (2018: 1198). According to Hope and Hall (2018), in recent times there has been a growing interest in the development of schools which are targeted specifically at pupils who identify as LGBTQ+, and while not exclusive to these pupils, these schools would be seen as safe spaces for pupils with an ambition to ensure inclusivity, thus protecting pupils against the homophobic bullying experienced in non-specialist schools. LGBTQ+ affirming schools arguably fit the remit of a heterotopia, which Foucault suggests are a critique to the rest of society; thus, where the norm does not meet the needs of a specific group, it becomes necessary to create that space for them.

While it could be argued that the creation of LGBTQ+ affirming schools could be viewed as a form of segregation, which arguably goes against civil liberties and human rights (Murray and Penman, 1996; Liasidou, 2012), Merry (2012) presents the idea that where such segregation is voluntary, as in the case of young people choosing a LGBTQ+ affirming school, then it forces us to consider how experiences might actually be enhanced within separate spaces. A young person who feels safe in the knowledge that they can be protected from the fear of homophobic bullying is more likely to enjoy a positive school experience. In writing about one such LGBTQ+ affirming school, the Harvey Milk High School in New York, the Hetrick-Martin Institute states:

> In an ideal world, all students who are considered *at-risk* would be *safely* integrated into all NYC public schools. But in the real world, *at-risk students* need a place like the Harvey Milk High School. HMHS is one of the many NYC small schools that provide *safety*, community, and high achievement for students not able to benefit from more traditional school environments.
>
> (Cited in Sadowski, 2016/17: 5)

Hope and Hall (2018) state that LGBT affirming schools fit Foucault's definitions of both heterotopias of deviation and of crises, since these can be seen as places in which 'individuals whose behaviour is deviant in relation to the required mean or norm are placed' (Foucault and Miskowiec, 1986: 25). Nevertheless, heterotopias of crises seems most fitting, since these represent places for those who are experiencing difficulties with the society or environment in which they live. Hope and Hall (2018) suggest that the LGBT affirming school exists as a safe place for those who have 'experienced bullying, alienation or marginalisation elsewhere' (2018: 1203), and present findings from the Pride School, whose founder justifies its existence as a result of the failure of mainstream settings to respond to the needs of LGBTQ+ children and their families.

Hope and Hall (2018) present the notion, therefore, that LGBTQ+ affirming schools can be considered as heterotopias, having an important function in the field of inclusive education and challenging educators to rethink provision for meeting the needs of all pupils. However, it could be argued that the creation of such spaces fails to address the fundamental issue of inclusivity, and perhaps more should be done to ensure that all schools provide a safe environment for all children. The next section will examine the ways in which mainstream schools might provide a safe space for LGBT pupils.

THE ROLE OF EDUCATIONAL SETTINGS IN PROMOTING INCLUSIVITY: SOME IDEAS FOR PRACTICE

Sadowski (2016/17) argues that, in the American education system, there exists a subset of LGBTQ+ students for whom the school experience focuses merely on the notion of their being safe in school. While few would question the importance of this, Sadowski (2016/17) goes on to suggest that the emphasis on safety of LGBTQ+ pupils has its foundations in the arguments made by activists in the 1980s and 1990s when LGBTQ+ issues were emerging, and in which gay and lesbian pupils were experiencing verbal and physical harassment on a daily basis. Under these circumstances, individual safety was paramount, necessitating a clear and focused response. However, twenty years on, it could be argued that the safety of LGBTQ+ pupils should be assumed, allowing schools to focus on the more pressing matter of inclusion and acceptance.

Sadowski (2016/17) observes that in order to make schools safe spaces for LGBTQ+ pupils, the following three components have been introduced: anti-bullying programmes, LGBTQ 'safe zones' and gay–straight alliances, with schools operating a combination of two or sometimes three of the components at any one time. A similar strategy has been adopted in the UK, with a report from the Government Equality Office (2018) outlining a strategy that focuses on tackling all forms of homophobic bullying, updating SRE policies and ensuring that schools have access to the necessary guidance to support LGBT pupils, as well as ensuring that LGBT teachers are supported. Nevertheless, as observed by Sadowski (2016/17), such policies may lead schools to assume that 'safe' is an acceptable standard, when actually much more can and should be done. Furthermore, it would seem opportune to capitalise on the strides already taken towards a more diverse community through reviewing provision from the ground up.

One project that sought to challenge heteronormative practices in schools and raise awareness of approaches to LGBT equality was the Economic and Social Research Council (ESRC) funded project 'No Outsiders'. Through collaboration between teachers in three areas of the UK and university researchers, the project sought to identify and disseminate examples of good practice. DePalma and Atkinson (2009: 839) observe that the project developed from a 'don't ask, don't tell tolerance' that served to perpetuate stereotypes and reproduce heterosexual assumptions. In order to address this, they present an argument that the introduction of anti-bullying discourse is insufficient as a means by which to eradicate these assumptions, and instead more proactive discussions around sexuality and gender are required. They advise that 'teachers need to reach beyond passive and disingenuous tolerance of "those LGBT people" to proactively incorporate discussions of sexuality and gender into their curriculum' (2009: 840).

While it could be argued that the aforementioned revised RSE curriculum has encouraged embedding gender equality into the curriculum, the No Outsiders study offers some practical ways in which these can be addressed, with a particular emphasis on challenging heteronormativity, while at the same time enhancing teacher development and autonomy through encouraging communities of practice. Sharing of experience and good practice was deemed particularly important as many teachers in the study expressed apprehension in tacking issues outside of the norm, with others citing a lack of secure knowledge as inhibiting their ability to tackle many of the issues. Goldberg and Allen (2018) suggest, however, that teaching about LGBTQ+ individuals is timely given the change in societal attitudes towards diversity and the growing acceptance of same-sex relationships. They go on to suggest that opportunities to teach about LGBTQ+ identities should be capitalised on. Moreover, this would offer a starting point for discussion around trans and non-gender confirming identities, which has not gained the same traction as same-sex relationships.

Given that a lack of information is cited as a major obstacle to delivering LGBTQ+ content (DePalma and Atkinson, 2009; Just Like Us, 2021; Stonewall, 2022) the No Outsiders project recommends that schools should be well resourced, particularly in respect of children's books that contain lesbian or gay characters, and that explore gender stereotypes and non-gender conformity. They suggest that these can be supported with video resources and posters. Within the study, books were used as a starting point for developing lesson plans and projects, including children writing their own stories using same-sex couples as the main characters and reinventing traditional tales with an LGBTQ+ perspective. DePalma and Atkinson (2009) advise that the use of stories have the advantage of positioning teachers as experts rather than individuals pushing their own agenda. Furthermore, they were seen as normalising non-traditional families, which provided comfort and reassurance to children with same-sex parents.

A further suggestion of good practice influenced by the No Outsiders project was through focused weekly assemblies, or tutor sessions for older children, in which children hear a message of equality at least once a week. Moffat (2020) observes that through the use of images showing diversity in different forms, children can be encouraged to discuss issues freely through the use of targeted questioning. Moreover, while the assembly might serve as a starting point, by making the image visible through the week, children are encouraged to allow the discussion to develop. Moffat (2020) suggests that this is an effective way of maintaining a regular focus on issues of diversity without encroaching on an already busy curriculum. This, too, has the added benefit of normalising issues of diversity, rather than presenting these as one-off lessons.

Drawing from the experiences of LGBTQ+ pupils, the Just Like Us (2021) report revealed that the most effective strategies that schools could employ were to increase the visibility of LGBTQ+ students and teachers, which again serves to normalise LGBTQ+ identities. Positive messaging about being LGBT was considered to engender a feeling of safety in schools, particularly if this was underpinned by secure anti-bullying policies. Furthermore, pupils reported improved mental health and well-being, and lower rates of depression and anxiety. Moffat (2020) debates the approaches that schools might take to ensure that issues of diversity are addressed sensitively in schools, documenting changes in his own policy from one of celebrating diversity to one of simple acceptance. He states:

> I want all children, including LGBT+ children, to explore who they are and know they belong in my class, and this means talking about LGBT+ identity alongside other identities.

(2020:18)

To conclude, while an overall ambition should be, as Moffat (2020) suggests, to strive for inclusivity for all, it can be argued that this remains a complex issue. As a starting point, therefore, Stonewall (2017) offers recommendations for schools which are shown in Table 8.1.

Table 8.1   Application of Stonewall recommendations to practice

Recommendations	*What this entails*
Get the basics right	Clear and consistent policies for addressing homophobic bullying – ensure that incidents are dealt with swiftly and in accordance with policies.
Show clear leadership	Have a clear and positive ethos for the creation of an inclusive learning environment for all. Lead from the front in delivering a clear message that any form of homophobic bullying and language is unacceptable.
Create an inclusive curriculum	Embed the experiences of LGBT people across the curriculum through celebrating diversity and making visible the LGBT community, including pupils and staff. Ensure that RSE reflects a full spectrum of identities.

(Continued)

Table 8.1   Application of Stonewall recommendations to practice (*Continued*)

Recommendations	*What this entails*
Equip staff	Ensure that staff are fully trained in tackling all forms of homophobic bullying and are able to address online safety, as well as understanding the mental health and well-being needs of LGBT pupils. Provide the necessary resources to enable teachers to deliver an inclusive curriculum.
Celebrate difference	Adopt a whole-school approach towards celebrating difference and creating an inclusive environment for all. Promote LGBT role models through inviting external speakers into school and enabling LGBT teachers to be open about their identity. Seek to support specific events targeted at the LGBT community – i.e., Pride Week.
Provide information and support	Direct LGBT pupils to appropriate support networks, including online resources and local youth groups. Provide resources and books that include LGBT characters and issues. Signpost information for parents and carers.
Provide specific support for trans pupils	Ensure that policies make specific reference to trans pupils, working with pupils themselves to ensure they have access to appropriate facilities – e.g., appropriate uniform, toileting facilities. Discuss levels of confidentiality and ensure that appropriate terminology is employed. Signpost to specific resources and support groups and organisations.
Protect health and well-being	Have a clear plan to support the health and well-being of LGBT pupils and ensure that staff with pastoral responsibility have received appropriate training, including mental health first-aid. Create a culture of openness in which pupils are aware of who they can talk to about gender identity and be clear on what support is available to them.
Involve LGBT young people	Include LGBT pupils in the creation and development of plans and policies. Make available opportunities for LGBT pupils to talk openly with staff, and facilitate the creation of support and equality groups. Encourage staff to reflect on their own preconceptions and seek to support young people in using words of their own choice to describe sexual orientation and gender identity.
Work with parents, carers and local organisations	Make visible to parents and carers plans and policies for combatting bullying and supporting LGBT pupils, and ensure that support is in place for them. Work collaboratively with external agencies and groups to share best practice in supporting young people.

Adapted from Stonewall, 2017: 38–9.

SUMMARY

The 2022 Stonewall Take Pride Report revealed a growing acceptance 'in LGBTQ+ people as neighbours, colleagues, friends and family' (Kelley and de Santos, 2022: 2), although they go on to suggest that a small minority of people in the UK still maintain feelings of disgust and fear of LGBT people, which arguably fuels the homophobic bullying which has been discussed throughout this chapter. Nevertheless, the findings revealed that in the period since the first gay rights marches held in London in 1970, there are far more positive feelings towards the LGBT community, and most especially from women and young people.

As we have seen from Chapter 4, education can and should be seen as an effective vehicle for social change, and since the repeal of Section 28 and the introduction of the revised SRE curriculum, it can be seen that in the area of LGBT rights, this is no different. Reports from Stonewall (2017) and Just Like Us (2021) indicate that young people have a positive attitude towards SRE, which incorporates more diverse relationships. However, experience of SRE remains one of heteronormativity. Equally, teachers recognise the importance of teaching about same-sex relationships, although the legacy of Section 28 has resulted in a climate of fear, with teachers still reticent about exploring relationships beyond what would be considered normal. Nevertheless, many teachers express a willingness to engage in training in order to deliver a more inclusive curriculum.

Projects such as No Outsiders (2009) have demonstrated that it is possible to break down some of the barriers that exist and, given that the most positive attitudes can be found among the younger generation (Stonewall, 2022), it could be argued that it is through education that inclusivity can be sought. Moreover, while tackling the homophobic bullying that still exists in schools and creating a safe space for learners is paramount, this can best be achieved through changing the cultures of our schools, rather than simply dealing with bullying as incidents in their own right (Sadowski, 2016/17). As seen earlier in the chapter, changing cultures can best be achieved through normalising the experiences of LGBTQ+ pupils, ensuring that resources reflect the diversity of school communities, that the school ethos is one of inclusivity and that policies are in place to protect all learners regardless of how they identify. It is hoped that in this way steps towards a fully inclusive curriculum, which embraces the rights of the LGBTQ+ community, might be taken.

GLOSSARY OF TERMS

Cisgendered

The antonym of transgender and a term that describes gender identity as someone who identifies with the sex assigned at birth. Often shortened to 'cis', the word came to prominence in the 1990s; the literal meaning of the prefix is 'on this side'.

Conversion therapy

Conversion therapy is a form of aversion therapy; a type of psychotherapy used to eliminate unwanted or undesirable behaviour patterns through a form of conditioning. Conversion therapy was widely used in the 1960s to 'cure' gay men of homosexuality and worked on the principle that if gay men became disgusted by acts of homosexuality, they would no longer wish to engage in them. Thus, men were shown images of homosexual activity while at the same time being subject to unpleasant experiences – i.e., vomiting induced by chemicals or electroshock therapy. Fortunately, the rise of the Gay Liberation Movement led to this being abolished in the mid-1970s.

Heteronormative

Refers to a default view of sexuality in which heterosexuality is the normal and natural expression of sexuality. Heteronormativity draws on the assumption that everyone is straight and relationships always exist between a man and a woman.

Heterosexual

Heterosexual people are naturally attracted to people of the opposite sex. People identifying as heterosexual are often referred to as 'straight'.

Homophobia

A fear, hatred or discomfort of those identified as LGBT, resulting in negative attitudes or beliefs. Homophobia can result in bullying or discrimination, which at its most extreme can lead to bullying and violence against LGBT individuals. Discrimination might result in exemption from groups or institutions, or being overlooked for jobs or promotion.

Protected characteristics

Introduced as part of the Equality Act 2010, protected characteristics refer to a set of characteristics that are protected by law against discrimination. There are nine characteristics in total: age; disability; gender reassignment; marriage and civil partnership; pregnancy and maternity; race; religion or belief; sex; sexual orientation. Individuals with one or more of the nine protected characteristics have the right to be treated equally and should not be subjected to unfair disadvantage as a result of that characteristic.

Section 28

Also referred to as Clause 28, Section 28 was introduced as an amendment to the Local Government Act 1986. It came into effect in 1998 and lasted until 2000.

Section 28 prevented authorities from promoting homosexuality or publishing materials with the intention of promoting homosexuality. Furthermore, maintained schools were prevented from teaching about homosexuality as an acceptable family relationship.

Transgendered

Refers to a person whose personal identify and gender does not match with their biological sex. The term is frequently shortened to trans, trans/male or trans/female. It is advisable to ask individuals how they would like to be referred to. Transgendered people may choose to express themselves in a way that represents how they identify – for example, through dress or mannerisms.

Transsexual

A transgender person who has sought to align with their gender identity through undergoing medical transformation such as surgery or hormone therapy. Where gender identity is inconsistent with assigned sex, a more permanent alignment with the identified gender is sought.

FURTHER READING

Baker, P. (2022) *Outrageous: The Story of Section 28 and Britain's Battle for LGBT Education*. London: Reaktion Books.

A background to Section 28, including first-hand accounts, the press reaction, the role of politicians and its eventual repeal. The text discusses the legacy of Section 28 and the prejudice it enacted.

Dellenty, S. (2019) *Celebrating Difference: A Whole School Approach to LGBT+ Inclusion*. London: Bloomsbury Education.

A practical handbook supporting schools in bringing about organisational change to ensure inclusion for all. Drawing from case studies and interviews, the text examines reasons behind prejudice and offers strategies to eradicate this.

Gates, J. and Buckler, S. (2020) *Lessons in Love and Understanding: Relationships, Sexuality and Gender in the Classroom*. London: SAGE.

Drawing on the 2019 revised SRE policy, the text offers comprehensive and practical guidance for teachers which goes beyond the statutory requirements. The text empowers teachers to tackle the complexities of delivering sex education in an increasingly diverse climate, breaking down some of the barriers that might otherwise impede inclusivity.

Hamilton, P. (2021) *Diversity and Marginalisation in Childhood: A Guide for Inclusive Thinking 0–11*. London: SAGE.

Chapter 7: Gender development and identities: intersex and transgender children.

The text offers an insight into the educational experiences of marginalised groups and the potential impact this has on outcomes. Drawing on case studies and reflective questions, readers are encouraged to reflect on policy and practice, and seek a way forward to more inclusive practice.

Tomlinson-Gray, D. (ed.) (2021) *Big Gay Adventures in Education*. Oxford: Routledge.

First-hand experiences of 'out' teachers documenting their experiences in schools with a view to empowering LGBT+ teachers to become much-needed role models in a bid to promote LGBT+ visibility and inclusion.

REFERENCES

Belmonte, L. (2021) *The International LGBT Rights Movement: A History*. Oxford: Routledge.

Bosche, S. (1983) *Jenny Lives with Eric and Martin*. London: The Gay Man's Press.

DePalma, R. and Atkinson, E. (2009) No outsiders: Moving beyond a discourse of tolerance to challenge heteronormativity in primary schools. *British Educational Research Journal*, 35(6): 837–55.

DePalma, R. and Jennett, M. (2010) Homophobia, transphobia and culture: Deconstructing heteronormativity in English primary schools. *Intercultural Education*, 21(1): 15–26.

Department for Education (DfE) (2019) *Relationships education, relationships and sex education (RSE) and health education: statutory guidance for governing bodies, proprietors, headteachers, principals, senior leadership teams, teachers*. London: Crown Copyright.

Dryden, S. (n.d.) *A short history of LGBT rights in the UK*. Available at: www.bl.uk/lgbtq-histories /articles/a-short-history-of-lgbt-rights-in-the-uk (accessed 16 March 2023).

Formby, E. (2015) Limitations of focussing on homophobic, biphobic and transphobic 'bullying' to understand and address LGBT young people's experiences within and beyond school. *Sex Education: Sexuality, Society and Learning*, 15(6): 626–40.

Forrest, S. (2018a) Straight talking. In M. Cole (ed.) *Education, Equality and Human Rights* (4th edn). Oxford: Routledge.

Forrest, S. (2018b) The making of sexualities. In M. Cole (ed.) *Education, Equality and Human Rights* (4th edn). Oxford: Routledge.

Foucault, M. and Miskowiec, J. (1986) Of other spaces. *Diacritics*, 16(1): 22–7.

Goldberg, A. and Allen, K. (2018) Teaching undergraduates about LGBTQ identities, families, and intersectionality. *Family Relations*, 67: 176–91.

GOV.UK (2015) *Equality Act 2010: Guidance*. Available at: www.gov.uk/guidance/equality-act-2010-guidance (accessed 16 March 2023).

Government Equalities Office (2018) *LGBT Action Plan: Improving the lives of lesbian, gay, bisexual and transgender people*. London: Crown Copyright.

Hall, J.J. (2020) The word gay has been banned but people use it in the boys' toilets whenever you go in: Spatialising children's subjectivities in response to gender and sexualities education in English primary schools. *Social & Cultural Geography*: 1–24.

History.com editors (2022) *Stonewall Riots*. Available at: www.history.com/topics/gay-rights/the-stonewall-riots (accessed 16 March 2023).

Hope, M.A. and Hall, J.J. (2018) 'Other spaces' for lesbian, gay, bisexual, transgendered and questioning (LGBTQ) students: Positioning LGBTQ-affirming schools as sites of resistance within inclusive education. *British Journal of Sociology of Education*, 39(8): 1195–209.

Just Like Us (2021) *Growing up LGBT+: The impact of school, home and coronavirus on LGBT+ young people*. Available at: www.justlikeus.org (accessed 16 March 2023).

Kelley, N. and de Santos, R. (2022) *Stonewall Take Pride Report. Public Sentiment towards Lesbian, Gay, Bi and Trans People in the UK*. Available at: www.stonewall.org.uk/system/files/take_pride_-_june_2022.pdf (accessed 16 March 2023).

legislation.gov.uk (1988) *Local Government Act 1988*. Available at: www.legislation.gov.uk/ukpga/1988/9/section/28/enacted (accessed 16 March 2023).

LGBT Lawyers (2021) *Section 28: History, response and future impact*. Available at: https://lgbtlawyers.co.uk/2021/02/08/section-28/ (accessed 16 March 2023).

Liasidou, A. (2012) *Inclusive Education, Politics and Policymaking*. London: Continuum.

Merry, M.S. (2012) Equality, self-respect and voluntary separation. *Critical Review of International Social and Political Philosophy*, 15(1): 79–100.

Moffat, A. (2020) *No Outsiders: Everyone Different, Everyone Welcome*. London: Routledge.

Monk, D. (2011) Challenging homophobic bullying in schools: The politics of progress. *International Journal of Law in Context*, 7(2): 181–207.

Murray, P. and Penman, J. (1996). *Let Our Children Be: A Collection of Stories*. Sheffield: Parents with Attitude.

Nicholls, J. (2021) Growing up in silence: A short history of Section 28. Available at: www.twentysixdigital.com/blog/growing-up-silence-short-history-section-28/ (accessed 16 March 2023).

Rivers, I. (2011) *Homophobic Bullying: Research and Theoretical Perspectives*. Oxford: Oxford University Press.

Sadowski, M. (2016/17) More than a safe space: How schools can enable LGBT pupils to thrive. American Educator: Winter.

Stonewall (2017) *School Report: The Experiences of Lesbian, Gay, Bi and Trans Young People in Britain's Schools 2017*. London: Stonewall.

Stonewall (2022) *Schools and colleges*. Available at: www.stonewall.org.uk/schools-colleges (accessed 16 March 2023).

Terrence Higgins Trust (2016) *No talking: LGBT inclusive sex and relationships education in the UK*. Available at: www.tht.org.uk/end the silence (accessed 16 March 2023).

Thatcher, M. (1987) Speech to Conservative Party Conference. Available at: www.margaretthatcher.org/document/106941 (accessed 16 March 2023).

Todd, M. (2021) *PRIDE: The Story of the LGBT Equality Movement*. London: Welbeck.

UNESCO (1994) *The Salamanca Statement and Framework for Action on Special Needs Education*. Available at: www.european-agency.org/sites/default/files/salamanca-statement-and-framework.pdf (accessed 16 March 2023).

9
CLIMATE CHANGE

LEARNING OUTCOMES

Having read this chapter, you should be able to:

- understand what is meant by climate change;
- recognise government policy on climate change;
- identify the role of education in mitigating against climate change;
- understand how the ethics of care theory can be applied to recent activism from young people.

KEY WORDS

benign neglect; cognitive dissonance; Global Climate Strikes; greenhouse gas emissions; Kyoto Protocol; OutRight Initiative; Paris Agreement; Student Climate Network.

INTRODUCTION

The World Health Organization (WHO) observes that 'climate change is the greatest health challenge of the 21st century', cautioning that it 'threatens all aspects of the society in which we live' (Campbell-Lendrum et al., 2018: 9), with UN Secretary General Ban Ki-moon proclaiming it to be the defining challenge of our time (UNESCO, 2010).

Climate change is not a new concept and has emerged over the past few decades as a matter of global concern. In 1992, Jamieson wrote about the catastrophic effect that rising temperatures would have on plants and non-human animals, going on to warn that problems associated with climate change were not just scientific, but problems of ethics and politics that would concern how humans live and relate to each other. Some 15 years later, he reiterated this message, stating that:

> Successfully addressing climate change requires long-term, sustainable changes in the way we live. This will only come about when we take responsibility for our actions and express our concern for future generations and the health of the Earth through our everyday actions. The transformation that is required is not only personal, but profoundly collective and personal as well.

> (2007: 8)

While Jamieson (2007) urged collective responsibility, Hansen (2009) cautioned that, despite the fact that the planet is in imminent danger of crashing, politicians were not dashing forward (cited in Cuomo, 2011); this is reflected in a 2010 report from the American Association for the Advancement of Science (AAAS) which found that at the time the public ranked global warming as the lowest of 21 government priorities (Bryce and Day, 2014). Nevertheless, the past two decades has seen worldwide acknowledgement that human activity is responsible for an increase in **greenhouse gas (GHG) emissions**, subsequently leading to global warming and climate change more generally (International Panel on Climate Change (IPCC), 2007). Moreover, these reports have mobilised governments worldwide into taking action, with the United Nations Climate Summit in Paris in December 2015 hailed as a major breakthrough in environmental governance and global policy-making (Walker, 2017).

Of particular note, and of relevance to this text particularly, is the way in which young people have been galvanised to act in respect of climate change, which was arguably prompted by the young Swedish activist, Greta Thunberg. Thunberg came to the attention of the media when, at the age of 15, she protested outside the Swedish parliament, holding a sign saying 'School Strike for Climate' (Kraemer, 2021). Subsequently, Thunberg's actions saw young people globally becoming actively involved in 'Climate Change Strikes' during 2018, walking out of lessons in order to pressure their governments to meet carbon emission targets. Observed by Grauer (2020), the great climate strikes saw young people drawing on their efficacy and sense of empowerment to insist on climate action. Grauer goes on to urge educators to 'teach [ing] them honestly and fearlessly and listening a whole lot more deeply. Today's and tomorrow's healthiest students will be those who are deeply aware, in a truly hopeful way, of the connections between people around the planet' (2020: 45–6).

The aim of this chapter is to consider how educational practice might build on the passion and fervour that young people have already shown in respect of climate change with a view to considering how this might be developed in the future. It will commence with a brief background to climate change and some of the policies underpinning provision, before exploring some of the theories that might help us to understand why young people have shown such investment in this subject.

WHAT IS CLIMATE CHANGE?

Article 21 of the United Nation's Framework Convention on Climate Change (UNFCCC) defines climate change as a 'change of climate which is attributed directly or indirectly to human activity that alters the composition of the global atmosphere and which is in addition to natural climate variability over comparable time periods' (United Nations, 1992a: 9). Signed in 1992 at the United Nations Conference on Environment and Development, the UNFCCC came into force in 1994 and has since been ratified by 197 countries (Kuh, 2018). Subsequently, it has provided the impetus for successive agreements, including the **Kyoto Protocol** (2005) and the **Paris Agreement** (2015). Sage (2003) posits that the principles of the framework recognised climate change as a serious problem and one that needed to be tackled with immediate effect, with developed countries taking a lead role in addressing the issues, which centred predominantly on stabilising greenhouse gas emissions.

Climate change, sometimes referred to as global warming, is not a new phenomenon, and while it can occur naturally as a result of variations in solar cycles, it is the actions of mankind that have been the main driver of climate change over the last two centuries. The first impact of climate change can be traced back to the Industrial Revolution of the 1800s, which saw the traditional agricultural and handicraft economy replaced by technological changes of machine manufacturing and industry. While for developed countries this resulted in a significant improvement in the standard of living, it also gave rise to the environmental pollution we see today 'beginning a slow but accelerating transformation of the Earth's surface and atmosphere' (UNESCO, 2010: 2). Moreover, rapid technological developments over the last century, coupled with an ever-increasing global population, has resulted in extensive use of the Earth's natural resources.

Arguably, it is the excesses of life in the twenty-first century that has contributed most significantly to what is now considered a climate crisis, since climate change is predominantly caused by the burning of fossil fuels, such as coal, oil and natural gases, to provide for the human requirements of mobility, power, heat and light. The burning of these fossil fuels leads to the production of greenhouse gas emissions which trap the sun's heat and raise temperatures. According to United Nations Climate Action (n.d.), greenhouse gas emissions, which are responsible for climate change, include carbon dioxide – for example, from transport, heating and clearing land and forests – and methane, a major source of which comes from landfill for rubbish.

The result is that the Earth's temperature is around 1.1°C warmer than it was two centuries ago. At the time of writing, record temperatures were recorded in the UK in July 2022, with the Met Office confirming a record-high temperature of 40.3°C at Coningsby, Lincolnshire, while both Scotland and Wales also saw record-high temperatures of 34.8°C and 37.1°C respectively (Met Office, 2022). While an increase in temperature is one very palpable consequence of climate change, accounting for the use of the term 'global warming', this is just one aspect of a far more complex picture. As noted by United Nations Climate Change (n.d.), 'Because the Earth is a system, where everything is connected, changes in one area can influence changes in all others' (para. 2). UNESCO outlines such changes as 'a reduction in seasonal sea ice at the Earth's poles, rising sea-level, shifts in precipitation patterns leading to extended droughts or flooding, and more frequent extreme weather events' (2010: 2). Furthermore, while developed countries are the ones most responsible for climate change, it is the developing countries that are most at risk of its effects (UNESCO, 2010). As observed by Cuomo (2011), inhabitants of Arctic settlements are facing unprecedented problems as erosion and melting permafrost results in the collapse and deterioration of land, making travelling perilous. Moreover, the loss of local species has a catastrophic effect on the native communities who rely heavily on subsistence traditions (Cuomo, 2011).

The WHO estimates that without action, climate change is expected to result in around 250,000 additional deaths per year between 2030 and 2050, with malnutrition, malaria, diarrhoea and heat stress being among the main causes (WHO, 2021). Furthermore, natural disasters caused by climate change, including cyclones, droughts, floods and wildfires, have devastating effects, including loss of homes, livelihoods and lives. For example, in March 2019, cyclone Idai led to the deaths of more than 1,000 people in Southern Africa, leaving millions more without food and services, while in South Asia, floods and landslides have forced people from their homes, with scientists reporting that the usual monsoon season rains typical in this area are worsened by the rise in sea surface temperatures.

Cuomo observes that:

> Climate change was manufactured in a crucible of inequality, for it is a product of the industrial and the fossil-fuel eras, historical forces powered by exploitation, colonialism, and nearly limitless instrumental use of 'nature'.

(2011: 693)

He goes on to observe that while the developed nations have built their fortunes on development and energy consumption, such actions have endangered everyone, but most especially those who have contributed least to the greenhouse effect, this being 'the least developed nations, the natural world and future generations' (2011: 693). Moreover, climate change presents itself as an issue of social justice, since it is those living in poverty who are most likely to be impacted by the effects of climate change (Cuomo, 2011; OXFAM, 2022).

GOVERNMENT POLICY ON SUSTAINABILITY

Hirst (2020) observes that 'at the start of the twentieth century climate change was largely seen as an esoteric study into a theoretical scientific phenomenon' (para. 1). However, he goes on to suggest that since then its profile has been raised, making it a permanent fixture on the political agenda. Furthermore, in 2019 the House of Commons declared a climate emergency; subsequently, it became the most pressing long-term, worldwide challenge (Hirst, 2020). While the first international environmental summit first took place in 1972, outlining a commitment to coordinating global efforts through the creation of the United Nations Environment Programme, climate change at this time was viewed as a scientific concern rather than as a political problem. Nevertheless, a decade later politicians began to take note of the warnings of scientists regarding the impact of greenhouse gases, leading to the first world climate conference in 1979, followed by the Toronto Conference on Changing the Climate in 1988 (Hirst, 2020).

As noted earlier in the chapter, the first real attempt to tackle climate change globally came through the establishment of the UNFCCC, which came about as a direct result of the first report published by the Intergovernmental Panel on Climate Change (IPCC) which warned that:

> emissions resulting from human activities are substantially increasing the atmospheric concentrations of the greenhouse gases carbon dioxide, methane, chlorofluorocarbons (CFCs) and nitrous oxide. These increases will enhance the greenhouse gases, resulting on average in an additional warming of the Earth's surface. The main greenhouse gas, water vapour, will increase in response to global warming and further enhance it.

> (IPCC, 1990: xi)

The subsequent establishment of the UNFCCC led to the first global agreement on climate change, which was the driving force behind the now annual Conference of Parties (Countries) (COP), which is the decision-making body of the UNFCCC. The first COP resulted in the Kyoto Agreement, which saw the setting of GHG reduction targets. This was followed by the Paris Agreement in 2015, in which ambitious goals were set to keep global temperature rises well below 2°C, with an attempt to limit temperature increase to 1.5°C (Hirst, 2020). The Paris Agreement took legal effect in 2020 and required agreement from all parties, including less developed countries, to submit nationally determined contributions or climate change action plans. In the UK, emission reduction targets of 'at least 68% (by 2030) and 78% (by 2035) below 1990 levels as recommended by the Committee on Climate Change' have been set (Climate Action Tracker (CAT), 2021), with strategies to include a ban on cars using fossil fuels to be implemented by 2030, construction of offshore wind capacity and removal of diesel-fuelled trains by 2040. Moreover, the government is seeking to fund new nuclear power capacity, as well as encouraging personal responsibility through allocating funding to encourage a modal shift away from personal vehicle travel and incentivising heat pump adoption (CAT, 2021).

Jakučionytė-Skodienė and Liobikienė (2021) suggest that to achieve climate change targets, it is necessary not only to raise concerns about climate change, but to promote climate-friendly behaviour. They go on to acknowledge that climate change mitigation has different costs and benefits that can have an impact on how far individuals accept personal responsibility for climate change. Bouman et al. (2020) present the notion that the more people feel worried about climate change, the more likely they are to support climate action, thus taking personal responsibility to reduce the impact of climate change. Nevertheless, Wood and Roelich (2019) argue that this presents a certain tension, since the use of fossil fuels that are responsible for GGE have well-being implications, and while individuals are aware of the impact of their actions on climate change, there may be a reluctance to modify behaviour if this requires sacrificing a way of life. The following section will explore this notion with an emphasis on the role of education in eliciting changes to behaviour.

CLIMATE CHANGE AND THE EDUCATIONAL CONTEXT: YOUNG PEOPLE AS AGENTS OF CHANGE

At the 1992 UN Conference on Environment and Development, Agenda 21 presented the notion that 'Education is critical for promoting sustainable development and improving the capacity of the people to address environment and development issues' (United Nations, 1992b: 320). They went on to propose education as a vehicle for promoting 'environmental and ethical awareness, values and attitudes, skills and behaviour consistent with sustainable development' (1992b: 320). This has since been reinforced through the United Nations Educational Social and Cultural Organization (UNESCO) sustainable development goals (SDG), with SDG 4 emphasising the need to make 'education accessible to all and the foundation for sustainable development and peace' (UNESCO, 2020, para. 1). Further reinforcing the role of education in sustainable development, the Secretariat of the UNFCCC through its 'Article 6, and the Convention's Kyoto Protocol, through its Article 10 (e), call on governments to develop and implement educational programmes on climate change and its effects' (Secretariat of the UNFCCC, 2012). Subsequently, parties have been required to report on the steps they have taken towards Article 6, with a number of parties reporting an increase in the number of university courses related to climate change, as well as an increased focus at primary and secondary level (Secretariat of the UNFCCC, 2012).

In the UK, Kulakiewicz et al. (2021) state that issues related to climate change are addressed through the national curriculum in England, predominantly through Science, which is compulsory at Key Stages 3 and 4, and Geography, which is compulsory at Key Stage 3. Similarly, in Northern Ireland the curriculum offers both statutory and non-statutory guidance on climate change, with a focus on delivery through Science and Geography at Key Stages 3 and 4. In Scotland, the Curriculum for Excellence promotes a cross-curricular delivery of climate change – for example, through a thematic approach. A similar approach is seen in the revised curriculum in Wales, which is to be divided into areas of learning, with suggestions as to how climate change might be addressed where appropriate. At tertiary level, Clark-Boyd and Hume (2015) argue that education, particularly at a higher level, should play a role in addressing existing and emerging ecological and socioeconomic challenges. Here they call for curricula reform, in which inter- and transdisciplinary learning spaces can be developed. Drawing from the United Nations Intergovernmental Panel for Climate Change, *Summary for Policymakers* (IPCC, 2014: 5), this reflects an approach that sees climate mitigation as interrelated to equity, justice and fairness, and in which delivery is associated with other societal goals. In this, they argue that learners from a range of disciplines might reflect on 'both the implications of decisions or practices and the positive contributions that their disciplines can make in addressing serious and complex issues' (2014: 67).

It can be argued, therefore, that education has already begun to play a significant role in the bid to tackle climate change and, given that children are presented with various environmental messages through compulsory education systems, it is important to consider their role as potential 'agents of change' in issues of sustainability and environmental policy (Walker, 2017: 74). Furthermore, when viewed against the recent call for action on climate change, inspired by Swedish activist Greta Thunberg, it can be seen that young people are already beginning to pick up the mantle, and while they have been talking about climate change for decades, it is this generation of young people who have been most vocal and more co-ordinated than previous generations (Marris, 2019). This is perhaps best illustrated through action in 2019 which saw young people from across the globe walking out of classrooms and taking to the streets for the **Global Climate Strike**. Bourn outlines the importance of this campaign in respect of encouraging policy-makers to address the emergency of climate change, and suggests that its success was a result of 'simple messages, the power of social media and the value of gathering an emotive response from young people' (2022: 181). Marris (2019) makes similar observations and argues that young climate change activists are capitalising on growing adult awareness through combining their moral authority as young people, alongside a social media savvy, in order to elicit change. Citing the work of environmental scientist Dr Harriet Thew, Marris goes on to state that for young activists climate change is a matter of global justice, with a focus on saving the most vulnerable.

According to Bourn (2022), it is timely to take the lead from young people, especially in respect of learning and social change, since the evidence suggests that they have a better awareness and understanding of other sectors in society. Moreover, as well as raising the profile of climate action, they have also demonstrated a capacity for social action. Actions have been further supported by a number of organisations, including UNICEF UK, the **OutRight Initiative** and the **Student Climate Network** in the UK (UKSCN). The UKSCN aims particularly to make connections between campaigning and education, setting out four demands in their mission statement – save the future, teach the future, tell the future, empower the future (UKSCN, 2022).

In their final demand, the UKSCN call for the inclusion of young people in policy-making, with no one excluded from participation in democracy. This too has a direct correlation with demand two – teach the future – in which they call for a reformed education system that 'teach [es] young people about the urgency, severity and scientific basis on climate change' (2022, para. 2). This reflects Walker's observation of young people as agents of change, stating that 'Children are central to the rhetoric supporting global climate agreements, yet they are also envisaged to play a strategic role in materialising such agreements' (2017: 72).

Nevertheless, White questions whether the curriculum in England is sufficiently focused on climate change, suggesting that treatment of the subject is 'sparse and uncoordinated' (2020: 869). He observes that climate change is mentioned only briefly in the Science curriculum, while climate is covered only generally as part of the Geography curriculum. Moreover, in response to the Global Climate Strikes, White proposes that schools and authorities in England have been critical of students taking direct action. Critics of the English education system are in agreement that the single discipline approach to the national curriculum, which has typified the approach since its introduction in 1988, is not conducive with tackling issues such as climate change (Waters, 2009; White, 2020). Furthermore, approaches are similarly limiting in tertiary education, with Wolff (2020, para. 9) suggesting that:

> Problems such as climate change or global inequality cannot be solved from within a single discipline. Making a valuable contribution requires painstaking acquisition of a variety of complex skills and knowledge.

Wolff (2020) proposes a reform of the undergraduate curriculum, with a move away from the typical single-discipline department to one that favours a multidisciplinary approach, a recommendation that was previously advocated by Ryan (2011) who, in his review of education for sustainable development and holistic curriculum change, emphasised the value of interdisciplinarity to mitigate the limitations of specialisation in a global context.

White (2020) observes that since its emergence, the curriculum in the UK has been under the control of politicians rather than professionals. Furthermore, while he argues that teachers as professionals have the credentials as transmitters of knowledge and skills, the same does not apply to their skills as ethical experts and proposes that decisions regarding what should be taught should be the responsibility of the democratic community. Waters (2009) advises that young people should have a say in what they are taught, since evidence from the Qualifications and Curriculum Authority signifies that what motivates young people the most is how relevant the curriculum is to their own lives and expectations for the future. As we have seen earlier in the chapter, the evidence would suggest that young people are motivated by climate change and in this respect educators should be supportive of actions taken by young people. Moreover, a reimagining of the curriculum that promotes interdisciplinary teaching may well be a way forwards in terms of allowing space in the curriculum for pressing issues such as climate change to be delivered, and in so doing support UNESCO's aim to

> Employ interactive, project-based, learner-centred pedagogy. Transform all aspects of the learning environment through a whole-institution approach to ESD to enable learners to live what they learn and learn what they live [and in so doing] Empower people to take responsibility for present and future generations and actively contribute to societal transformation.
>
> (UNESCO, 2020: 8)

While practical suggestions as to how this might be achieved will be addressed later in the chapter, it is pertinent at this juncture to consider why young people appear so invested in the climate change emergency.

ETHICS OF CARE AND THE CAPABILITIES APPROACH

The National Framework for Sustainable Schools, introduced by the Department for Children, Schools and Families (DfCSF) in May 2006, comprises three interlocking parts: a commitment to care, an integrated approach and a selection of 'doorways' or sustainable themes (2006: 2). In the first, a commitment to care, the DfCSF states that: 'Sustainable schools have a caring ethos – care for oneself, for each other (across cultures, distances and generations), and for the environment (far and near), (2006: 2). They go on to observe that since a culture of care already exists in educational institutions, this should be readily extended to new areas, such as energy consumption, waste management, food and acknowledgment of the difficulties faced by the community it serves and the wider community. While this caring ethos sought to identify ways in which stakeholders might support the school in becoming a more sustainable environment, the evidence suggests that an ethics of care philosophy has since been extended further to address the wider issue of climate change.

Ethics of care, or care ethics, refers to a way of thinking that combines the nature of morality and the ethics of decision-making. Educational philosopher Nel Noddings considers that care is basic in human life, which she proposes consists of two distinct strands: 'the cared for' and 'the one caring for' (Aubrey and Riley, 2021: 169). Moreover,

Noddings (1984) proposes that individuals are guided by an ethics of care, which is a natural propensity to caring and which she sees as being inbuilt to the human psyche. In respect of the moral obligation to caring, Noddings goes on to identify a further two dimensions – caring for and caring about – with caring about being most applicable to the climate change crisis. In her earlier writing, Noddings proposed that caring about held less of a personal dimension than caring for – for example, in demonstrating care through carrying out charitable work such as raising money for poorer communities. Initially, she implied that this type of caring could potentially be tokenistic, suggesting that the lack of reciprocity in this caring encounter diminished its scope. Nevertheless, she later revised her theory and proposed that caring about could serve as an important vehicle for local and global justice. This was similarly observed by Held (2004) who observes that moral theory is beginning to influence how individuals see their global responsibilities.

While early writings on ethics of care saw it as being built around relationships between people in close proximity – for example, between parents and their children – Held (2004) observes that it is not exclusive to private contexts, and suggests that it is quite possible to develop caring relationships for people in remote parts of the globe who may be experiencing hardship. Held (2004) goes on to propose that emotions play a key role in helping an individual to behave in a moral way, suggesting that 'empathy, sensitivity, and responsiveness to particular others may often be better guides to what we ought to do than are highly abstract rules and principles about "all men"' (2004: 145). According to Held, 'the ethics of care has gone *far* beyond its earliest formulations' (2004: 146) and, as proposed by Gibson-Graham (2008), economic actions too can be reimagined in order to reflect care and responsibility for the ecosystem. It could also be argued that what began as a predominantly feminist theory, based on the principle that it was women who traditionally adopted the caring role (Noddings, 1984; Held, 2004), it is now young people who have picked up the mantle of care from an environmental perspective.

In considering how people respond to care in the environment, Moriggi et al. question what motivates a person's desire to nurture 'the life sustaining webs of the worlds they live in' (2020: 284) and ask how they learn to care. They draw from three lenses of care which they see as important points of enquiry in the debate for care in the environment: practice, responsibility and emotions. In appreciating why young people appear so invested in climate change action, it is worth considering the notion of practice and responsibility, since arguably they are aware more than other generations of the ways in which the exploitative actions of humans have led to the destruction of the environment. Thus, the motivation to engage in eco-friendly behaviours might in some way atone for the sins of the past or, as Haraway (2016) observes, such behaviours are a trade-off for the exploitative use of resources, offering accountability for breaking environmental rules, in the face of the guilt felt for the ecological destruction man has created. Mariss (2019) suggests that young activists appear to demonstrate a level of responsibility for the actions of their predecessors, quoting 22-year-old activist Vanessa Nakate who states, 'the older generation messed things up... we are doing the clean up' (2019: 472). Furthermore, Marris (2019) draws from statistics that reveal that adults are also showing an increasing awareness and concern for the environment, but from the perspective of the impact on the next generation if action is not taken. Studies show that people demonstrated a willingness to make financial contributions towards preventing the negative impacts of climate change in order to protect the needs of the next generation, which in itself reflects a caring about ethos.

Nevertheless, there is a concern that within an ethics of care perspective, people could become overburdened by the magnitude of the issue, leading to a feeling of despondency and fear that small actions such as recycling household waste are insignificant in impacting on the fate of the planet (Cuomo, 2011; Moore, 2017). However, Hamilton (2017) observes that for some there is a refusal to believe what the scientists are telling them, and he argues that, in their view, 'humans are too puny to change the climate ... so it is outlandish to suggest we could change the geological timescale' (para. 4). Arguably, from a care perspective, this could be seen as a form of **benign neglect**, however, it is necessary to consider why people might hold these views. Moriggi et al. (2020) propose that caring practices should be motivated by a feeling of relational responsibility in which people can see how their ethically responsible actions might contribute to sustaining and regenerating the environment. Nevertheless, it could be argued that the lack of reciprocity in a caring-about relationship makes it difficult to see the results of these actions. Cuomo (2011) observes that feelings of disempowerment and disillusionment can be psychologically and cognitively debilitating, leading to a form of **cognitive dissonance**, with avoidance and denial proving to be a better alternative than the reality of climate change.

Kronlid (2009) proposes that one way of viewing the moral landscape of climate change is through the capability approach, a theoretical approach first pioneered by Amartya Sen in the 1970s and later developed by social science and humanities scholars, most notably Martha Nussbaum (Robeyns and Moreton, 2021). The capabilities approach holds that of primary importance is the freedom to achieve well-being, and that well-being is typified in terms of a person's capabilities and functionings. Capabilities are defined as what a person can achieve if they so choose, with an emphasis on the importance of being in order to achieve these things – i.e., being well fed and educated. Functionings, therefore, are those capabilities that have been achieved – for example, getting a good job on the basis of being well educated. This relies on a person being able to convert means into functioning, which subsequently depends on personal, sociopolitical, and environmental conditions, or conversion factors (Robeyns and Morten, 2021).

Capabilities are seen as an indicator of well-being (Kronlid, 2018), with Nussbaum identifying a core list of 'central human functional capabilities' which she proposes are the bare minimum for which human dignity requires (Nussbaum, 2006) (see Table 9.1).

Table 9.1   Nussbaum's capabilities

Life	To live to a normal length human life – not dying prematurely or having a reduction in the quality of life.
Bodily health	To enjoy good health, including: • reproductive health; • adequate nourishment; • adequate shelter.
Bodily integrity	Freedom to move. Protection of bodily rights, freedom from all forms of assault, including sexual assault, child sexual abuse, domestic violence. Freedom for sexual satisfaction and reproduction.
Senses, imagination and thought	Freedom to use the human senses to imagine, think and reason through access to an adequate education, with literacy, mathematics and science as a bare minimum. Freedom of expression through religion, literary, political and musical endeavours. Freedom of speech and the ability to search for one's own meaning of life. Opportunity for pleasure and avoidance of pain.
Emotions	Freedom to have attachments to things and people outside of ourselves, and express to ourselves accordingly through love, grief, longing, gratitude and anger. Not be inhibited by fear or anxiety by traumatic events of abuse or neglect.
Practical reasoning	To create a personal definition of what good entails and to critically reflect on the planning of one's own life.
Affiliation	Living in harmony with others, recognising and showing concern for mankind. To have the freedom to engage in social interaction, and to show empathy and compassion. Having self-respect and humility, and dignity through being treated as an equal, with protection from discrimination. Working on an equal footing with colleagues.
Other species	Showing respect for and in relation to animals, plants and the world of nature.
Play	To laugh, play and enjoy recreational activities.
Control over the environment	To participate in political choices that govern one's life, including political participation, and the protection of free speech and its association. Owning property (both land and movable goods), which affords opportunity and equality with others. The right to seek employment on an equal basis with others. Freedom from unwarranted search and seizure.

Adapted from Holland, 2008: 322–3.

Kronlid maintains that the capability approach can be employed to 'produce a temporary, selective and complementary map of the moral landscape of climate change' (2018: 28), especially in view of the fact that climate change might threaten people's capabilities which Cuomo (2011) observes are of intrinsic value to us being at the core of freedom, integrity and dignity. Moreover, where capabilities are threatened, then life chances are negatively impacted and the less people have, the greater the threat to capabilities.

There is little doubt that climate change impacts on an individual's capabilities. However, it could be argued that the impact is situational – for example, as noted previously, it is people living in developing countries who are most impacted by climate change. Thus, from a capabilities perspective, quality of life is seriously impacted. However, people in the developed world might argue that the pressure to change lifestyle and consumption behaviour to mitigate against climate change will impact on personal well-being, potentially resulting in a reluctance to do so. This might also account for the cognitive dissonance, as noted earlier, as individuals seek to justify their inertia; as expressed by Kleist (n.d.), a possible conflict arises when flourishing of the environment impedes human flourishing. Regardless, in order to tackle climate change it is necessary to make significant changes to how we live, necessitating a change to everyday actions to secure the world for future generations. Moreover, given that young people have an invested interest, education would seem to be a practical way forward. The next section will offer some suggestions as to how this might proceed.

THE ROLE OF EDUCATIONAL SETTINGS IN ADDRESSING CLIMATE CHANGE

Research suggests that there is a consensus among pupils and teachers that global learning is essential for the future of the world. Furthermore, where pupils have experienced global learning in school, the more likely they are to take action against climate change (Shah and Young, 2009). This is reinforced with the introduction of the Education for Sustainable Development (ESD) 2030 Roadmap in which UNESCO outline education is a top priority on which to build peace and drive sustainable development. UNESCO Assistant Director-General for Education, Stefania Giannini, stresses that ESD

> was born from the need for education to address growing sustainability challenges. ESD employs action-oriented, innovative pedagogy to enable learners to develop knowledge and awareness and take action to transform society into a more sustainable one.
>
> (2020: 1)

Priority action areas outlined in the road map include transforming learning environments in order that learners can become change agents who are able to take transformative action for sustainable development, including within their own environments. Of importance is the role of educators in facilitating this, who should also be empowered, through appropriate training, to guide and empower learners through being equipped with the relevant knowledge, skills, values and behaviours.

Priority Action 4 promotes the empowerment and mobilisation of youth, especially given that it is their future which is at risk. Additionally, as we have seen earlier in the chapter, young people are becoming increasingly vocal and active around climate change. The ESD initiative recommends that young people should be enabled to empower each other, and one such initiative to encourage this is through the DFID Global Schools Partnership which 'encourages the development of educational and sustainable school partnerships between schools in the UK and schools in Africa, Asia, Latin America and the Caribbean' (Think Global, 2018, para. 1). Lewis (2009) observes that participation in such an initiative presents children with the opportunity to learn about different cultures through sharing experiences, understanding challenges and seeking similarities that bind everyone together. Teachers involved in the programme recognise its benefits as it allows pupils to become personally invested in issues rather than seeing them as remote, theoretical concepts that do not affect them.

On the other hand, Clarke-Boyd and Hume (2015) draw from a 2015 study undertaken by Reicher Newstadt which revealed that secondary school participants expressed that they were not concerned about climate change for the following reasons: it is not local; it is happening somewhere else; it is happening in the future; it was not impacting on the learners but it was impacting on animals and the environment (2015: 69). It is proposed, therefore, that the most effective way to change such a mindset is through 'cultivating compassion [by which] individuals will develop a more sophisticated emotional literacy in duality with critical literacy which might impel them to intervene more rigorously for social change as a compassionate global citizen' (Murphy et al., 2014: 53). However, as seen previously, in England the current approach to addressing climate change issues is through subjects within the national curriculum, which arguably fail to enable learners to see the interconnections between different aspects of climate change. It is recommended, therefore, that an interdisciplinary approach might be taken to facilitate deeper learning with a more problem-centred, collaborative approach (Clarke-Boyd and Hume, 2015).

Conversely, Skamp et al. (2012) propose that science education can play a key role in empowering students, since through teaching the science of climate change students will feel personally empowered to effect change. Nevertheless, this requires a shift from the current passive approach of independent enquiry to one that is targeted towards sociopolitical action which contributes to education for citizenship (Hodson, 2003). White (2020) observes that through education students are able to put pressure on those in positions of power to act. Furthermore, he suggests that multidisciplinary already exists, in as much as

It [education] draws on chemistry and physics, given the role of CO2 and other substances in the greenhouse effect; on biology, seeing the dangers to biodiversity and on geography, in connection with such things as uncontrollable wildfires and the social effects of sea-level rises in different areas.

(2020: 868)

White (2020) goes on to express that different disciplinary perspectives are interconnected through related global, social, economic and historical factors, such as population increase, social inequalities and the development of the free market economy, all of which can be addressed through citizenship in the national curriculum across Key Stages 1–4.

While citizenship remains non-statutory at Key Stages 1 and 2 (DfE, 2013), delivery of it does encourage children to reflect on themselves as individuals and as part of the wider community. In relation to Education for Sustainable Development (ESD), this is first introduced at Key Stage 1, with a focus on recognising their responsibility to others and understanding what harms local, natural and built environments, and how they might look after them. At Key Stage 2, specific reference is made to sustainability with a focus on the allocation of resources and how economic choices can affect individuals, communities and the sustainability of the environment. Citizenship at Key Stages 3 and 4 is statutory, and while no direct reference is made to ESD, the teaching of it requires that pupils are equipped with 'the skills and knowledge to explore political and social issues critically, to weigh evidence, debate and make reasoned arguments' (DfE, 2013, para. 1). Walker (2017) sees citizenship as a means by which to deliver ESD and proposes that pupils should work with other actors on local sustainable initiatives. Moreover, she draws from studies that see the utilisation of educational interventions that encourage pro-environmental actions – for example, through encouraging children to monitor energy usage in the home, which resulted in families adopting energy-saving behaviours. Child agency offers an effective way of carrying pro-environmental messages and, combined with their social media savvy, children are able to share pro-environmental messages. White (2020) observes that social media was central to the mobilisation of pupils in the climate change action and draws from the work of Andersson and Öhman (2017) in suggesting that online conversations might generate discussion which allows young people to engage in moral and political arguments.

It is without question that climate change education can enrich the current curriculum, particularly through the identified areas of science, geography and ESD, although this is most empowering when conceptualised across disciplinary boundaries and delivered in a participatory and creative way (Læssøe et al., 2009). Rousell and Cutter-Mckenzie-Knowles (2019) argue, however, that new modes of thinking around climate change education is preferable, which draws on more radical and visionary alternatives and capitalises on the current trends and developments, including 'environmental activism, social and political intervention, digital innovation, citizen science, and the creative arts' (2019: 15). Moreover, Rousell and Cutter-Mckenzie-Knowles call on policy-makers to make climate change more meaningful for children, moving away from the scientific basis of study and drawing on the more pressing aims of climate change mitigation. Furthermore, they suggest that researchers should be working with children themselves to develop what could potentially be a transdisciplinary field of environmental education.

SUMMARY

Grauer (2020) refers to climate change as the 'thief of childhood', offering a bleak outlook on the future of the planet, drawing from Mckies's (2017) work that suggests that 50 per cent of the world species will be extinct by the end of the century. Grauer goes on to observe that the combination of natural and human causes of climate change can lead to 'feelings of anxiety, pessimism, helplessness, eroded sense of self and control, stress, distress, sadness, loss, and guilt' (para. 6). Nevertheless, despite his reservations of burdening young people with these looming environmental catastrophes, he observes that this is unavoidable given that news of climate change is 'permeating their minds' (2020, para. 11). Furthermore, as this chapter has shown, there seems to be a genuine desire among young people to play an active role in mitigating against the impact of climate change. In view of this, it could be argued that education is a fitting vehicle for capitalising on this plea for change.

As seen in the chapter, while climate change is certainly not a new issue, the past two decades has seen it growing in significance on a global scale, with governments worldwide committing to take action to reduce GHG emissions. Importantly, however, is the way in which young people have been mobilised to act, particularly in relation to the pressure placed on governments to take action, which can be viewed through the lens of an ethics of care. Young people have demonstrated that they care about the environment and are prepared to be proactive in securing the future of our planet.

While policy-makers have sought to use the curriculum as a channel for young people to secure their knowledge of environmental issues, most specifically through the Science and Geography curriculum, as has been shown here there remains a question mark over how effective this is in allowing young people to make connections (Waters, 2009; White, 2020). White (2020) calls for a more interdisciplinary approach to education in which different kinds of understandings are promoted, enabling young people to mobilise opinion and force governmental response. He suggests that the best way to achieve this is through a new approach to curriculum development, more appropriate to a democracy and that allows young people to explore issues that have meaning to them.

Rifkin (2011) posits that the world is entering a third industrial revolution, necessitating a vision for change in education culture. This is validated by Barry (2012) who argues for changes in educational structures and cultures, without which we are faced with the prospect of living unsustainably and the subsequent global inequalities and ecological crises. This chapter has sought to identify some of these challenges, but also offers some suggestions as to how education might elicit change, particularly in a climate where there appears to be a genuine desire for action.

GLOSSARY OF TERMS

Benign neglect

An intentional form of neglect, or lack of attention, which has the intention of helping someone over offering direct assistance. This often relates to a delicate or undesirable situation. Noddings saw 'caring about' as a form of benign neglect, suggesting that this involved engaging in charitable work, but failing to offer further practical assistance.

Cognitive dissonance

Cognitive dissonance refers to an uncomfortable mental state in which a person holds one or more conflicting belief at any one time. In climate change this would refer to the knowledge that human actions are adversely impacting on the environment, but continuing to engage in such actions because the alternative would require making significant lifestyle changes.

Global Climate Strikes

Coordinated strikes undertaken by hundreds and thousands of young people across the world with the aim of pressurising governments to take urgent action to tackle climate change. Initially inspired by the actions of Swedish activist Greta Thunberg in 2018, strikes have since become regular events.

Greenhouse gas emissions

Emissions from human activities that serve to strengthen the greenhouse effect and contribute to climate change. Greenhouse gas emissions arise from the combustion of natural gases and petroleum products required for heating, cooking, travel, etc., emitting carbon dioxide, methane and nitrous oxide.

Kyoto Protocol

An international treaty formulated by industrialised nations and signed in 1997 by more than 150 countries, the Kyoto Prtocol set mandatory limits on greenhouse gas emissions.

OutRight Initiative

Promoted by UNICEF UK, the OutRight Initiative seeks to support children and young people in realising their own rights, while speaking out for the rights of children in less fortunate circumstances.

Paris Agreement

Also known as the Paris Climate Accord, the agreement was adopted by 196 parties at COP21 held in Paris in 2015. The agreement came into force in 2016 and was a binding treaty in which parties agreed to limit global warming to below 2° Centigrade, compared to pre-industrial levels. The agreement has been seen as a landmark agreement, as it is the first time that nations have been united in a common cause.

Student Climate Network

A group of young people who have sought action against what they perceive to be a lack of action from the government in respect of climate change. The group have organised a significant number of demonstrations, such as Global Climate Strikes, with a view to mobilising young people to spread the message.

FURTHER READING

Gore, A. (2007) *An Inconvenient Truth: The Crisis of Global Warming*. New York: Viking Books for Young Readers.

An adaptation of Gore's bestselling book, this text is designed for young people to help them to understand global warming and inspire them to action.

Held, V. (2007) *The Ethics of Care: Personal, Political and Global*. Oxford: Oxford University Press.

An explanation of the moral and feminist roots of the ethics of care perspective, with an exploration of what it means to be a caring person. The latter section of the text shows the application of the ethics for care philosophy, with an emphasis on how it might apply to issues of global inequality.

Robeyns, I. (2017) *Wellbeing, Freedom and Social Justice: The Capability Approach Re-Examined*. Cambridge: Open Book Publishers.

An examination of how the capability approach can be applied to policy making in different academic disciplines. A critical evaluation of the approach is offered alongside discussion relating to theories of justice, human rights, basic needs and the human development approach.

Tanzi, V. (2022) *Fragile Futures: The Uncertain Economics of Disasters, Pandemics, and Climate Change*. Cambridge: Cambridge University Press.

An examination of how governments globally should be addressing unpredictable and uncertain events that have previously been viewed as uncontrollable acts of God. The author argues that in the modern, interconnected global society, governments should be better equipped to deal with the harms, risks and crises that threaten mankind.

Walsh, E.M. (ed.) (2022) *Justice and Equity in Climate Change Education: Exploring Social and Ethical Dimensions of Environmental Education*. Oxford: Routledge.

An exploration of the relationship between climate change education and issues of justice, equity and social transformation. The text explores how climate change impacts on social injustices and examines how education reform might mitigate against this.

REFERENCES

Aubrey, K. and Riley. A. (2021) *Understanding and Using Challenging Educational Theories* (2nd edn). London: SAGE.

Barry, J. (2007) Spires, plateaus and the infertile landscape of Education for Sustainable Development: Re-invigorating the university through integrating community, campus and curriculum. *International Journal of Innovation and Sustainable Development*, 2(3/4): 433–52.

Bouman, T., Verschoor, M., Albers, C.J., Böhm, G., Fisher, S.D., Poortinga, W., Whitmarsh, L. and Steg, L. (2020) When worry about climate change leads to climate action: How values, worry and personal responsibility relate to various climate actions. *Global Environmental Change*, 62: 1–11.

Bourn, D. (2022) *Education for Social Change: Perspectives on Global Learning*. London: Bloomsbury.

Bryce, T.G.K. and Day, S.P. (2014) Scepticism and doubt in science and science education: The complexity of global warming as a socio-scientific issue. *Cultural Studies of Science Education*, 9: 599–632.

Campbell-Lendrum, D., Wheeler, N., Maiero, M., Villalobos Prats, E. and Nevelle, T. (2018) *World Health Organization COP24 Special Report on Health and Climate Change*. World Health Organization. Available at: www.who.int/publications/i/item/cop24-special-report-health-climate-change (accessed 16 March 2023).

Clark Boyd, M. and Hume, T. (2015) Addressing the challenges of climate change: The potential role of development education in the tertiary sector. *Policy and Practice: A Development Education Review*, 21: 63–86.

Climate Action Tracker (CAT) (2021) *United Kingdom: Country Summary*. Available at: https://climateactiontracker.org/countries/uk/ (accessed 26 March 2023).

Cuomo, C.J. (2011) Climate change, vulnerability and responsibility. *Hypatia; Responsibility and Identity in Social Justice*, 26(4): 690–714.

Department for Children, School and Families (DfCSF) (2006) *National Framework for Sustainable Schools: Eight Doorways*. London: Crown copyright.

Department for Education (DfE) (2013) *National Curriculum in England*. London: Crown copyright.

Gibson-Graham, J.K. (2008) Diverse economies: Performative practices for 'other worlds'. *Progress in Human Geography*, 32(5): 613–32.

Grauer, S.R. (2020) Climate change: The thief of childhood. *Climate Change*. Kappanonline.org., pp. 42–6.

Hamilton, C. (2017) The great climate silence: We are on the edge of the abyss but we ignore it. Available at: www.theguardian.com/environment/2017/may/05/the-great-cmate-silence-we-are-on-the-edge-of-the-abyss-but, we-ignore-it (accessed 16 March 2023).

Hansen, J. (2009) *Storms of my Grandchildren: The Truth about the Coming Climate Catastrophe and Our Last Chance to Save Humanity*. New York: Bloomsbury.

Haraway, D. (2016) *Staying with the Trouble: Making Kin in the Chthulucene*. Durham, NC: Duke University Press.

Held, V. (2004) Care and justice in the global context. *Ratio Juris*, 17(2): 141–55.

Hirst, D. (2020) The history of global climate change negotiations. House of Commons Library. Available at: https://commonslibrary.parliament.uk/the-history-of-global-climate-change-negotiations/ (accessed 16 March 2023).

Hodson, D. (2003) Time for action: Science education for an alternative future. *International Journal of Science Education*, 25: 645–70.

Holland. B. (2008) Justice and the environment in Nussbaum's 'capabilities approach': Why sustainable ecological capacity is a meta-capability. *Political Research Quarterly*, 61(2): 319–32.

IPCC (1990) *Climate Change: The IPCC Impacts Assessment: Policy Makers Summary*. Australia: Imprimatur Press.

IPCC (2007) *Climate Change 2007: Impacts, Adaptation and Vulnerability*. Cambridge: Cambridge University Press.

IPCC (2014) *Climate Change (2014): Synthesis Report. Contribution of Working Groups I, II and III to the Fifth Assessment Report of the Intergovernmental Panel on Climate Change* (core writing team: R.K. Pachauri and L.A. Meyer (eds). IPCC, Geneva, 151pp.

Jakučionytė-Skodienė and M. Liobikienė, G. (2021) Climate change concern, personal responsibility and actions related to climate change mitigation in EU countries: Cross-cultural analysis. *Journal of Cleaner Production*, 281: 125–89.

Jamieson, D. (1992) Ethics, public policy and global warming. *Science, Technology, & Human Values*, 17(2): 139–53.

Jamieson, D. (2007) The moral and political challenges of climate change. In: S. Moser and L. Dilling (eds) *Creating a Climate for Change: Communicating Climate Change and Facilitating Social Change*. Cambridge: Cambridge University Press.

Kleist, C. (n.d.) *Global Ethics: Capabilities Approach*. Available at: https://iep.utm.edu/ge-capab/ (accessed 16 March 2023).

Kramaer, D. (2021) Greta Thunberg: Who is the climate campaigner and what are her aims? Available at: www.bbc.co.uk/news/world-europe-49918719 (accessed 16 March 2023).

Kronlid, D.O. (2009) Sigtuna think piece 2: Climate capabilities and climate change education research. *Southern African Journal of Environmental Education*, 26.

Kronlid, D.O. (2018) The capabilities approach to climate change. In D. Kronlid, *Climate Change Adaptation and Human Capabilities: Justice and Ethics in Research and Policy*. London: Palgrave Macmillan.

Kuh, K.F. (2018) *Climate change*. Available at: www.sciencedirect.com/topics/earth-and-planetary-sciences/united-nations-framework-convention-on-climate-change (accessed 16 March 2023).

Kulakiewicz, A., Long, R. and Roberts, N. (2021) *Inclusion of sustainability and climate change in the national curriculum*. House of Commons Library. Debate Pack 25.

Læssøe, J., Schnac, K., Breiting, S. and Rolls, S. (2009) *Climate Change and Sustainable Development: The Response from Education*. International Alliance of Leading Educational Institutes.

Lewis, I. (2009) Preparing young people for global citizenship. *Education Review: Schools on the Global Stage*. 21(2): 23–6.

Marris, E. (2019) Why young climate activists have captured the world's attention. *Nature.* 573(7775): 471–72. DOI: 10.1038/d41586-019-02696-0. PMID: 31551545

McKie, R. (2017) Bioligists think 50% of species will be facing extinction by the end of the century. Available at: https://www.theguardian.com/environment/2017/feb/25/half-all-species-extinct-end-century-vatican-conference (accessed 29 March 2023).

Met Office (2022) Record high temperatures verified. Available at: www.metoffice.gov.uk/about-us/press-office/news/weather-and-climate/2022/record-high-temperatures-verified#:~:text=The%20UK's%20new%20record%2Dhigh,of%20analysis%20and%20quality%20control (accessed 16 March 2023).

Moore, K. D. (2017) *Great Tide Rising: Towards clarity and courage in a time of planetary change.* Counterpoint Press.

Moriggi, A., Soini, K., Franklin, A. and Roep, D. (2020) A care-based approach to transformative change: Ethically-informed practices, relational response-ability & emotional awareness. *Ethics, Policy & Environment,* 23(3): 281–98.

Murphy, C., Ozawa-de Silva, B. and Winskell, M. (2014) Towards compassionate global citizenship: Educating the heart through development, education and cognitively based compassion training. *Policy & Practice: A Development Education Review,* 19: 52–69.

Noddings, N. (1984) *Caring: A Feminist Approach to Ethics and Moral Education.* Berkeley, CA: University of California Press.

Nussbaum, M. (2006) *Frontiers of Justice: Disability, Nationality, Species Membership.* Cambridge, MA: Belknap Press of Harvard University Press.

OXFAM (2022) 5 natural disasters that beg for climate action. Available at: www.oxfam.org/en/5-natural-disasters-beg-climate-action (accessed 16 March 2023).

Rifkin, J. (2011) *The Third Industrial Revolution: How Lateral Power is Transforming Energy, the Economy and the World.* Basingstoke: Palgrave Macmillan.

Robeyns, I. and Morten F.B. (2021) The capability approach. *Stanford Encyclopedia of Philosophy* (Winter). Edward N. Zalta (ed.). Available at: https://plato.stanford.edu/archives/win2021/entries/capability-approach/ (accessed 16 March 2023).

Rousell, D. and Cutter-Mckenzie-Knowles, A. (2019) A systematic review of climate change education: Giving children and young people a 'voice' and a 'hand' in redressing climate change. *Children's Geographies,* 18(2).

Ryan, A. (2011) *Education for Sustainable Development and Holistic Curriculum Change.* York: Higher Education Academy.

Sage, C. (2003) The scope for North/South co-operation. *Environmental Policy in an International Context,* 3: 167–96.

Secretariat of the UNFCCC (2012) Climate change education as an integral part of the United Nations Framework Convention on Climate Change. *UNESCO Special Section on the ESD Response to the Three Rio Conventions,* 6(2): 237–9.

Shah, H. and Young, H. (2009) Global learning in schools and the implication for policy. *Education Review: Schools on the Global Stage,* 21(2): 15–22.

Skamp, K., Boyes, E. and Stannisstreet, M. (2012) Beliefs and willingness to act about global warming: Where to focus science pedagogy? *Science Education.* Wiley OnLine Library.

Think Global (2018) Global Schools Partnership – British Council. Available at: https://think-global.org.uk/member/gloabal-schools-partnership-british-council/ (accessed 16 March 2023).

United Kingdom Student Climate Network (UKSCN) (2022) *We the students demand …* Available at: https://ukscn.org/our-demands/ (accessed 16 March 2023).

United Nations Educational, Scientific and Cultural Organisation (UNESCO) (2010) *The UNESCO Climate Change Initiative.* Available at: www.unesco.org/en/climatechange (accessed 16 March 2023).

United Nations Educational, Scientific and Cultural Organisation (UNESCO) (2020) *Education for Sustainable Development: A Roadmap.* France: UNESCO Education Sector.

United Nations (n.d.). Climate action. Available at: www.un.org/en/climatechange/what-is-climate-change (accessed 16 March 2023).

United Nations (1992a) *United Nations Framework Convention on Climate Change.* Available at: https://unfccc.int/files/essential_background/background_publications_htmlpdf/application/pdf/conveng.pdf (accessed 16 March 2023).

United Nations (1992b) *United Nations Conference on Environment & Development Rio de Janerio, Brazil, 3 to 14 June 1992.* Incheon, South Korea: United Nations Division for Sustainable Development.

Walker, C. (2017) Tomorrow's leaders and today agents of change? Children, sustainability education and environmental governance. *Children and Society*, 31: 72–83.

Waters, M. (2009) Climate change: Global warming or global yawning. *Education Review: Schools on the Global Stage*, 21(2): 60–73.

White, J. (2020) The climate emergency and the transformed school. *Journal of Philosophy of Education*, 54(4): 867–73.

Wolff. J. (2020) In the 2020s universities need to step up as a central pillar of civil society. Available at: www.theguardian.com/education/2020/jan/07/2020s-universities-need-to-step-up-central-pillar-civil-society (accessed 16 March 2023).

Wood, N. and Roelich, K. (2019) Tensions, capabilities, and justice in climate change mitigations of fossil fuels. *Energy Research and Social Science*, 52: 114–22.

World Health Organization (WHO) (2021) Climate change and health. Available at: www.who.int/news-room/fact-sheets/detail/climate-change-and-health (accessed 16 March 2023).

10

REALIGNING EDUCATION WITH SOCIAL JUSTICE IN CHANGING TIMES

LEARNING OUTCOMES

Having read this chapter, you should be able to:

- identify the possible lessons learned from events, crises and the political shift in education;
- evaluate the rationale for revisiting the purpose and nature of education in uncertain times;
- critically appraise alternative progressive educational concepts for the future;
- identify possible ways to utilise progressive concepts for a changing and uncertain world.

KEY WORDS

critical pedagogy; cultural capital; deschooling; education renewal; progressive education; traditional education; transformative learning.

INTRODUCTION

This chapter seeks not only to identify the lessons to be learned from the crises, events and phenomena that have been explored in this book, but also to attempt to consider the wider political and societal shifts which have, or will, perhaps have an impact on education. The focus is for the most part on statutory education in the UK, but the main emphasis will be on England and the DfE. Education has witnessed increasing marketisation, an emphasis on assessment and a drive for more traditional (sometimes referred to as 'formal' for the purposes of this chapter) teaching methods. Furthermore, the events covered in this volume have exposed high levels of inequality and marginalisation; as such, there is an argument for repurposing education to prepare young people to cope and thrive in times of uncertainty. At the time of writing, in the UK there have been ten education secretaries since the Conservative-led coalition government came to power in 2010 (GOV.UK, 2022a). During the events that surrounded Boris Johnson's attempt to stay in power, there were three education secretaries in post in three days, before he announced on 7 July 2022 his decision to step down. Between the 7 July and 5 September, Johnson remained as the caretaker prime minister presiding over a government in a state of limbo. It was also a period in which the two remaining prime ministerial candidates displayed an increasingly right-wing, populist and culture war agenda to appeal to the Conservative Party membership. The new prime minister, Liz Truss, took office on 5 September 2022, with Kit Malthouse named as Education Secretary on 6 September 2022 (GOV.UK, 2022a). After a short, tumultuous period, Liz Truss stood down and Rishi Sunak took over as prime minister with Gillian Keegan as Education Secretary.

The UK is now witnessing a political shift that could possibly be harmful for the long-term economy and society at large, leading to an ever-widening regional gap in learning and attainment. Some events are also concerns for the international community, such as the continuing recovery from COVID-19, the Russian invasion of Ukraine with its appalling humanitarian crisis, rising energy costs, and difficulties in food production and supply. The UK is still grappling with the result of the 2016 Brexit referendum, ever-increasing rates of inflation, a rise in child poverty, collective industrial unrest which has seen many sectors such as law, communications, transport, education and NHS staff either striking or threatening to strike for better working conditions and to ensure their wages keep pace with rising inflation. Education and schools are affected by these events. It is contested that the continuing government call for traditional schooling is not helping to prepare for future uncertainties that students may face. This is evident on at least two fronts, which is mainly apparent in England. First, by the ideological rhetoric that increasingly seeks to return to the passive and nostalgic notion of schooling, the return of grammar schools, narrowing of the curriculum for 'academic' subjects at the expense of the arts and humanities, mainly for the acquisition of skills for the global marketplace. Second, by using a business model for a measurable academic education rather than for developing not only learning, but also a means of nurturing social justice in such turbulent and uncertain times.

Such passivity and unquestioning nature of schooling with its fixation on grading pupils from an early age is exemplified by Danny Dorling in the Foreword to Brighouse and Waters's contemporary seminal text, *About Our Schools: Improving on Previous Best* (2021).

> At some times and in some schools, we are told that other people are our betters, often others not at our school. We learn to behave and to be disciplined, so that later in our lives our apparent superiors will find that we have been well trained; that we are respectful; compliant; that we know our place. This still occurs in England today. Not everywhere, of course, but the idea that different children are of different rank and worth is still endlessly stamped into young minds in ways that do not often occur so forcefully elsewhere in Europe.
>
> (Dorling, 2021: i)

This chapter will explore the lessons learned from the events, crises, phenomena and the political changes by the UK government. It will then briefly review the shifts between progressive and **traditional education** in UK state education from the start of the second half of the last century when teachers were very involved with curriculum content, pedagogy and assessment. It will offer ideas for re-establishing **progressive education**, and consider different progressive themes of thought and the key contemporary thinkers involved. Finally, it will consider options for the future in dealing with the events outlined in the book and other possible unexpected occurrences.

LEARNING FROM EVENTS, CRISES AND POLITICAL INTENTIONS

The events, crises and phenomena explored in this text are a reminder that policy-makers need to ensure that schools and other educational establishments are prepared for what the future may bring, such as the global population shift, the increasing developments in artificial intelligence, as well as the ongoing advances in the internet and associated new technologies (Brighouse and Waters, 2021). Preparing young people for an ever-changing and uncertain world requires a change in the way we think about, and practise, education. This requires **education renewal** rather than reform. A renewal will obviously need to take into account the specifics of the events, crises and phenomena. However, developing confident, democratic and questioning citizens has been, and still is, the aim of progressive education.

Schools in England focus on narrow, mostly subject-based academic content, with the emphasis on instrumental forms of assessment, and increasingly promote didactic forms of pedagogy. However, schools are also places where pupils learn to be part of society where they develop mutual respect and acquire beliefs, values and biases (Dorling, 2021). Although academic attainment is a very important acquisition for pupils, they also need the ability to cope and thrive in uncertainty, to appreciate and value differences, engage in dialogue, challenge dominant thinking and work democratically with others. Another limiting factor in dealing with uncertainty is what Illich termed 'commodification', promoted by neoliberal thinking, where learning and the curriculum is packaged like any other merchandise (Illich, 1971).

A brief overview of the contents of each of the chapters covered in this text is offered here as a recap of the main points to reflect upon and help start the process of what can be learned. Knowledge proffered by the curriculum pays scant attention to the realities of everyday life for many sections of society. Rather, knowledge in the curriculum has become what Michael Apple (2000) termed 'official knowledge', which has been created by policy-makers who wish to reproduce either the status quo or exacerbate the inequities of those who are not of the dominant social class or culture. These aspects of the curriculum have implications for raising social mobility. This has been the focus of progressive thinkers such as Basil Bernstein who maintained that the social class structure in British culture will always favour the middle-class students at the expense of those with a working-class background. However, there have been initiatives to narrow the gap between the two, such as pupil premium funding for the most disadvantaged students and the inclusion of **cultural capital** as a focus for inspection to celebrate different cultures.

Populism, particularly right-wing populism with its emphasis on neoliberalism, is a worldwide phenomenon. Policy-makers in England have, since the election of the Conservative-led coalition government in 2010, employed populist rhetoric promoting traditional teaching methods, the importance of examinations, league tables and competition, as well as a narrow curriculum that focuses on 'academic' subjects. There has also been a noticeable separation between education and social justice matters – for example, the demise of Every Child Matters (ECM) and the reduction in funding of Sure Start centres, all of which limits the opportunity for preparing young people for the future. Regarding the Black Lives Matter movement, the UK government has made a tentative response which suggests a reluctance to acknowledge that there is a serious problem with racism in society. However, there are more positive steps from an educational viewpoint in relation to decolonising the curriculum in addressing the harm done in past social injustices, although there needs to be even more progress on this to raise awareness and to celebrate students' cultural heritage.

The COVID-19 pandemic has caused tremendous disruption to education throughout the world and has exposed huge inequalities such as levels of poverty differences in culture in some parts of society. In the UK, there were errors in school closures, the handling of algorithms and examinations, and the lack of advice and resources for schools. However, the UK was not alone in ignoring early advice and its paucity of planning for unexpected and uncertain events that might occur (Tanzi, 2022). There were, however, some positive outcomes such as the use and development of online learning, home-schooling and the innovative pedagogy by many teachers. Unfortunately, the resultant 'catch-up' programmes have tended to focus on academic points rather than the students' well-being, which again limits the roundness of education needed for future uncertainties (Breslin, 2021). Although positive progress has been made in inclusive initiatives evidenced in the revised Sex and Relationships Education (SRE) guidance since the repeal of Section 28, the SRE focus remains very much one of heteronormativity. It is considered that normalising the experiences of LGBTQ+ students and using resources that mirror the diversity of the school communities will advance the ethos of inclusivity which respects and protects all students regardless of how they identify.

Climate change has enormous implications for the planet and is a heavy burden for children and future generations for many reasons. Young people wish to play an active part in alleviating the impact of climate change, and they have shown their voice and determination in caring for the environment. However, while currently climate change is part of the Science and Geography subjects in the national curriculum in England, perhaps now is the time that it becomes a topic in its own right to prepare students for active and engaged citizenship living in an environment that may be unsustainable with the consequent worldwide inequalities. Young people have been emancipated by their desire to make a difference in tackling climate change; they have questioned, debated and advanced their concerns. Such democratic participation is welcomed and aligned with the progressive educational thinking.

SHIFTS IN PROGRESSIVE AND TRADITIONAL EDUCATION

The 'golden age' of progressive education in the UK was epitomised by the Plowden Report published in 1967. However, the rise and influence of the radical right began to dominate the politics of education, starting in earnest with Thatcherite thinking and its focus on prescription and measurable outcomes (Lowe, 2007). This shift from progressive education has now accelerated even further and is driven by ideology rather than being thoroughly informed by theory, or research-based evidence (Breslin, 2021), a situation that would be unthinkable in any other professional sector. Yet, Rosenshine's 'Principles of instruction: Research-based strategies that all teachers should know' (2012) is a form of traditional teaching that has seen a rise in popularity in schools over the last ten years. It takes its ideas from cognitive psychology, which is a move away from the behaviourism often linked with traditional teaching methods. Rosenshine's work focuses on student achievement, teacher performance and instruction. It is popular because it gives structure to lessons and is seen by many to be a format for good teaching practice, fitting well with the limitations of the current objectives-based national curriculum. There is no doubt that Rosenshine's principles of instruction is popular among some teachers because of the reasons made above. However, his work has attracted criticism such as the danger of overgeneralising the background theory, using the ten principles as a checklist, a return to didactic teaching with the memorising of facts over experimentation, discovery and creativity, and whether it is suitable for all types of learners. Furthermore, and in context with this chapter (and volume), it is focused very much on learning processes and takes little regard of matters of democracy and social justice (Aubrey and Riley, 2022).

Before exploring further the origins of progressive education, it is fitting to consider the differences between progressive and traditional or formal education which is clearly outlined by Thomas (2013) in Table 10.1. It is strongly contended that, despite the increasing calls for a shift to more traditional education, in practice both traditional and progressive methods are employed at the discretion of teachers' professional judgement.

Table 10.1 Progressive versus formal (traditional) education

	Progressive education	*Formal (traditional) education*
Also known as …	Informal; child centred; discovery learning; integrated day; new education; learning by doing.	Traditional; teacher directed; didactic; 'back to basics'; essentialism; 'chalk and talk'.
Achieves aims by …	Problem solving; activity; discovery; play.	Instruction; learning facts, established ideas, rules and traditions; compliance.
Aims to …	Teach the child to think, to be independent, to be critical.	Teach the child the skills and knowledge necessary for life.
Assumes that children, above all, need …	Freedom.	Structure.
Curriculum is …	Project based or topic based, with the integration of 'subjects'.	Subject based, with subjects taught separately.
Emphasises …	Activity, freedom, and the growth of understanding; individuality; the nature of the child.	Teaching; reception and acquisition of knowledge and skill; conformity to establish principles of conduct and enquiry; the nature of knowledge.
Motivation by …	Absorption in the work itself; the satisfaction gained by working with others – cooperation.	A desire to comply with teacher demands; competition for better grades; rewards and punishments.
Motto (after Dewey, in *Experience and Education* …)	Development from within.	Formation from without.
Students and pupils, relating with the teacher mainly by …	Group or individual work, with teachers and pupils in a mentor-apprentice relationship.	Mainly class work, with the teacher primarily in an instructional position.
What to be learned …	How to think independently; critical thinking; a questioning disposition.	Basic skills; factual information and principles; respect for authority.

Source: Thomas (2013: 30–1).

Prior to considering the reasons for the rise and demise of progressive education in the UK, it is pertinent to briefly reflect on the changes taking place in society and following the end of the Second World War to give it further context. The latter half of the twentieth century saw massive changes in international power and order. People had had enough of suffering and the horrors of the war, and were seeking a better and just society. European countries were handing over their colonies at a pace and the Cold War concentrated the mind on the horrors of the possibility of a nuclear conflict up until the Berlin Wall was brought down in 1989. In the USA, there was a rise in the civil rights movement, a demand for gender equality and mass protests against the involvement in the Vietnam War. In the UK, the period witnessed the Abortion Act, the decriminalisation of homosexuality and the end of capital punishment; the 1960s was a period of openness and social tolerance principally promoted by Harold Wilson's Labour government (Howlett, 2013; Aubrey and Riley, 2021).

Yet, in contrast, in the latter half of the twentieth century governments were also promoting traditional learning educational practices as a way of enhancing skills to compete in the international markets. When considering the debate between progressive and traditional education, and reflecting on the idea of Plato's Academy in relation to current education, Thomas posed a few thought-provoking questions on the purpose of schools which are still unresolved:

> Should schools principally be about passing on knowledge and skills to a new generation, and if so which knowledge and which skills? Or should they put the emphasis on the transmission of manners, habits, and traditions of a culture? Should education be about encouraging compliance with the existing ideas and norms of a society or should it concern the promotion of a questioning, challenging, free thinking disposition.
>
> (Thomas, 2013: 16)

There is little doubt that the debate between traditional and progressive education is divisive. Ted Wragg (2005) emphasises the acrimony involved: a mention of traditional education will resonate with 'solid British values such as industry, determination and thoroughness' with one group, yet to another group 'people will assume you are out of date, … [and] … backward looking' (p. 260).

Chapter 3, 'The curriculum Part 2', explores the significance of the 1944 Education Act, otherwise known as the Butler Act, in structuring education into primary, secondary (tripartite system) and further education sectors (Bartlett and Burton, 2020). Interestingly, the 1944 Education Act legislation did not mention the curriculum or pedagogy because it was widely understood at the time that whatever happened in classrooms was the concern of teachers themselves and 'the question of what teachers actually did (or should be doing) was taken for granted' (Lowe, 2007: 2). Although politicians focused mainly on the contentious matter of selection for secondary school, the curriculum was seen as a mystery by politicians, particularly the role of teachers in its content and control. This concern was raised by David Eccles, Minister for

Education in 1960, who coined the famous term for the curriculum as 'a secret garden'. 'Secret garden' was used by Prime Minister James Callaghan in the 'Great Debate' on education in his 1979 Ruskin College speech. Politicians felt that the curriculum was a carefully guarded domain by education professionals and teachers, and not the remit for politicians, parents or the public. Callaghan thought that central government needed a greater say in the curriculum and that statutory state education should be accountable to ensure that value for money was achieved (Lowe, 2007; Thomas, 2013). It was also the overt and systematic start of education being seen as a key part of the nation's economy, and this view has been sustained by successive governments since.

This reversal from teacher to government-led control of the curriculum, and much else of statutory education including pedagogy and assessment, heralded 'the draconian 1988 Education Reform Act … [which] … resulted not only in a national curriculum … testing … publication of league tables of school performance … reports on school inspections … [and very quickly] … teachers were made answerable to their political masters' (Lowe, 2007: 3). In a critical commentary about the 1988 Education Reform Act, Wragg (2005) stated that the Act did not have the people's assent that was afforded to the 1944 Education Act, and he suggested what was needed was 'another such Act to unscramble it, if its market-mad dogma has not ruined schools beyond redemption in the meantime' (p. 213). Such limitations and competitiveness of the 1988 Education Reform Act has led, it is argued, to an increase in traditional teaching and learning methods that value knowledge and skills rather than creativity, innovation, discovery and experimentation.

However, in the latter part of the last century and the very beginning of the twenty-first century, there were positive initiatives aligned to progressive education which have come to the forefront, even if they have not endured the passing of time. First, the 1967 Plowden Report epitomised progressive educational thinking and practice, and promoted the idea that 'activity and experience, both physical and mental, are often the best means of gaining knowledge and acquiring facts' (Plowden Report, 1967: 195). The second is ECM (DfES, 2003), a policy that aligned education and social justice to enhance the outcomes of children and young people. The policy was in response to the tragic death of Victoria Climbié in 2000. The inquiry into her death led to the Laming Report which called for shared working between professional agencies, such as education, health, social services, probation for children and young people age 0–19. The outcomes were embedded into the 2004 Children Act and reinforced by an integrated inspection framework to ensure that services worked in unison (Wallace, 2008). Unfortunately, the ECM policy was withdrawn by the Conservative-led coalition government as soon as it came to power in 2010.

Since 2010, the shift to traditional education has intensified using increasingly populist rhetoric to dismiss any notion of progressive teaching and learning. This was exemplified at first by Michael Gove and was followed by Gavin Williamson, who, despite their interventions, have shown little vision or awareness in building an education that prepares young people for uncertainties or future threats. At the time of writing, it is difficult to evaluate the initiatives of the successive secretaries of state for education as they have been afforded little chance to make a difference. Although this section has briefly navigated the shifts in the thinking and practice between progressive and traditional education, much of it has been driven by politics. Lowe (2007) cautions about being precise about the timing and the political ideology:

> It is a mistake to think issues around schooling suddenly become politicised during the 1970s and 1980s in response to the emergence of a 'new right' politically. The reality of the matter is that provision of popular education has always been a sensitive and controversial issue and this was no less true of the 1940s and 1950s than it has been of other historical periods.
>
> (p. 39)

THEMES OF THOUGHT: PROGRESSIVE EDUCATIONAL CONCEPTS

Progressive education is a contested concept with a broad range of ideas underpinned by an amalgam of educational thought. Rowntree (1981) defines progressive education as

> a movement towards a more flexible, democratic and learner-centred approaches to education that began in the late 19th century as a reaction against the formal curriculum, methods, and human relations then prevailing in schools.
>
> (p. 231)

Wallace (2008), on the other hand, offers a contrasting definition:

> [Progressive education is] taken to mean anything from a principled opposition to corporal punishment to allowing pupils complete freedom to learn as and when they please. It is often employed to indicate the opposite of 'traditional' ... [education] ... it has been used in very positive sense by those advocating education reform such as abandoning of rote learning in favour of discovery and understanding, which was seen as progress against draconian methods of 19th – and early 20th – century educators. Under the Conservative governments of the 1970s and 1980s, 'progressive education' became a regular target for criticism.
>
> (p. 235)

These two definitions offer a fair notion of progressive education. However, there are two points of commentary to add. First, it is argued that the criticism of progressive education has intensified following the 2010 UK general election, and progressive education has now become a weapon in the Conservative government culture wars. Second, although it is acknowledged that the nineteenth century witnessed the rise of progressive education (Rowntree, 1981), the democratic, learner-centred and social justice aspects of progressive education have been in existence since ancient times. Howlett (2013) contends that there were many progressive thinkers, including Confucius, Jesus, Plato, through to John Amos Comenius, John Locke, Jean-Jacques Rousseau, Friedrich Froebel, Robert Owen, the McMillan sisters and (of course) John Dewey, as well as the constructivists such as Lev Vygotsky, Jean Piaget and Jerome Bruner, and the humanists Abraham Maslow and Carl Rogers. All of these thinkers' ideas have made a huge contribution to progressive education.

Some of the more contemporary thinkers coming under the broad spectrum of progressive education cover a wide range of educational themes. Certain aspects of their ideas are somewhat far-reaching and even possibly subversive, and could appear to be not commensurate with education as we perceive it. Nevertheless, their ideas focus on matters of social justice, emancipation, democracy, inclusion and well-being, as well as student-centred learning – all matters that are needed for an education in changing and uncertain times. A note of caution regarding the themes of thought below: they are somewhat nebulous as some ideas cross boundaries. However, they are our interpretation and are offered in the context of the chapter. For example, critical educators such as Henry Giroux, Michael Apple, Paulo Freire and bell hooks were all anti-racist commentators and called for the decolonisation of the curriculum. Briefly, then, the themes of thought and a small example of the thinkers who champion them are listed in Table 10.2.

Table 10.2 Progressive themes of thought and the relevant thinkers

Themes of thought	*Relevant thinkers*
Freedom in childhood, home-schooling/unschooling and deschooling	A.S. Neill John Holt Ivan Illich
Social class, gender and race	Basil Bernstein bell hooks Gloria Ladson-Billings
Relationship between power and knowledge	Michael Apple Pierre Bourdieu Paulo Freire
Caring education	Nel Noddings bell hooks
Critical and transformative pedagogy	Henry Giroux Jack Mezirow Michael Apple

The ideas of the thinkers explored in this chapter are included because they offer alternative education approaches for such changeable and indeterminate times. Given such uncertain times, what is not needed is more of the same type of traditional education, or not even education reform, particularly if the reform is based on an ideological viewpoint. Rather, what is needed is what John Goodlad, the eminent American educator, called education renewal, arguing that education reform was politically driven and was 'a nasty concept that suggests bad people and bad conditions that must be reformed in somebody else's image' (2000: 86). Furthermore, Goodlad was highly critical of education reform as it epitomises all that is wrong with existing traditional education, which he argued was:

> a linear model of inputs and outputs, prescribed by well-meaning outsiders, whose initiatives show just how out of touch they are with our present realities and future threats … [instead Goodlad preferred] … the term 'renewal' … an essential characteristic of a robust democracy … a comprehensive overall.
>
> (Goodlad, 2008, cited in Coffield and Williamson, 2012: 70)

Goodlad's notion of education renewal embodies the key themes of progressive education, being focused on learner-centred pedagogy and in educating the whole child so they can develop into a caring person in the broadest sense (Goodlad, 1984; Aubrey and Riley, 2021). These key themes of thought encompass and complement those concepts explored in the previous chapters. An overview of the themes and their thinkers' ideas are discussed below.

FREEDOM IN CHILDHOOD, HOME-SCHOOLING/UNSCHOOLING AND DESCHOOLING

A.S. Neill's main idea was freedom in childhood. He was a radical, and controversial, educator whose ideas on the free and self-regulating child have had a major impact on the thinking around education and child development. His ideas can be aligned with Freud and Rousseau. He is firmly associated with Summerhill School which he set up in 1921 (the school is still thriving today and so is his philosophy). Critical of traditional schooling, arguing that repression by adults hindered children's natural development, Summerhill's pupils were allowed to decide what lessons they attended, as well as being given the option of non-attendance, and they were involved in the democratic running of the school (Neill, 1960).

Another educator with similar ideas was John Holt and his notion of home-schooling, which was very popular in the USA during the 1960s and 1970s, a time of progressive social reform, and promoted through two influential books: *How Children Fail* (1964) and *How Children Learn* (1967). He later coined the term 'unschooling' to describe a form of home-schooling that did not rely on a set curriculum and traditional teaching methods, and where children were allowed to learn at their own pace according to their interests by exploring creative ideas. It is interesting that children registered for home-schooling has risen in England considerably since the start of the COVID-19 pandemic: there were 60,500 registered pupils in March 2019 and 81,200 in October 2021 (Long and Danechi, 2022).

Like Neill and Holt, Ivan Illich was critical of traditional education and set out his ideas in his seminal text *Deschooling Society* (1971). For Illich, the reason why schools fail is because of poverty rather than the fundamental abilities of the child (Thomas, 2013). His philosophy for education was: '*learning*, as opposed to schooling; *conviviality*, as opposed to manipulation; *responsibilisation*, as opposed to deresponsibilisation; *participation*, as opposed to control' (Finger and Asun, 2001: 13). His key idea of **deschooling** is the utilisation of technology using learning webs that provide access to learning resources and allow access to knowledge, skills and dialogue (Illich, 1971). His ideas on the use of technology for learning webs was well before its time and pertinent to what was evident during the COVID-19 pandemic.

SOCIAL CLASS, RACE AND GENDER

Educator and sociologist Basil Bernstein explored the effects of social class in the British education system. His work on language codes found that the elaborate code with its more formal language with a broad vocabulary and reasoning power related to middle-class students, while the restricted code which related to working-class students was evident in public language and lacked sophistication. The difference between the two codes indicated the variance of the levels of achievement. He also championed the cause for democratic education and student rights among other progressive ideas (Bernstein, 1971).

bell hooks was an activist, feminist and anti-racist who saw education as a practice of freedom. She called for a democratic pedagogy where students and teachers play an equal part in the learning process by empowering the voice of students – a concept she termed as 'engaged pedagogy'. Her idea of critical thinking is where students and teachers build meaningful learning communities regardless of class, race or gender. The trilogy of her education texts are: *Teaching to Transgress: Education as a Practice of Freedom* (1994); *Teaching Community: A Pedagogy of Hope* (2003), and *Teaching Critical Thinking: Practical Wisdom* (2010).

Gloria Ladson-Billings, an educator, created the concept of culturally relevant pedagogy that draws upon Vygotsky's ideas on social learning and interaction. The concept emerged from her research with African American students and the use of their own home/culture to build upon their learning. It asks teachers to see student actions as positive rather than something requiring control. Culturally relevant pedagogy allows students to celebrate their cultural identity and develop critical perspectives that contest inequality in schools and in life, as described in her 2021 book, *Culturally Relevant Pedagogy: Asking a Different Question*.

RELATIONSHIP BETWEEN POWER AND KNOWLEDGE

Michael Apple, educator and activist, challenged the neoliberal marketisation of education. One of his main concerns was the curriculum in conservative countries such as the USA, arguing that it was biased towards the powerful dominant middle class to the disadvantage of the working class, and matters of gender and race. This included the textbooks that were created, approved and marketed in favour of right-wing thinking. This bias, underpinned by official knowledge, was created by those responsible for education policy as a way of reproducing the status quo and inequality. His two texts that are relevant to knowledge and power are: *Ideology and the Curriculum* (1979) and *Education and Power* (1982).

Pierre Bourdieu, a social philosopher, like Apple, was concerned with the idea that inequality is reproduced from generation to generation. Those with the greatest cultural capital maintain their position in society through symbolic violence, which denotes that those of the dominant class wield power over the subordinate class, which in turn normalises and legitimises the existing state of affairs. Those lacking in cultural capital are hindered because the language used in education is an obstacle to engage fully in the learning process. His seminal text, *Reproduction in Education, Society and Culture* (1990), co-authored with Jean-Claude Passeron, is the most popular work on social reproduction relating to education.

Paulo Freire's main thrust was the influence of power over knowledge, set out in his seminal work *Pedagogy of the Oppressed* ([1970] 1996). He had a great impact on global education, with an emphasis on the empowerment of learners and society. He criticised traditional teaching, which he termed a 'banking concept of education'. He called for critical and culturally based teaching, using dialogue and problem-posing education. His ideas were at a time of political unrest in Brazil. Following a military coup in 1964, he was arrested and exiled to Chile. Brazil's recently desposed right-wing populist leader Jair Bolsonaro has challenged Freire's ideas, calling for traditional and didactic teaching methods (Knijnik, 2021). Just before Freire died in 1997, he was writing a book on environmental justice and global sustainability (Bourn, 2021).

CARING EDUCATION

bell hooks also advanced the ideas of spirituality, care and love in education. She believed that conventional schools fail to respect students' spirit, deepening their feeling of being detached from learning: 'No wonder then that black students, students of color, and working-class kids of all races often enter schools, especially colleges, with a learned experience of interconnectedness that places them at odds with the world they have entered' (hooks, 2003: 180). She emphasised the importance of well-being for students and teachers alike, aligning matters of love, care, spirituality and imagination as fostering personal growth and well-being (Sewell, 2010), all qualities that help to create a meaningful learning community. hooks sees many similarities between the teaching and caring professions that she felt were unappreciated (Aubrey and Riley, 2021).

Nel Noddings, a renowned philosopher of education and feminist ethics, championed the cause of caring which she thought was an educational goal in itself. For her, ethical caring was a moral responsibility, an ability fostered from early experiences at home and positive student–teacher relationships. She campaigned to borrow Goodlad's (2000) 'word', for a renewal of education through caring. She challenged the school curriculum, feeling it concentrated on standardised testing, rather than taking into account the needs and aptitudes of individual students. Like many progressive educators, she highlighted the importance of dialogue and practice. Two of her early texts set out her philosophy: *Caring: A Feminine Approach to Ethics and Moral Education* (1984) and *The Challenge to Care in Schools* (1992) (Aubrey and Riley, 2021).

CRITICAL PEDAGOGY AND TRANSFORMATIVE LEARNING

For Henry Giroux, the aim of **critical pedagogy** is to expose the disparities that are often concealed in educational establishments and to empower students. He argued that education is driven by neoliberal ideology focused on economic growth, whereas it should be focused on matters of social justice, fairness, democracy and an instrument for change. He contested that with the current educational system, students are 'shamelessly reduced to "cheerful robots" through modes of pedagogy that embrace an instrumental rationality in which matters of justice, values, ethics, and power are erased' (Giroux, 2011: 3). The system advantages the middle class and overlooks diverse members of society; the system also fails to look to the future such as the multicultural changes in society, and shies away from issues of class, race and gender (Giroux, 2011).

Jack Mezirow's notion of **transformative learning** focused on using experience, critical reflection, discourse and personal change, and hence emancipation had a significant impact on adult, and later, higher education. Previously, adult education pedagogy (andragogy) was very instrumental and focused on the mastering of skills and theoretical aspects were gained through self-directed learning (Brookfield, 2005). Mezirow's research found that critical reflection of learners' beliefs and the use of emotion were important aspects of transformative learning (1998). Like many progressive educators, his work was about fostering social justice, social cohesion and the inclusion of marginalised learners. Mezirow was influenced by Thomas Kuhn's book, *The Structure of Scientific Revolutions* ([1962] 2012).

Michael Apple was a renowned advocate of critical pedagogy, particularly in response to the increasing influence of right-wing ideology. He saw critical pedagogy as a way to empower students to question the social origins of the knowledge they are offered to expose the bias and inequalities evident in society. The purpose of critical pedagogy for Apple is to create a democratic learning environment that encourages a discussion between student and teacher, and between other students in an equally shared and valued environment. Apple contested the neo-liberal, market-focused belief that shaped education policy, misrepresenting what actually happens in society for the benefit of the dominant classes (Aubrey and Riley, 2021).

These ideas can play a significant part in underpinning the options for the future in shifting towards a fair renewal of education to help young people manage events, crises and changes in society in the times ahead.

OPTIONS FOR THE FUTURE

All the events, crises and matters of social justice discussed in this book have had an impact on young students' education, well-being and aspirations. It has also affected in many ways school staff, families and communities. There have been issues of inequality, marginalisation and exclusion, and wide gaps in learning have been exposed, as well as a feeling of helplessness and uncertainty about the future. These are indeed of great concern, yet what is also disturbing is that some sections of society have been more adversely affected than others. Reasons for such disparity emanate from issues of social justice and include poverty, gender, race, culture, disability and access to resources. However, there have also been positive outcomes and experiences that point towards hopeful possibilities in tackling future occurrences and threats. These possibilities include increased levels of skill in using online learning, and the greater connectivity between schools and families during the COVID-19 pandemic. There has been increased awareness and active participation in matters of gender, race and climate change. There is also a growing consciousness regarding the populist right-wing intentions towards education. All these positive outcomes should be built upon for the future.

It is not intended to repeat at length the ideas which have been included, where appropriate, in each of the chapters. Nevertheless, a very brief recap of examples from practice is offered as they are founded on principles of social justice and in developing young people to face future challenges. They are set out in Table 10.3.

Table 10.3   Brief example of positive ideas from practice

Chapter topic	*Brief examples of positive ideas from practice*
The curriculum	Options for teaching and learning within the constraints, of a narrow and overly 'academic' national curriculum. The promotion of active and discovery learning, and the use of critical reflection.
Education as a vehicle for social mobility	The need for high levels of parental engagement and a recognition that children who attend settings will have very different experiences. The inclusion of cultural capital as a focus inspection helps celebrate learners' different cultures.
Rise of populism	Using methods that encourage reason and discussion, involve topics that are of cultural interest to them, and which foster student real-life experience.
Black Lives Matter	The use of an awareness of students' cultural heritage to plan teaching and learning activities which are of cultural interest and relevance.
The COVID-19 pandemic	Amid all the calls for 'catching-up' for lost time in learning during lockdown, Breslin, (2021: 176) appealed for 'putting well-being first'. His six themes for post-pandemic schooling are of significant value for practice and for future government education policy.
LBGTQ+	Initiatives such as 'No Outsiders' (2009) has shown its potential to break down barriers (Stonewall, 2022). Setting up safe spaces for learners is very important in helping change cultures of schools, rather than in just dealing with bullying as a stand-alone incident (Sadowski, 2016/17).
Climate change	Young people have demonstrated that they care about the environment and a genuine desire to play an active role in mitigating against the impact of climate change. This has been achieved through active learning and discussion.

These ideas for practice are encouraging and for the most part focus on teaching methods that stimulate discussion, challenge conventional thinking on important topics and matters of inequalities. Educational practitioners have shared ideas, cooperated between schools and been involved in research activities, all of which will be of benefit in facing future unforeseen events. Brighouse and Waters (2021), writing during the COVI9-19 pandemic, celebrate the role of educators:

> Most schools and teachers will find a way to unlock the minds and open the hearts of their pupils and inspire them to realise enough of their limitless potential to live fulfilled lives and help our society solve the many issues that COVID-19 and other developments have thrown in our path.

(p. 11)

There is a central role for the DfE and devolved governments to implement, communicate and fund education policy. This should be done by seeking guidance and consensus from educators and professional bodies relevant to the crises and events that occur. There is common ground in seeking solutions in crises such as the COVID-19 pandemic. An excellent text by Marilyn Leask and Sarah Younie, *Education for All in Times of Crisis: Lessons from Covid-19* (2022), considers the experiences of different education systems, and outlines challenges and possibilities, as well as offering options for the future drawing from the findings of global research; its findings are a valuable foundation source for dealing with future emergencies. From a governance point of view, it stresses the importance of pre-planning and contingency planning, and the cooperation with international agencies like the United Nations and the World Health Organization. It also addresses matters of isolation, marginalisation, inclusion and equality of learning opportunities. The outcomes of the UK COVID-19 inquiry chaired by Baroness Hallett, a former High Court judge, will no doubt highlight the preparedness of the UK for the pandemic. The findings will offer options for the future when dealing with pandemics and other emergencies that affect, among other areas, 'education and early years provision, as well as the impact on children and young people, including health, wellbeing and social care' (GOV.UK, 2022b).

SUMMARY

Seeking ways to create an education for a changing and uncertain world is a complex and problematic undertaking at the best of times, but in the current national and international turbulence, it is even more difficult. In the UK, there have been a number of changes in the role of secretary of state for education, and recently a change of Conservative prime minister. Furthermore, there is increasing inflation, a cost-of-living crisis, child poverty, industrial unrest and an energy emergency. Internationally, countries are still coping with and recovering from the COVID-19 pandemic, the Russian invasion of Ukraine is a huge humanitarian crisis that is affecting the rise in energy costs and causing disruption to the supply of food. All of these issues, along with the topics covered in the text, have had a detrimental impact on young people's learning and well-being. The events, crises and phenomenon have further exposed inequalities, marginalisation and an ever-widening gap in learning.

Lessons have been learned from dealing with each of the topics discussed in the chapters of this book, not only highlighting areas for development, but also positive areas of innovation and creativity which will be beneficial for the future. Overall, though, it is felt that education systems, particularly in England, focus too much on learning processes and assessment, and are restrained by an ever narrow subject-based curriculum that relies heavily on a traditional method of teaching increasingly promoted since the election of the Conservative-led coalition government in 2010.

It is argued that this impedes students from being prepared to challenge and take an active part in society in coping and thriving in the face of future changes and uncertainties; what is needed is a renewal, not just a reform of the current systems of education. A renewal would embrace a more student-centred progressive teaching that values critical thinking skills, discovery, integrated learning and independent thought (Thomas, 2013). Progressive education in the UK was evident in the 1960s, a time of social tolerance, and was epitomised by the 1967 Plowden Report. The ideas of some of the contemporary progressive thinkers are particularly helpful in the seeking for this renewal of education as they amalgamate learning with democracy, social justice, emancipation, and matters of race, gender and social class. They also challenge the orthodoxy and unfairness of current educational systems.

Although an imprecise task, an attempt has been made at locating different thinkers with broad themes of progressive thought relevant to this chapter. The themes reflect an array of ideas that challenge the status quo and include the thoughts of A.S. Neill, John Holt and Ivan Illich (freedom in childhood, home-schooling and deschooling); Basil Bernstein, bell hooks, Gloria Ladson-Billings (social class, race and gender); Michael Apple, Pierre Bourdieu, Paulo Freire (relationship between power and knowledge); Nel Noddings and bell hooks (caring education); Henry Giroux, Jack Mezirow, and Michael Apple (critical and transformative pedagogy). There are options for good practice which could be utilised for future events both for practice and governance which need to be taken into account in planning for the future. The UK COVID-19 inquiry into the preparedness and management of the pandemic will embrace the impact on children, their education, well-being and mental health (GOV.UK, 2022b).

GLOSSARY OF TERMS

Critical pedagogy

The purpose of critical pedagogy is to encourage and empower students by creating a democratic learning environment that advances social justice through active and questioning discourse. Michael Apple and other critical pedagogy thinkers encouraged students to challenge the source of the knowledge the come across to reveal any inequalities that are inherent in education.

Cultural capital

Pierre Bourdieu thought that cultural capital denoted an understanding and experience of society's dominant culture, and he believed that families actively passed cultural capital on to their children. The more cultural capital a person possesses, the more power they have.

Deschooling

Although it might appear as such, Ivan Illich did not mean that he wished to ban schools. A better term to use would be to disestablish schools so that attendance would not be legally compulsory. As an alternative, he advocated the idea of a democratic learning community with a network of informal but knowledgeable tutors, shared resources and technology-based learning webs, all of which would be shared with the local community.

Education renewal

A term used by John Goodlad as a counter to education reform. He thought that 'reform' offered only a deficit and narrow meaning where students, schools and teachers needed improving. Instead, for him education renewal was a greater ambition as it embraced democracy and social justice for students, teachers, and the whole school community.

Progressive education

A contrast to traditional education where students are encouraged to be creative, think critically and to use active methods of discovery and experimentation. It is often understood as a child-centred and informal approach to learning. Pupils are taught either individually or in small groups where subjects are integrated into activities rather than whole-class single subject teaching.

Traditional education

The focus is on the acquisition of facts, knowledge and skills, normally didactic in nature with the formation of learning directed by the teacher sometimes through whole-class lessons. It is usually subject-based.

Transformative learning

Jack Mezirow proposed that transformative learning could be developed through the use of experience, critical reflection, discourse and personal change. It is a term more often used for adult learning where he observed that students developed through a number of stages, including self-awareness, change of attitudes and learner identity, leading to a reformation of their meaning perspective.

FURTHER READING

British Educational Research Journal (BERJ) (2021) Special Section – Right-wing populism and education: Interrogating politics, policy and pedagogic resistance. *British Educational Research Journal,* 47(2).

Some ten articles in this special section explore the associations and the effects between right-wing populist politics and pedagogy. The articles also include the links between populism and religion, the populist reasoning in Conservative school reforms in England, as well as international perspectives from Israel and Brazil.

Brown, A. and Wisby, E. (eds) (2020) *Knowledge, Policy and Practice in Education and the Struggle for Social Justice: Essays Inspired by the Work of Geoff Whitty*. London: University College London Press.

A collection of essays by some of the most influential contemporary educational thinkers in the celebration of the life of the education sociologist Geoff Whitty, such as Michael Apple, Michael Young, David Gillborn, Hugh Lauder, Sharon Gewirtz and Alan Cribb.

Ranson, S. (2019) *Education and Democratic Participation: The Making of Learning Communities*. London: Routledge.

A significant progressive education text that explores the value of education in the face of neoliberal ideology. It calls for creating a democratic education that fosters empowerment and social justice, in the form of inclusive and tolerant learning communities.

Tisdall, L. (2020) *A Progressive Education?: How Childhood Changed in Mid-twentieth Century English and Welsh Schools*. Manchester: Manchester University Press.

This is a detailed critical analysis of the rise and fall of progressive education. It includes a thorough review of the works of progressive educational thinkers and the increasing involvement and control of politics in pedagogy and the curriculum.

REFERENCES

Apple, M. (1979) *Ideology and Curriculum*. Boston, MA: Routledge & Kegan Paul.

Apple, M. (1982) *Education and Power*. New York: Routledge.

Apple, M. (2000) *Official Knowledge: Democratic Education in a Conservative Age* (2nd edn). New York: Routledge.

Aubrey, K. and Riley, A. (2021) *Understanding and Using Challenging Educational Theories* (2nd edn). London: Sage.

Aubrey, K. and Riley, A. (2022) *Understanding and Using Educational Theories* (3rd edn). London: Sage.

Bartlett, S. and Burton, D. (2020) *Introduction to Education Studies* (5th edn). London: Sage.

Bernstein, B. (1971) *Class, Codes and Control: Theoretical Studies Towards a Sociology of Language*. Vol. 1. London: Routledge & Kegan Paul.

Bourdieu, P. and Passeron, J-C. (1990) *Reproduction in Education, Society and Culture* (2nd edn). London: Sage.

Bourn, D. (2021) Ecopedagogy: Critical environmental teaching for planetary justice and global sustainable development. *Policy and Practice: A Development Education Review*, 32: 147–9, Spring. Available at: www.developmenteducationreview.com/issue/issue-32/ecopedagogy-critical-environmental-teaching-planetary-justice-and-global-sustainable. (accessed 16 March 2023).

Breslin, T. (2021) *Lessons from Lockdown: The Educational Legacy of COVID-19*. London: Routledge.

Brighouse, T. and Waters, M. (2021) *About Our Schools: Improving on Previous Best*. Carmarthen: Crown House Publishing.

Brookfield, S. (2005) *The Power of Critical Theory for Adult Learning and Teaching*. Maidenhead: Open University Press.

Coffield, F. and Williamson, B. (2012) *From Exam Factories to Communities of Discovery: The Democratic Route*. London: Institute of Education, University of London.

Department for Education and Skills (DfES) (2003) *Every Child Matters*. Green Paper. London: Crown copyright.

Dorling, D. (2021) Foreword. In: T. Brighouse and M. Waters, *About Our Schools: Improving on Previous Best*. Carmarthen: Crown House Publishing.

Finger, M. and Asun, J. (2001) *Adult Education at the Crossroads: Our Way Out*. London: Zed Books.

Freire, P. ([1970] 1996) *Pedagogy of the Oppressed*. London: Penguin.

Giroux, H. (2011) *On Critical Pedagogy*. New York: Continuum.

Goodlad, J. (1984) *A Place Called School: Prospects for the Future*. New York: McGraw-Hill.

Goodlad, J. (2000) Education and democracy. *Phi Delta Kappan*, 82(1): 86–9.

GOV.UK (2022a) *Secretary of State for Education*. Available at: www.gov.uk/government/ministers/secretary-of-state-for-education (accessed 16 March 2023).

GOV.UK (2022b) *UK COVID-19 Inquiry: Terms of Reference*. Available at: www.gov.uk/government/publications/uk-covid-19-inquiry-terms-of-reference/uk-covid-19-inquiry-terms-of-reference (accessed 16 March 2023).

Holt, J. (1964) *How Children Fail*. London: Penguin Books.

Holt, J. (1967) *How Children Learn*. London: Penguin Books.

hooks, b. (1994) *Teaching to Transgress: Education as the Practice of Freedom*. London: Routledge.

hooks, b. (2003) *Teaching Community: A Pedagogy of Hope*. London: Routledge.

hooks, b. (2010) *Teaching Critical Thinking: Practical Wisdom*. London: Routledge.

Howlett, J. (2013) *Progressive Education: A Critical Introduction*. London: Bloomsbury.

Illich, I. (1971) *Deschooling Society*. London: Marion Boyars Publishers.

Knijnik, J. (2021) To Freire or not to Freire: Educational freedom and the populist right-wing 'Escola sem Partido' movement in Brazil. *British Educational Research Journal*, 47(2): 355–71.

Kuhn, T. ([1962] 2012) *The Structure of Scientific Revolutions* (Fiftieth Anniversary Edition). Chicago: Chicago University Press.

Ladson-Billings, G. (2021) *Culturally Relevant Pedagogy: Asking a Different Question*. London: Teachers College Press.

Leask, M. and Younie, S. (2022) *Education for All in Times of Crisis: Lessons from Covid-19*. London: Routledge.

Long, R. and Danechi, S. (2022) Home education in England. House of Commons Library (28 March). Available at: https://commonslibrary.parliament.uk/research-briefings/sn05108/ (accessed 16 March 2023).

Lowe, R. (2007) *The Death of Progressive Education: How Teachers Lost Control of the Classroom*. London: Routledge.

Mezirow, J. (1998) Transformational learning and social action. *Adult Education Quarterly*, 49(1): 70–3.

Neill, A.S. (1960) *Summerhill: A Radical Approach to Child Rearing*. New York: Hart.

Noddings, N. (1984) *Caring: A Feminist Approach to Ethics and Moral Education*. Berkeley, CA: University of California Press.

Noddings, N. (1992) *The Challenge to Care in Schools*. New York: Teachers College Press.

Plowden Report (1967) *Children and their Primary Schools: A Report of the Central Advisory Council for England*. London: HMSO.

Rowntree, R. (1981) *A Dictionary of Education*. London: Harper & Row.

Rosenshine, B. (2012) Principles of instruction: Research-based strategies that all teachers should know. *American Educator*, 12–39, Spring.

Sadowski, M. (2016/17) More than a safe space: How schools can enable LGBT pupils to thrive. *American Educator*. Winter.

Scott, D. (2008) *Critical Essays on Major Curriculum Theorists*. London: Routledge.

Sewell, A. (2010) Review: Teaching community: A pedagogy of hope. *International Journal of Children's' Spirituality*, 15(2): 341–3.

Stonewall (2022) *Schools and Colleges*. Available at: www.stonewall.org.uk/schools-colleges (accessed 16 March 2023).

Tanzi, V. (2022) *Fragile Futures: The Uncertain Economics of Disasters, Pandemics, and Climate Change*. Cambridge: Cambridge University Press.

Thomas, G. (2013) *Education: A Very Short History*. Oxford: Oxford University Press.

Wallace, S. (2008) *Oxford Dictionary of Education*. Oxford: Oxford University Press.

Wragg, E.C. (2005) *The Art and Science of Teaching and Learning: The Selected Works of Ted Wragg*. London: Routledge.

INDEX

Note: Page numbers followed by "n" denote notes.